TAKING FLIGHT

TAKING FLIGHT

THE NADINE RAMSEY STORY

RAQUEL RAMSEY & TRICIA AURAND
FOREWORD BY MAJ. GEN. JEANNIE M. LEAVITT, USAF

UNIVERSITY PRESS OF KANSAS

Published by the University Press of Kansas (Lawrence, Kansas 66045), which was organized by the Kansas Board of Regents and is operated and funded by Emporia State University, Fort Hays State University, Kansas State University, Pittsburg State University, the University of Kansas, and Wichita State University

Cover: Aviatrix and former military aircraft pilot Nadine Ramsey stepping out of the cockpit of her own fighter aircraft, the P-38 Lockheed Lightning, ca. 1946

All images courtesy of the Ramsey family unless otherwise noted.

Library of Congress Cataloging-in-Publication Data

Names: Ramsey, Raquel, author. | Aurand, Tricia, author. | Leavitt, Jeannie M., writer of foreword.
Title: Taking flight : the Nadine Ramsey story / Raquel Ramsey and Tricia Aurand.
Description: Lawrence, KS : University Press of Kansas, [2020] | Includes bibliographical references and index.
Identifiers: LCCN 2020007597
 ISBN 9780700629800 (cloth)
 ISBN 9780700629817 (ebook)
Subjects: LCSH: Ramsey, Nadine, 1911–1987 | Women Airforce Service Pilots (U.S.)—Biography. | Air pilots, Military—United States—Biography. | World War, 1939–1945—Aerial operations, American. | World War, 1939–1945—Participation, Female. | Women veterans—California—Long Beach—Biography. | Women air pilots—United States—Biography. | Secretaries—California—Long Beach—Biography. | Wichita (Kan.)—Biography. | El Dorado (Kan.)—Biography.
Classification: LCC D790.5 .A94 2020 | DDC 940.54/4973092 [B]—dc23
LC record available at https://lccn.loc.gov/2020007597.

British Library Cataloguing-in-Publication Data is available.

Printed in the United States of America

10 9 8 7 6 5 4 3 2 1

The paper used in this publication is recycled and contains 30 percent postconsumer waste. It is acid free and meets the minimum requirements of the American National Standard for Permanence of Paper for Printed Library Materials Z39.48–1992.

To the Women Airforce Service Pilots, whose indomitable courage enabled them to serve their country unselfishly though unrecognized. With this book, we remind others of their sacrifice and service.

* * *

To my darling Ed, my loving husband of thirty-four years, my hero.
This book is my promise to you.
To Nelle Ramsey, a true inspiration as a woman ahead of her time and as a mother loved by her two children, Ed and Nadine.
And to my sweet Nadine, whose love and affection really touched me.
I'm so proud of your accomplishments as a woman aviator and cherish the memory of the loving care you gave to your mother, Nelle, and to Ed.
Despite all odds, the bonds with your family were never broken.
—Raquel Ramsey

* * *

To Stephen J. Rivele, mentor and friend
—Tricia Aurand

Oh! I have slipped the surly bonds of Earth
And danced the skies on laughter-silvered wings;
Sunward I've climbed, and joined the tumbling mirth
Of sun-split clouds,—and done a hundred things
You have not dreamed of—wheeled and soared and swung
High in the sunlit silence. Hov'ring there,
I've chased the shouting wind along, and flung
My eager craft through footless halls of air . . .

Up, up the long, delirious burning blue
I've topped the wind-swept heights with easy grace
Where never lark, or ever eagle flew—
And, while with silent, lifting mind I've trod
The high untrespassed sanctity of space,
Put out my hand, and touched the face of God.

—John G. Magee Jr., "High Flight," September 3, 1941

CONTENTS

FOREWORD

I am honored Raquel Ramsey asked me to write the foreword to this book about her sister-in-law Nadine Ramsey. She and Tricia Aurand have done an amazing job painting a vivid picture of Nadine's exciting life, including the special time she spent as part of the Women Airforce Service Pilots (WASP). I can relate to Nadine's passion for flying and her "ready for anything" personality. She flew some of the most iconic aircraft of World War II, including the P-51 Mustang and the P-38 Lightning. Also, I think it is truly remarkable that Nadine bought her own P-38 after the war and named her "Lucky."

The authors have captured the bold, adventurous spirit of Nadine and the other incredible women pilots who served their country as WASPs during World War II. These women were smart, talented, and driven. They seized every opportunity and pushed on any door, whether open or closed. They became the first women in history to fly US military aircraft. For far too long, their story as part of our Air Force history and the critical role they played in the war effort was overlooked.

These pioneers were ahead of their time—it was as if a portal to the future opened for a few years and then closed again. On December 7, 1944, the last WASP training class graduated at Avenger Field in Sweetwater, Texas. General Henry "Hap" Arnold, commander of the Army Air Forces, spoke at the final WASP graduation. He said he was skeptical of the program at first but called the operation a complete success. He stated, "It is on the record that women can fly as well as men." The WASP program was disbanded later that month. More than thirty years passed before women flew US military aircraft again. In September of 1977, the first Air Force Undergraduate Pilot Training (UPT) class with women graduated at Williams Air Force Base, Arizona.

March 10, 2010, was a significant day. It was a Wednesday, and I had received permission to miss my classes at National War College that day in order to attend a historic event: the Congressional Gold Medal ceremony for the WASPs. It was nearly impossible to get a ticket. Luckily, my friend Col. (ret.) Nicole Malachowski was able to get one precious ticket for me—though I had hoped for two so I could go with my husband, Col. (ret.) Craig

Leavitt, who was a graduate of the United States Air Force Academy and an F-16 fighter pilot.

With more than two thousand people in attendance, it was standing room only for the WASP Gold Medal ceremony in Emancipation Hall at the US Capitol. I found a place to stand near the back where I could see the stage and considered myself extremely lucky to be in the crowd. The ceremony finally provided a level of recognition commensurate with the actions of these amazing women. Afterward, I was honored to shake hands with some of those who attended and thank them for blazing a trail for so many women military aviators to follow. Their recognition was long overdue.

My journey as an Air Force fighter pilot would not have been possible if it were not for the incredible women who went before me, beginning with the WASPs. Being first at anything is never easy, and everyone is watching you to see if you will fail. As the first, you can never give up or quit because you would not clear a trail for others to follow. In my case, I wanted to be a fighter pilot before Department of Defense (DoD) policy allowed women to fly fighters. The WASPs provided the example I needed to find the courage to stand up and ask for the F-15E Strike Eagle assignment after pilot training, knowing the answer would be no. While I was nervous at the time, I felt the strength of all the women pilots who went before me. I knew women were capable of flying fighter aircraft—the WASPs flew every fighter, bomber, transport, and trainer aircraft in the inventory during World War II. These daring women set the precedent for women to fly fighter aircraft. When DoD policy changed a few months after I graduated from pilot training in 1993, the Air Force remembered my request and changed my assignment to the F-15E.

It is now forty-three years since women were allowed to go into pilot training and twenty-seven years since we were permitted to fly fighter air-craft. There are almost nine hundred female pilots in the US Air Force and about 10 percent of them are fighter pilots. The numbers are increasing, but there is more progress to be made. In the US Air Force, we recognize diversity as a competitive advantage over any potential adversary. There are many efforts underway to ensure we engage with a diverse audience to highlight the many opportunities available. Today, the Air Force wants a diverse pilot force, which was not always the case.

This book does a wonderful job of adding to the mosaic that is the story of the WASPs. These women served their nation during some of its darkest hours, yet their story was a missing chapter in US history for many years. It is important to continue to recognize them for the heroes they are and to inspire the generations that follow.

Nadine Ramsey can rest in peace, knowing that her story will encourage future generations. I wish I had the opportunity to meet her—I would have loved to hear her tell me about her many flying adventures. I hope readers will draw from Nadine's example the strength to be bold, dream big, and believe in themselves. Readers should also be inspired to believe nothing is out of reach.

Aim High!

Major General Jeannie M. Leavitt, United States Air Force
Director of Operations and Communications,
 Headquarters Air Education and Training Command
Joint Base San Antonio–Randolph, Texas
July 2020

PREFACE

It is thrilling to finally see my sister-in-law, pilot Nadine Ramsey, come to life in the pages of this book, for the journey to tell her story has spanned nearly thirty years. Her brother, Edwin P. Ramsey, my late husband, first expressed the desire to tell it in the early 1990s, when his memoir, *Lieutenant Ramsey's War*, was published, documenting his harrowing escape into the jungles of Luzon in the Philippines during World War II and his covert command of guerrilla forces there. Why, he insisted, should his bravery be so honored and not his sister's, when her courage and conviction were equally deserving and, he believed, exceeded his?

A decorated war hero, Ed led the last mounted cavalry charge in US Army history during the Japanese invasion of the Philippine Islands. Throughout the Japanese occupation, he and his guerrilla troops provided intelligence that allowed General Douglas MacArthur to keep his famous promise: "I shall return." When Ed passed away on March 7, 2013, at the age of ninety-five, I made my own promise: to tell Nadine's story and the Ramseys'. How, I marveled, had this one family produced two such committed and patriotic citizens who fought so fearlessly for their country?

Making this promise gave me the resolve to overcome the many challenges we faced while striving to keep it. Early attempts to interview Nadine in the 1990s were not productive. Living in a nursing home, only a handful of years before her death, she could not answer an interviewer's questions; her memory and confidence had failed. At that time, nothing could come of Ed's vision.

After Nadine's death in February 1997, Ed and I received many letters of remembrance from family and friends. We collected them and put them in an envelope for safekeeping. At my urging, Ed made an audiotape of his own memories of his sister. These tributes to Nadine's memory were the beginning of our Nadine Ramsey collection, and of this book.

When we fully embarked on our journey to tell Nadine's story, there arose an unexpected obstacle. Nadine's struggle to find meaning in her life after her wartime job as a ferry pilot of fighter aircraft resulted in the destruction and disappearance of key documentation: logbooks, personal letters,

memoirs, and scrapbooks. Without her voice, how could we re-create the character of this beautiful, strong-willed, and fun-loving woman?

Diligent research accomplished by a team of authors, scholars, archivists, publishing professionals, family members, and friends uncovered many aspects of Nadine's life we had never known or had only glimpsed. We studied her military records. We examined her personal effects—newspaper and magazine articles, photographs, and objects—about her family and the war. We interviewed members of the Ramsey clan, even one approaching a hundred years old. We spoke with other Women Airforce Service Pilots family members, as well as WASPs who were still alive and eager to share their stories and memories of Nadine. We accessed institutional, museum, and newspaper archives across the country and pursued many leads.

What we initially considered a hindrance became a mountain of discoveries. From it emerged the portrait of a woman at once confident and insecure, outgoing and retiring, free in the air and constrained on the ground—and always dependent on her family's love and support. Above all, Nadine Ramsey was an individual of resilience, self-determination, and dedication toward a singular purpose yet a free spirit who scaled heights to follow her dreams.

Working with a screenwriter, my coauthor Tricia Aurand, enabled us to include imaginings of what Nadine would think, say, and do while embracing danger, celebrating success, surmounting hurdles, and fulfilling her own promise. We hope readers will see her as we do, even in her postwar years of disappointment and illness: a woman who overcame conflict to find her calling.

While Nadine's life achieved its pinnacle during the war, she searched relentlessly afterward for a similar sense of purpose. Her struggle was shared by many of her contemporaries who were relegated to the societal and gender norms of the day, when, it seemed, men owned the sky, sea, and land. And, I believe, that struggle is recognizable to women today—those fighting to break glass ceilings, earn equal pay, and eliminate sexual harassment at home and in the workplace.

Whatever vicissitudes characterized Nadine's life, she is and forever will be among those heroic WASPs who proved the aptitude of women pilots for flying military aircraft and who fought for recognition, each in her own

way. These many decades later, their efforts are finally acknowledged as the shoulders on which today's women combat pilots stand.

I am thankful that this book has reached publication during the centennial anniversary of the ratification of the Nineteenth Amendment, which granted women the right to vote. Breaking gender barriers is part of our national story; despite burdens and disappointments, these efforts are uplifting and inspirational all the same. It is this dichotomy we have sought to both honor and convey in this book.

Raquel Ramsey
Los Angeles, California
January 2020

ACKNOWLEDGMENTS

Our deepest gratitude goes to the many people and organizations that have made this book possible.

First and foremost, thanks to Ramsey family members, including Ed Ramsey Jr., Doug Ramsey (a constant source of counsel and support), Barbara Stuntz, and Richard and Jeanette Powell. Barbara's journals and her communications by phone and letters vastly helped our understanding of the Ramsey family in Illinois and Kansas before and during the war. She and her daughter, Jeanette Powell, also kindly shared photos from their family albums.

Thank you to the inspirational London family: Barbara (B. J.) Erickson London and Terry Rinehart. We especially acknowledge and appreciate B. J.'s friendship with Nadine, which extended until Nadine's death in 1997; her leadership as Nadine's commanding officer at Long Beach Army Air Field; and the special role she played in WASP history and women's aviation.

Our appreciation extends to the gracious and remarkable WASPs who granted us interviews during the course of our research, including Iris Cummings Critchell, Jean Landis, and Dawn Seymour.

Thanks also to Shelby Jean Lutz for speaking with us about her father, Jack Gardner.

Special acknowledgment goes to WASP historian and author Sarah Byrn Rickman, whose professional review of our WASP chapters, as well as her insights and encouragement, were invaluable in writing this book.

We are grateful for the support of the following history keepers and historians at their homes and at archives and institutions across the country: Danette Boyle and Dewey Wilson, Rogers State University, Claremore, Oklahoma; Carol C. Cain, National WASP WWII Museum, Avenger Field, Sweetwater, Texas; Civil Air Patrol National Archives and Historical Collections, Washington, DC; Marilla J. Cushman, Women in Military Service for America Memorial Foundation (Women's Memorial), Arlington, Virginia; Kimberly Johnson, director of Special Collections, Woman's Collection, Texas Woman's University Libraries, Denton, Texas; Kelly Kalcheim and Steve Blake, P-38 National Association and Museum, Riverside, California;

Barb Kramer, Kansas Aviation Museum, Wichita, Kansas; Major Colleen McCormick, Civil Air Patrol National History Program, Archives Division, Maxwell Air Force Base, Alabama; Kimberly T. McMahon and Lindsey Phillips, Public Affairs, Long Beach Airport, California; Brian Nicklas, National Air and Space Museum, Washington, DC; Ken Spurgeon and Tiya Tonn, Kansas Oil Museum, El Dorado, Kansas; Barbara Stuntz, Wichita, Kansas; Brandon Werts and John Royce, Historical Society of Long Beach, California; Tim Weinschenker, Society of Air Racing Historians; Sarah White, Textron Aviation Business Aircraft, Wichita, Kansas; and Lieutenant Colonel Barbara C. Willis, Kansas Wing, Civil Air Patrol, Salina, Kansas.

We thank the following museums, archives, collections, and individuals whose images shed visual light on Nadine's story: Amy Barnard; Ben Franklin Collection; Butler County History Center; Gil Cohen; Kansas Aviation Museum; Dan Kelly; Library of Congress, Carol M. Highsmith Archive; LIFE Picture Collection/Getty Images; Long Beach Airport Archives; Los Angeles Public Library; P-38 National Association and Museum; Saint Louis University Archives and Digital Services; Smithsonian Air and Space Museum; Barbara Stuntz; Texas Woman's University, Woman's Collection; US Air Force; US Cavalry Association; US Department of Defense; US Post Office; Vanilla Fire Productions; Wichita-Sedgwick County Historical Museum; Wichita State University, Special Collections and University Archives; and Women in Military Service for America Memorial.

Additional thanks for their support, consultation, and review of the manuscript go to Sheri Aurand, James Charleton, Dorothy Cochrane, Lieutenant Commander Tom Cutler, Rick Flaherty, Kevin Grantham, Glenn Griffith, Ted Hamady, William Kidstone, Doug Ramsey, Ed Ramsey Jr., Janine Ramsey, Sarah Rickman, Stephen J. Rivele, Victoria Sams, and Thadd Turner. For their testimonials, we thank Janet Bednarek, professor of history, University of Dayton; Rabbi Abraham Cooper, Associate Dean, Simon Wiesenthal Center Museum of Tolerance, Los Angeles; Lieutenant Commander Tom Cutler, US Naval Institute; WASP author and historian Sarah Byrn Rickman; and San Diego State Professor Lisa Shapiro.

This book was supported at every step by the extensive research of Corynthia Dorgan, with assistance from the staff of the Women Airforce Service Pilots Records collection (also known as the WASP Archive) at Texas Woman's University, Denton, Texas.

We are especially indebted to Editor-in-Chief Joyce Harrison, Acquisitions Editor Bethany R. Mowry, and the editorial board of the University Press of Kansas for their guidance and shared vision of the press as the natural home for a book about an accomplished Kansas pilot, her family, and their place in the state's historical record. We appreciate the efforts of the press's editorial, design, production, marketing, and sales staff to produce and distribute the book, especially Kelly Chrisman Jacques, managing editor; Michael R. Kehoe, marketing and sales director; and Karl Janssen, art director and webmaster. Thank you to the initial manuscript's three peer reviewers, who provided both encouragement and constructive critique. Margaret Weitekamp's comments were particularly useful to us as we refined Nadine's story.

We are truly grateful to Major General Jeannie M. Leavitt, Director of Operations and Communications, Headquarters Air Education and Training Command at Joint Base San Antonio-Randolph, Texas, for honoring Nadine's memory through her foreword to our book. As the first female fighter pilot in Air Force history and the first woman to command a USAF combat fighter wing, Maj. Gen. Leavitt's trailblazing experience brings special relevance to Nadine's story. We also appreciate Christine Cuttita of the Air Force Recruiting Service Public Affairs office for her diligence in obtaining the necessary approvals and facilitating the process. Thanks also to the US Air Force Book Support Program for its assistance with our book project.

Sam Griffith, Richard Kale, and the spirit of Edwin Price Ramsey have seen us through.

Finally, we thank our editor and publishing consultant— our "sister"— Shelly Kale. Editor of *Lieutenant Ramsey's War* and Ramsey family friend since the memoir's publication in 1990, her dedication to telling Nadine's story, begun even before her death in 1997, steadfastly guided us throughout the development and editing of this book.

PROLOGUE

Nadine Ramsey took a deep breath of sharp fall air as she lowered herself back into the Mustang's single-seat cockpit. Other pilots—male pilots—complained that there wasn't any elbowroom in the P-51 Mustang, but Nadine's petite frame fit in here fine; she was snug but not uncomfortable. This little peashooter, she thought, is a dream of a ship. *In fact, it was a thirty-two-foot, sleek, cutting-edge warbird with a wingspan of thirty-seven feet. Definitely compact for a fighter, but not little, Nadine knew. She waved at the mechanic, flashing him a broad, scarlet-lipped smile, and slid the P-51's bubble canopy closed. It was October 1944, Nadine was thirty-three, and this—Evansville, Indiana—was the last refueling stop before New Jersey. From Newark, this Mustang would be sent overseas to Europe, into the hands of some young male American pilot facing the bullets of the Luftwaffe.*

Before taking off, Nadine checked the rudders, toe brakes, and control stick, gauging their sensitivity to her touch. Then she tested the radio and carefully ticked through her mental checklist of dials and gauges. She cracked the throttle and the 1,490-horsepower Merlin engine roared to life, driving the four-bladed Hamilton Standard propeller and creating a deafening cacophony sounding from the exhaust stacks barely ten feet from her ears. After a standard series of S-turns on the taxiway to ensure visibility, she steered the plane into position and requested clearance from the tower.

As she waited in that brief moment before takeoff, Nadine thought about the vastness of the world and about her tiny place within it, in a hotel suite in Wichita, Kansas, with her mother and brother. A brief ache pulsed in her heart as she noticed the line of trees at the far end of the runway, ablaze with crimson, rust, olive, and ochre, patched and undulating like an artist's brushstrokes.

Then she got her clearance and pushed the throttle all the way forward toward the brilliant forest ahead. Her body was pressed back into the seat as she pulled back on the stick, and the Mustang surged and leaped into the air, climbing to ten thousand feet and more than three hundred miles per hour in what felt like the blink of an eye. Her heart soared as she climbed further still, the expanse of the heavens opening around her. Her place wasn't really in that tiny hotel apartment; it was here, in the driven blue of an autumn sky, high above the panorama

of her country in green and gold, tracing the snaking Ohio River far below. Her mother and brother knew that, for they too were in their own places and finding their own way. In any case, it was a glorious day. Nadine willed the three-hour flight to last forever.

She didn't hear the hiccup in the Mustang's Merlin engine until she was nearly ready to descend into Newark, but the sudden sputter sent a bolt of panic through her happiness. The Mustang jolted and shuddered, and Nadine hastily radioed the tower that she was having engine problems. The Merlin was going to die, she thought, and as she went into a downwind turn to scrub off her speed, she whispered a quick prayer that she would make it down in time. Sure enough, just as the Mustang's tail wheel touched the runway, the engine cut into silence, and Nadine fought the controls to keep the deadweight of the plane between the lines. At last, she pulled the P-51 to a stop. Her hands were shaking. She forced herself to release the stick, unbuckled, and thrust back the canopy.

"You okay?" a young flight officer shouted, jogging up as Nadine shook her soft auburn curls loose of the headphones.

"Fine," she said, impressed at the bravado in her own voice. "But I think you boys will have to tow this pony in."

At last, after Nadine and the Mustang had been towed to the hangar, she climbed down, longing for a drink at the Officers' Club to steady her nerves. But as she finished filing the paperwork for the Mustang, she received new orders: to ferry a P-39 Airacobra into Great Falls, Montana, where it would then be sent into Russia. Nadine's stomach turned over. Though she'd flown the P-39 before, the pursuit aircraft was known for being accident prone, and she was surprised at how the Mustang's engine failure had rattled her.

Oh well, *Nadine thought, drawing a breath.* Better to die in the sky, free, than live scared on the ground. *She grinned to herself, shouldered her parachute, and walked back out onto the tarmac.*

Irrepressible, redheaded Nadine was a descendant of our nation's heartland settlers, of log-cabin homesteaders, a young girl raised on the edge of the Dust Bowl in the midst of the Great Depression. Yet she was destined, quite literally, to rise above adversity.

As a young woman in Wichita, Kansas, Nadine dreamed of flying. In secret and with her own meager earnings, she devised a strategy to learn to

fly—one undeterred by the economic trials of the Depression and the rigid social norms of the 1930s. The era in which she lived brought her unexpected opportunity as a pilot: the gathering storm clouds of World War II.

Even before the Japanese invaded Pearl Harbor, thrusting the United States into war, the US government recognized that the country needed more pilots for the war effort, including women. Nadine answered the call. She became one of only 303 women to ferry military aircraft as part of the Women Airforce Service Pilots (WASP) of the US Army Air Forces (AAF)—an elite corps of fearless women pilots who transported aircraft to bases across the nation for use in the theaters of war.

Along the way, her achievements stood as milestones of success: soloing to earn her pilot's license after six and a half hours of instruction (half the time usually required, even of men); becoming the first woman in Kansas to receive a commercial pilot license and the first licensed woman pilot of the National Aeronautic Association (NAA) Wichita chapter; being celebrated as a pilot during the 1938 National Air Mail Week; joining the ranks of stunt and racing pilots across the country; working her own aircraft dealerships; commanding a squadron of thirty young women for the Civil Air Patrol (CAP); serving as a flight instructor for the federal Civilian Pilot Training Program (CPTP); ferrying military aircraft in the Fifth and Sixth Ferrying Groups of the AAF's Air Transport Command (ATC); obtaining certifications from the AAF's Pursuit and Officer Training Schools; distinguishing herself as the only woman in the country to instruct male pilots to fly army fighter planes after the war; and making headlines as the first woman pilot to own her own Lockheed P-38 Lightning fighter aircraft.

But these were not solitary pursuits. Throughout, Nadine was guided by the inspiration of a strong nuclear family: an entrepreneurial single mother and a brother who became a decorated World War II hero. The Ramsey family's unconquerable American spirit was evident throughout Nadine's life.

During the war years, Nadine helped to prove that women pilots were as competent and resilient as their male counterparts. Then and in the years after, she and the other 1,101 WASPs who had flown for the US military endured years without formal recognition. Finally, after decades of campaigning for treatment equal to their male counterparts, these women—including the thirty-eight WASPs who died in defense of their country—

were recognized as military veterans. Today, they are celebrated for their historical role in our country's military history, with monuments, museums, films, and publications testifying to their service and patriotism.

From the start of her flying career in the 1930s to her death in the 1990s, Nadine Ramsey was a pioneer and role model, a woman of skill and achievement, and a heroic fighter against a great darkness. This is her story.

PART I
STRONG ROOTS

Nelle Ramsey swung her big yellow car around a sharp bend in the dirt road, sending Nadine and Ed crashing into each other in the back seat, laughing. As Nelle glanced at her children over her shoulder and resumed her cheerful singing, Nadine shoved her brother off and, shaking her buoyant auburn curls, resumed her post looking out the car's rattling window. This was summer in Illinois, and, humid though it was, Nadine relished it, drinking up the passing landscape.

She was a teenager now. She and her brother could roam wild in the summer, both on foot and on horseback; she could wear slacks and good, sturdy boots. Smoked ham awaited them, and Grandma's pies, and an abundance of hot fried chicken. They would hear Grandpa's rumbling voice again, spinning some yarn or even scolding; Nadine didn't care. They were bound for the Ramsey farm, far from the life of the bustling Kansas city where the three of them—well, the four of them, sometimes—lived. Nadine frowned, then put thoughts of her father out of her mind. She took up the song her mother was singing and found a harmony.

Ed burst like a bird out of the back seat as the car stopped, finally, in front of a hand-built clapboard farmhouse. This house, bedecked with three massive rambling porches and many additions, stood only feet from an old, unshakable log cabin that no one really used anymore. Nadine got out of the car too and stretched. Already Grandma Margaret and Aunt Winnie were coming down the steps to the packed-earth yard, calling bright hellos. Nadine was caught up in Winnie's arms, in a hug that smelled like freshly baked bread. Her little cousin Barbara toddled up on stubby legs, squealing with pleasure and sending a handful of Margaret's chickens squawking.

It has always been like this, *Nadine thought, looking around. She drew a deep breath, trying to believe that. It was hard to imagine that her father, now a man of shadows, had come from such a sunny place. Nadine walked past Margaret's garden, ablaze with color and humming with bees. She saw scarlet tomatoes ready to be picked and the bony green joints of beans. Under the earth, she knew, turnips and potatoes waited to be dug. It seemed impossible that her father could have lived here and been unhappy.*

By the time Nadine's annual self-guided farm tour brought her to the stables, Ed was already there, thrusting an apple at one of Grandpa Hiram's big work-horses. He grinned at her, and Nadine punched him playfully on the shoulder. These horses weren't for riding, but that would come later. Nelle's family didn't live far, and they had horses of their own. There would be plenty of time all sum-mer for Ed and Nadine to leave hoofprints across the countryside, to come back in the evenings with the pungent, outdoor smell of horse. And there would be time to wash, after hauling buckets out to Grandpa Hiram's smokehouse, which he usually used to smoke bacon and ham but which in the summer became a bath-house with a cold steel washtub. Time for playing with Barbara and other Ramsey cousins, time for scraping plates clean, time for catching fireflies.

Nadine could see the whole delicious summer spread out ahead of them. She turned and walked back toward the house where her father had been born. There would be time.

CHAPTER 1

FARMERS AND OILMEN

In the early 1870s, Hiram Eugene Ramsey bought a 160-acre farm across the road from his mother, Amanda. A lean, leather-faced man of Irish ancestry, he had been looking after Amanda and his sister, Dora, since their father died in 1862. At twelve, he had become the man of the family, the boot-and-trousers wearer in a house full of petticoats.

As the Civil War raged in the East, pioneers from southern Indiana and Illinois—the Ramsey family among them—headed west. After Hiram came of age, Amanda remarried, and the whole family moved from the area around the small Illinois town of Cairo to the outskirts of an even smaller village known as Odin, a little more than a hundred miles south of the famous Springfield home where Abraham Lincoln had lived.

In Odin Hiram met Margaret Jane Young, an austere beauty nine years his junior. Margaret was a brunette whose great-grandfather, Captain Samuel Young, had fought at the Battle of Yorktown in the Revolutionary War. Born in Pennsylvania, Young later became the first white settler in Marion County, Illinois. One of his six children, James Wiley Young, married a woman of Native American descent, Sarah Ann Copple. They had seven children, all raised in the tradition of hard work. One of them was Margaret, who possessed a rare blend of imagination and grit. Margaret and Hiram married in October 1872, bought the flat, fertile property across the road from Amanda's, and set about putting up a log house.

That house soon became the birthplace of Hiram and Margaret's first daughter, Daisy, in 1879, and their first son, Claude, in 1881. It would remain in the Ramsey family for more than a hundred years.

As a boy, Claude Ramsey sprouted like a thorny, out-of-place weed in an immaculately kept garden. He despised his chores, primarily picking fruit from the apple, cherry, and peach orchards Hiram had planted; lacking Margaret's discipline, he preferred to roam as his moods compelled. Sometimes at night, Hiram and Claude went fox hunting with the hounds they kept tied up by the house during the day. In the heavy, cloud-dampened dark, they

James Wiley Young and Sarah Ann Young (Courtesy Barbara Stuntz)

Margaret Jane Ramsey (née Young) and Hiram Ramsey (Courtesy Barbara Stuntz)

The Ramseys at the family farm, Odin, Illinois, ca. 1907. Claude is at far right; seated to his left on the porch are his mother, Margaret, and father, Hiram (Courtesy Barbara Stuntz)

turned the dogs loose to pick up the scent of a fox, and Hiram mounted his small, gray horse to follow their baying. If the dogs were several miles away and had lost the fox's scent, Hiram would blow on his horn (made of a cow's horn) to summon the hounds back to him.

Sometimes, on these nights, Hiram's neighbors were out on their own hunts, and the men would sit around a campfire, listening to the hound music. Their ears were so sharp that each man could single out his own dog's bark. Among these patient men, Claude began to realize that he simply didn't have the steady temperament of a farmer. But what he wanted to do he didn't exactly know.

Odin, meanwhile, was a growing community. Central Illinois is flat and glacier carved, the soil made rich with deposits from the last ice giant that moved through the region more than thirteen thousand years ago. When the Ramsey family moved into the area, land was cheap to buy (between eight and twelve dollars per acre) and quick to yield its bounty.

When the first building was erected in Odin in 1855, the town's population was about five hundred. By the turn of the century, that number had tripled, transformed by the arrival of the Illinois Central Railroad, which stretched 705 miles, at that point the longest railroad in the world.[1] Hiram and his family worked in the orchards during the day picking fruit and then hauled it down by horse and wagon to the Odin railroad depot about three and a half miles away. There, Ramsey peaches, apples, and cherries were loaded onto boxcars and shipped overnight to Chicago to be ready for buyers in the morning. The Ramsey farm and the ever-spreading patchwork of farms around it were feeding one of the fastest-growing cities in America.

However, it wasn't Odin's destiny to become a great metropolis. The town's population crested at around 1,800 in 1940 and would never surpass 2,000.[2] Odin was a rural village of people who knew one another and each other's business, who saw each other on Sundays at one of a half-dozen churches or at the dry goods store or at the newly built bank. Life revolved around the land. The industries were coal and corn; the seasons brought floods and fireflies.

But none of it was enough for Claude Ramsey. Finally, when he was a teenager, his best friend's family felt the pull west and decided to move to the state of Washington. They offered to take Claude along with them in their wagon train, temporarily, as extra help. By that point, Hiram had fathered seven more farmhands, and he must have realized that Claude would end up wayward one way or another. He gave his assent, and Claude left Illinois, not to return until he was grown and full of the knowledge of the trail.

On May 22, 1891, Rebecca Harris Cozad gave birth to her seventh child, Nelle Brown Cozad, with her husband, Joseph. The Cozads also had settled near Odin, having arrived in the area from West Virginia in a covered wagon. Joseph's mother was a relative of General Robert E. Lee, and the family was staunchly Baptist. Many prayers were said and many tears wept when Rebecca, then an older mother at forty-nine, died just three years after Nelle was born. The third-youngest Cozad, John, only ten at the time, later became a Baptist minister.

At three, though motherless and the youngest Cozad, Nelle had no desire to be babied. She grew up to be an assertive, pretty young woman, with a broad, smooth face, auburn hair, and dark, sparkling eyes. She was strong—

Rebecca Cozad (née Harris) and Joseph Alexander Cozad, married 1866

stronger than her slim frame suggested—and she strove to be her own person and make her own place, darting out from under the canopy of her siblings.

Nelle had the advantage of a sharp mind, so she committed herself to her own education. She could learn anything, she realized, and be or do whatever she wanted. The first job she took was as a schoolteacher in a quaint, 720-square-foot building simply called the Brick School, one and a half miles from the Ramsey family farm.

By now, Claude was pushing thirty. When he came home from the Pacific Northwest, he'd gone back to helping Hiram run the farm, tending the cherry orchard by pruning trees and clearing brush. But farmwork was still farmwork, and in the meantime the oil boom had come to Illinois. By 1910 Carlyle, Illinois—a town only eighteen miles from Odin—was drawing clamoring oil prospectors. To Claude (as to many at that time), oil represented the future. Along with several other Ramsey brothers, he talked about moving to Carlyle.

But first Claude met Nelle. In those days, events at school buildings were an invitation to the whole community. It was common for rural schools to host fundraisers for books and supplies, such as pie suppers in which the boys bid on pies baked by the girls. Some winters, schools in Odin Township hosted concerts for fiddlers, guitar and banjo players, and singers like Nelle, who had a naturally musical ear. Since all of Claude's younger siblings (the youngest of whom was two years older than Nelle) attended the Brick School and most settled down in the immediate area, it's likely that some of Claude's nieces and nephews were Nelle's students when Claude walked into one such community event at the Brick School in 1910.

Nelle was beautiful, confident, and kind. At only nineteen, she was already being courted by bankers' and doctors' sons. Claude saw himself as an uneducated roughneck and knew Nelle was far out of his league, yet he determined to try to win her. Nelle loved poetry, so Claude courted her with verse. He gave her flowers and showered her with attention—all of which fascinated her. She was young, and the Ramseys weren't rich, but she was after adventure and independence, not money. Claude, a stormy-tempered man with stories from the west, a man with perpetually dirty hands, was simply not the kind of man she *should* have wanted, and yet he was some-

thing different and exciting. Nelle impulsively allowed herself to be swept away by the tide of Claude's frantic affection.

Nelle and Claude fell in love, however unwisely. Then, in early 1911, Nelle realized she was pregnant. Accepting responsibility for the baby and wishing to avoid causing the family any disgrace, they were married in a small service on Saint Patrick's Day 1911. Their daughter was born on August 28 of that year. Nelle called her Nadine Berniece.

Nelle and Claude settled down in Carlyle, and Claude went to work in the oil fields. Nelle kept busy raising Nadine and keeping house. She became particular friends with Claude's second youngest sister, Winnie, who was just a few years older than she. Both Nelle and Claude thought Winnie should have a boyfriend, so they arranged for her to meet "a nice young man" who worked for the railroad. With free rail passes from her new beau to travel from Odin to Carlyle, she began visiting Nelle quite often, helping her with Nadine and with Nelle's second baby girl, Treva Eileen.

As a child, Nadine displayed her personality early. She was fun loving, restless, impulsive, and fearless. When her hair came in, it was red—not copper red, but decidedly more auburn than brown, a trait she inherited from her Cozad ancestors. Nelle must have seen in her young daughter a mixture of herself and Claude: her own strength, intelligence, and ambition and Claude's stubborn dissatisfaction and passionate volatility. For his part, Claude may or may not have recognized himself in Nadine or liked oil drilling, but he worked determinedly to provide for his growing family.

Then, just as the Great War threw the world into chaos, another tragedy struck, this one closer to home. While unattended one day, Treva Eileen, who was just a toddler, pulled a kettle of boiling water onto herself. She died from extensive burns and was buried in the Fredonia Cemetery, about ten miles from the Ramsey farm.

She was not the first family member the Ramseys had lost. The family's matriarch, Hiram's mother, Amanda, had passed away in 1892, and one of Claude's sisters, Gertrude, had died from appendicitis in 1907 at age twenty-two. But the loss of one as young as Treva Eileen stung bitterly. Nadine, herself a young child, was suddenly bewildered and lonely, and one can only imagine the depth of Nelle's grief.

Nelle, Claude, and Nadine Berniece Ramsey (age one), 1912

So when Nelle gave birth to her third child, Edwin Price Ramsey (Ed, or Buddy, as he came to be called), on May 9, 1917, everything changed for the Ramseys. Claude at last had a son, Nadine was a big sister again, and though the oil boom was slackening in Carlyle, it was taking off in Kansas. Perhaps the family needed to make a fresh start; perhaps Claude's restlessness or Nelle's ambition or both were tugging at them; or maybe they no longer wanted to live in the house where Treva Eileen had died. In any case, they decided to leave Illinois behind. They packed their things and—with Nelle holding baby Ed tightly in her arms and rambunctious Nadine, now nearly six, firmly by the hand—headed south for El Dorado, a burgeoning Kansas oil town.

El Dorado (said by locals with a long *a*), about thirty-three miles from Wichita, is the geographical center of Butler County in southeastern Kansas, at the time the region's wealthiest farming and stock-raising county. As a book published in 1916, a year before the Ramseys moved there, described this "Garden of the West":

> It is beautifully located on the west bank of the Walnut River and sits like a queen on her throne, overlooking the picturesque and fertile Walnut valley, one of the richest portions of the country east of the Rockies, and teeming with rural life and wealth, the result of nearly a half century of the toil, frugality, and economy of the people who in all these years have called this "Garden of the West" home.[3]

El Dorado was thriving, with a population of about twenty-three thousand, quadruple that of Odin. It boasted good roads, "one of the most complete and efficient systems of water works to be found in the west," and a network of tungsten street lamps furnished by the Kansas Gas and Electric Company. More important to Nelle, it also offered schools with high academic standards, including a high school, so Nadine and Ed—who both had inherited their mother's intelligence—would get a good education.

Most important of all, there was lots of oil in El Dorado. The strike at Stapleton Oil well No. 1 on October 6, 1915, was one of the Midwest's most important oil finds. Celebrated as the discovery oil well for the El Dorado Oil

Oil Hill in El Dorado, the world's largest "company town," 1916–1917 (Butler County History Center)

Field, it was called "the oil field that won World War I." The largest single field producer in the United States, the El Dorado Oil Field was responsible for nearly 13 percent of national oil production and 9 percent worldwide.[4] There would be plenty of work for Claude—and for a few of the other Ramsey brothers too.

El Dorado had much to offer, but it didn't have sufficient housing for all of its new residents. By 1920 the population had doubled, and more oil companies had bought up land in the area, drawing still more workers like Claude Ramsey and his siblings. Some 8,500 oil field employees lived on Oil Hill, a "company town" of cookie-cutter houses founded by the Empire Gas and Fuel Co. However, there wasn't room there or anywhere else for the Ramsey family, so Claude built a temporary home for Nelle and the kids. The lower part of this structure was a wood frame, with a tarpaulin stretched over the top, serving as the roof. During this crowded, competitive time in Kansas, Claude wasn't the only desperate driller to build and live in such a house.

El Dorado Oil Field, ca. 1917 (Wichita State University Libraries, Special Collections and University Archives)

In fact, his sister Winnie had by this point met and married a man named Dennis Branch. Dennis was an oil "wildcatter" like Claude, who saw the same opportunities to the south. Winnie and Dennis also moved to El Dorado, settling in a wood-frame building with a partition down the middle. The youngest Ramsey brother, Verbie, and another man from Illinois lived on the other side. A third Ramsey sibling, Hiram R., or Hizy, also moved to El Dorado, drawn by the oil business.[5]

Thus, Nadine and Ed grew up among this troop of displaced Ramsey kin. When their family finally moved to a permanent home, Claude and Nelle took the downstairs and Winnie and Dennis Branch moved in upstairs. Hizy and his wife, Dilla, lived next door. The other Ramseys, too, had and were having kids of their own, and there were always cousins for Ed and Nadine to play with.

One day, Winnie was hanging washing on the clothesline in the yard and saw Ed with Hizy's boy, Francis, coming around the corner of the house with something heavy wrapped in a blanket. They were half-dragging it, Ed on one end of the blanket and Francis on the other. Suspicious, Win-

nie decided to investigate and then nearly tanned them both: the bundle was Francis's baby brother, Maurice. Winnie never did find out where the boys were planning on taking him, but it seemed clear that Ed shared the Ramsey children's penchant for getting into trouble.

Eventually, in the early 1920s, the Branches moved—first to Peabody, Kansas, where Winnie's only child, Barbara, was born in 1923, then to Chicago, where Dennis worked in the Pullman railroad car shops, making railcars. Finally, when Hiram's health began to fail, they returned to Illinois to take over the Ramsey farm. Despite all this moving, Nelle and Winnie's friendship held firm. In fact, Nelle, Ed, and Nadine were visiting the Branches in Peabody when Winnie went into labor with Barbara. She was born in the home, as was still common at the time, and both Nelle and twelve-year-old Nadine got to hold her. In the summers, there were those visits to the Ramsey farm to reunite them.

Nadine grew into adolescence. At school, she was vivacious, pretty, and popular, well liked by both girls and boys for her fun-loving personality. Like Nelle she loved to read and learn, but she was also irrepressibly adventurous. She had a knack for foreign languages and a musical gift she had inherited from her mother. Nelle encouraged and helped teach Nadine to play the organ.

In El Dorado Nelle was no idle mother and housewife. It was the twenties, and she became passionately interested in one of the hottest beauty trends at the time: Marcel waves. Unlike the now-iconic finger waves of the decade, Marcels involved specialized equipment: heavy iron tongs, imported from France, that were originally heated over a gas burner. This process made it incredibly hard to regulate the irons' heat (often resulting in burned hair) and required expert handling to make the hair wave and not curl. When electric irons came along, making the process somewhat easier, the best hairdressers were still sought after and kept busy by anyone who could afford them.

Nelle, with shrewd curiosity and her customary determination, taught herself to do Marcels. From there, she started working in a beauty parlor, and a whole new career opened before her.

All in all, life in El Dorado was productive for the Ramseys, as it was for

middle-class families in most growing cities after World War I. The war had created an economic boom, and new industries flourished across the country. America's factories hummed, oil and gas fed the flourishing automobile industry, and the expanding entertainment industry put a movie theater in every reasonably sized town (El Dorado's opened in 1921).

This was the Jazz Age, and one of its most significant results was the social liberation of women, who had done all kinds of jobs during the war, as they would in the next war two decades later. By 1920 women could vote; it was a new world. They bobbed their hair, wore slacks, drank alcohol, and spoke their minds. It became possible for girls like Nadine to dream that they could go to college and have careers outside of secretarial, teaching, or homemaking work. There were women in science and medicine now, women in business, and—most significantly for Nadine—women in aviation. It was the age of aviators and aviatrixes, including many who would influence and even alter the course of Nadine's life: Amelia Earhart, Louise Thaden, and Jacqueline Cochran.

While some of these positive changes in society became permanent, the United States couldn't prosper forever. Clouds gathered across the nation on the economic horizon; the Depression was coming, and it would rock and devastate many families. In El Dorado, in the Ramsey household, the approaching storm was of a different nature—less tangible but more present.

Despite all the growth, excitement, and bustle of the time, Claude wasn't well. In the early 1920s, there was plenty of work to do but not a lot of money for an uneducated man like him to make. Ed recalled that his father worked harder than any man he'd ever seen, yet others reaped the profits of his tireless labor in the oil fields.[6] Early in their marriage, Nelle's lyrical spirit and grace had sustained Claude through the long graceless hours and the grime of drilling. Later, as the oil business changed, he was forced to spend more and more time away from home, following the black gold to Texas and Oklahoma.

Though the distance from Nelle tormented Claude, it didn't soften his nature or feelings toward her. Instead, his underlying belief about himself and Nelle—that she was much too good for him—drove him to furious jeal-

ousy. He began to believe that she was unfaithful, sure that she was cheating with one of the many men in El Dorado who admired her. Whenever he returned home from the oil fields, he crashed into the house, determined to find some signs of Nelle's infidelity. Finding none, he grew madder still. Ed wrote:

> It was all in his mind, of course, which was warping. To Nadine and me as small children, the transformation was a puzzle, and I tried for a time to think of it as a game he was playing. After his trips he would return from the fields with exotic gifts, arrowheads or lumps of turquoise or the intricate silver carvings of the Indians. Nadine and I would buzz around him, happy that he was home and eager for the prizes he brought.
>
> But as time went on, I watched him become sullen, then angry, then isolated. This was no game, I began to understand; it was a frightening intrusion in our lives, an alien presence we were helpless to understand or control. We tried to ignore it, distancing ourselves from him and hoping that it would end of its own accord, but it only grew worse. He began to rail at Mother and to accuse her, and despite her tearful denials he refused to believe her. Then he began to beat her.[7]

Claude's fury whenever he was home slowly turned the Ramsey home into a nightmare. Nadine and Ed quickly decided not to cower or hide from their father when he was in one of his rages; rather, they intervened as best as they could, crying and pulling at him, desperately trying to protect Nelle from his violence. Still, they were only children when his outbursts began. Nadine was in middle school; Ed was younger than ten.

Terrible as Claude became, his fits drew Nadine and Ed together. They had always liked each other and had more or less gotten along. Now, in crisis, they became a close-knit team, forming a tight little unit of two soldiers on a two-pronged mission: to keep their mother as safe as possible and to prevent anyone from finding out. As Nelle's social standing rose and she bought the beauty parlor where she worked, Nadine was sure that El Dorado society would not accept any of them if Claude's behavior became known. She and Ed together schemed to keep up the family's appearances and the monster within Claude at bay. Sadly, this wasn't possible. Their father's temper grew worse.

One October night in 1927, the siblings were awakened by shouting in

their parents' room. It wasn't the first time. Ten-year-old Ed and sixteen-year-old Nadine crept into the hallway, listening, nauseated with dread. Then they heard the word *gun.* Together they ran to their parents' room and burst in—just in time to see Claude struggling to pull his shotgun from behind the bed's headboard. Nelle saw her children and yelled at them to run, but Nadine and Ed instead immediately threw themselves at Claude, wrestling with all their strength, and at last managed to drag him away. "He stared at us in a horror of recognition," Ed remembered. "He was gripping the barrel of the shotgun, his hands white and trembling. He glanced down at it, gave an animal groan of anguish and shame, thrust it aside, and shoved his way heavily out of the room. . . . Mother was trembling so badly that she could not speak."[8]

When they were sure Nelle hadn't been hurt, Nadine hastened to call the police, who found Claude outside near the house and arrested him. They took him to the police station, where they only intended to hold him overnight, but something had broken within Claude beyond reparation. He was found dead the next morning, hanging in his cell.

Claude's father, Hiram, had died only five months earlier, and the Ramsey family had traveled back to Odin for the funeral. Already grief stricken, Nelle, Nadine, and Ed now went through the process again, and this time it was much worse. They put Claude's body on a train home to Illinois—home to Margaret, Winnie, and the others, home to the fields and orchards he had never figured out how to love. Once again, brother and sister climbed into Nelle's big yellow car, and the three made the familiar drive north, this time very quietly, to bury their father in the land where he grew up.

The night before Claude's funeral service, neighbors came over and "set up" all night in the Ramsey farmhouse, grieving with the family. Some helped Winnie and Margaret prepare sandwiches, pie, and coffee for everyone who watched that night bleed into a wan morning. Then more mourners arrived, and more chairs were brought, and many experienced the eerie echoes of Hiram's recent death. There were hymns and prayers. There was talk of Claude's life. Finally, as Nadine and Ed approached their father's casket to say goodbye, their cousin Barbara, who was only four at the time, watched them carefully. She never forgot what she saw: "Ed was quiet and serious. Nadine was very sad and held her brother's hand."[9]

* * *

Claude's death was devastating, but it was also, terribly, a relief. Nadine and Ed now didn't have to worry about coming home to find their mother bruised or weeping. Nelle was strong, and the father they had known in childhood had been lost to them for a long time. The strain of their long-standing mission to protect their mother was at an end, as was the pressure of keeping their family problems hidden. There was no concealing now what Claude had been, and there was certainly scandal in the immediate wake of the suicide. As Ed later recalled, the pernicious whispers around town stung him almost as much as Claude's death did.[10]

Moreover, the loss of Claude's meager income created real financial problems, as he left no pension behind for his wife and children. To Nelle, however, these were merely logistical issues, exactly the kind of hardships she knew how to conquer. A widow at only thirty-six, Nelle was still beautiful, enterprising, and respected by many in El Dorado's social circles. In fact, her beauty parlor business was so successful that she started traveling around the region, helping to set up other businesses like it. Her kids could work too, and she determined that they both would.

Ed was quickly approaching eleven, and he was now suddenly forced to face adolescence without a man in the house. He wanted to be that man, to take over, as his Grandpa Hiram had done at nearly the same age, and look after his mother and sister—though Nelle and Nadine were far from stereotypical helpless women who needed a male breadwinner.

Still, he did his best to contribute. He took up a paper route, trudging the streets with a heavy sack before dawn. It was isolating work for an already lonely boy. With every step he walked hauling his load, Ed resented Claude's absence. At the same time, he worried that he was restless and moody, like Claude, and this made him even more resentful. He grew sullen and aimless. Then he discovered girls and, eventually, liquor. Claude had been a drinker, so perhaps his children were destined to inherit this habit. It was Prohibition, and rebellion ran hot in the blood of city-dwelling Americans, young people included.

Claude's death also affected Nadine deeply. She coped in the ways typical of irresponsible teenagers at the time; in Ed's words, she was "pretty rambunctious." Her misbehavior was also surely influenced by her boyfriend, a dark-haired, broad-shouldered football player named Harold Honn, called

Nadine's El Dorado High School yearbook picture, 1929

Lefty or Honn by his peers. She had met him in glee club during her sophomore year of high school, though he was in the grade above her.

Harold was a bold, outgoing tenor, Nadine a soprano who couldn't help but notice him as she played the organ for the glee club. She tended to be

drawn to boys who were rakish, reckless, and not altogether safe—in other words, men who were a lot like her. She was crazy about him, and the two started going steady. They were a popular couple. Nadine was fun loving and jolly; Harold was well regarded by his teachers and coaches, a member of the school's E Club, indicating proficiency in scholarship as well as athletics.

When Nadine graduated in 1929, she right away enrolled in El Dorado Junior College, studying music and foreign languages. Then, fatefully, that October, the stock market crashed, and she reluctantly dropped out of school and worked as a secretary to help support the family.

If at the time Nelle saw parallels between Nadine's passionate, youthful romance with Harold and her own experience as a young woman falling for Claude, she kept her worries to herself, realizing that they just didn't matter to bullheaded Nadine, who always did exactly what she wanted. If Nelle did warn her to be careful running around with Harold, Nadine didn't listen.

Then, early in 1930, Nelle decided to move her little family of three out of El Dorado to the big city: Wichita. There were probably a variety of reasons behind her decision, including better business opportunities, Ed's education, and ongoing social fallout from Claude's suicide. Nonetheless, it couldn't have hurt that a move would also get Nadine away from Harold.

CHAPTER 2

A FAMILY OF THREE IN WICHITA

In 1930 Wichita, Kansas, was home to about 110,000 people, and it's not a stretch to say that most of them were obsessed with aviation. Of course, this phenomenon was hardly unique to Wichita. Flying was a national fascination: it was glamorous, and famous pilots were as well-known as movie stars. Charles Lindbergh had made his world-altering transatlantic flight a few years earlier, in 1927, becoming an industry leader and a household name overnight; Hollywood was busy churning out flying pictures for the public's frenzied consumption.

By 1929, when the World War I epic *Wings* became the first film ever to win the Academy Award for best picture, wealthy young prodigy Howard Hughes was already bragging about spending a fortune on making *Hell's Angels*, billed as a "thrilling, multi-million dollar air spectacle." Hughes's money turned out to be well spent. Even a year later, in the midst of the Depression, American audiences couldn't buy their tickets to see *Hell's Angels* fast enough.[1]

Wichita was uniquely positioned within the exploding aviation industry. The natural topographical features of the region as well as the city's geographic location made it an ideal fit for early commercial aviation tycoons, and men had already begun building factories and manufacturing aircraft there.

Founded on the broad alluvial plains east of the Arkansas River, Wichita was level and well cleared by wind, flood, and tornado. It was practically a natural airport. Conveniently, it was also right in the middle of the country, where any potential coast-to-coast flights would need to stop to refuel. In fact, several large tracts of farmland had already been used as runways for years, since Wichita's first air show in 1911.

Wichitans were proud of their city and the nickname it had earned, the Air Capital City, so dubbed in 1929 by the National Aeronautical Chamber of Commerce—thanks to some of the aviation industry's greatest businessmen and pioneers who set up shop there in the 1920s. It would not be long before the title was expanded to Air Capital of the World.

Wichita Municipal Airport, Air Capital of the World, ca. 1931 (Wichita-Sedgwick County Historical Museum)

One of the earliest major players on the aviation scene was Pennsylvanian Jake Moellendick, who, like the Ramseys, had been drawn to the region in 1917. While Claude Ramsey was slicking his hands and arms pumping oil, Moellendick had bigger ideas and sank his life savings into establishing the Okmulgee Producing and Refining Company. Then forty-five, he was wealthy within a few years. In 1920 he teamed up with Matty Laird, a young Chicago businessman, who had been building planes since 1912. Together, they formed America's first commercial airplane enterprise, the E. M. Laird Airplane Company, building their plant in Wichita.

Thus began the founding of a series of aircraft manufacturing heavyweights in the Wichita area. Shortly after its formation, the Laird company lured a talented young assembler named Lloyd Stearman away from an architect's company and brought him on to design planes. Moellendick and Laird then hired a test pilot who had served in World War I, a brash, mischievous hotshot named Walter Beech.

Born in early 1891, Beech was the same age as Nelle. Like her, he was largely self-taught and as a young man had taken responsibility for his own education, learning mechanics by repairing farm equipment. He had a

quick, analytical mind that was well suited to engineering, yet he turned down the chance for a college education at Vanderbilt University to work for White Motor Corp. in Minneapolis as a technician and chauffeur. In his biography of Beech, *The Barnstormer and the Lady*, Dennis Farney writes: "Studio photographs of Walter as a young man show an impeccable dandy, five feet, nine inches tall, with an erect carriage and striking, light colored eyes. His jaw is set determinedly, his lips in a firm line."[2]

In Minneapolis Beech had soloed in a Curtiss Pusher biplane that he and a friend had bought and refurbished. "He apparently was a self-taught pilot," Farney writes, "just barely capable of flying at all; aviation writer Edward H. Phillips concluded that he 'just stumbled into the air.'"[3]

Beech was also like Claude Ramsey in some ways. Though he was born on a farm in Pulaski, Tennessee, he knew he wasn't suited to farmwork. Following his fateful "stumble into the air," he became a barnstormer and later a sergeant in charge of repairing airplane engines at a base near Waco, Texas, during World War I.

Within three years of establishing the company, Matty Laird left Wichita, but Beech and Lloyd Stearman remained, running for Moellendick what became the Swallow Airplane Manufacturing Company. Several more shake-ups, separations, and short-lived ventures followed. In 1925 Stearman and Beech teamed up with Clyde Cessna and others to form the Travel Air Manufacturing Company. There Beech met Olive Ann Mellor, then twenty-one and a cool, efficient secretary. She was levelheaded, stubborn, and whip smart; she'd had a head for numbers all her life and had been in charge of her family's finances since age eleven. Mellor was a wonder, and she was never afraid to stand up to loudmouthed Walter Beech. He fell for her, hard.

Travel Air made a major name for itself in the second half of the decade, but it, too, eventually broke up. Beech, Cessna, and Stearman nonetheless stubbornly stayed in the airplane business, eventually becoming the presidents of their own companies: Beech Aircraft, Cessna Aircraft, and Stearman Aircraft. The latter ultimately became Boeing.

Beech and Olive Ann married in February 1930 and were promptly dubbed the "aristocrats of the air" by the press. Two years later, they set up shop in an old Cessna factory, founding their own company, Beech Aircraft. With Walter as the president and Olive Ann as treasurer, they were ready to climb to new heights in the aviation industry.

Stearman Aircraft Company, Wichita, ca. 1935 (Wichita State University Libraries, Special Collections and University Archives)

These three men broke new ground in aircraft design throughout the 1920s, and by the end of the decade the Wichita area was producing a quarter of the nation's planes. As an article in the August 1927 edition of *The Wichita* reported, the city of Wichita alone had six significant airplane factories. "Wichita," the article claimed, "once famous because of the cattle that passed through the city over the Chisholm Trail, and again as she became the hard wheat center of America, and again when she gained recognition as the oil center of the great Kansas fields, now is blessed with world-wide recognition because of her air activity."[4]

All the while, Wichitans eagerly reveled in their city's shiny, bustling new industry. Each day, five hundred passengers flew in and out of Wichita's many small airports. There were regular air shows and exhibitions throughout the Roaring Twenties, drawing the attention and imaginations of people countrywide. Thanks to all this air activity as well as periodic visits from

Kansan Amelia Earhart, Charles Lindbergh, and other famous fliers, Wichita became well-known as an aviation hub—again, in no small part because of its fine weather and natural runways.

The most famous and well-trafficked of these "airfields" was a 640-acre—or one-square-mile—hayfield southeast of downtown known as the California Section (because its owners lived in California). Lindbergh himself, speaking to reporters at the *Wichita Beacon*, had called the California Section one of the finest fields in the country.[5] Even so, city leaders realized that in order to keep Wichita at the center of the commercial airline business, they would need to build a real airport.

In 1929 the City of Wichita bought the California Section and set about planning the Wichita Municipal Airport. The vision for the property included a large hangar and a two-story administration building, fashioned in the Beaux Arts style. The administration building was designed to be passenger-friendly and would house a waiting room, a restaurant, ticket offices, airmail offices, and, on the roof, a garden and observation deck.

Construction of the airport became a plodding affair, a six-year wrestling match over budgets and city funding in the midst of the Depression. After ground broke in 1929 some parts of the airport were built immediately, but the erection of the administration building was largely put on hold. When the Ramseys arrived in Wichita in early 1930, the airport had a brick and steel hangar, a concrete apron, and fencing around the cleared hayfield, but no real runways.

Nonetheless, Wichitans kept flying. Whatever the red-tape-entangled bureaucrats couldn't accomplish, men like Clyde Cessna and Walter Beech did on their own to lead the way skyward.

By April 1930 Nelle, Nadine, and Ed had settled down in a small house just east of downtown Wichita, about five miles from what was soon to be the Beech Aircraft Company. The move to Wichita didn't have a settling effect on Nadine. Obediently, she began attending the American Business College, taking a two-year secretarial and bookkeeping course to further her career options, but she didn't stop seeing Harold Honn. The situation quickly became a deadlock between stubborn Nadine and her equally insistent mother. Nelle had tolerated Harold for long enough, she felt, and now

that they were living in another city, this whole childish fling ought to have been over. It seemed to Nelle that Nadine was determined to throw her life away on this boy, but the more Nelle objected, the more Nadine wanted him.

As for Nadine, she knew her mother would never give her blessing to a marriage to Harold, so she decided to take matters into her own hands. To Nelle's utter horror, she and Harold ran off and got married. The date was August 23, 1930, five days before Nadine's nineteenth birthday.

Nelle was furious and insisted that Nadine get an annulment before she had children and it would be too late to do so. It must have been painful, that conversation, mother to daughter, about Nelle's hopes and disappointments in Nadine. Maybe Nadine knew that if she stayed married to Harold, her relationship with Nelle would be forever changed, perhaps ended. In any case, she agreed to end her relationship with him; it seemed the marriage was over just as soon as it had begun. Her divorce was finally legalized, almost two years to her wedding day, in August 1932.

Unlike Nadine, Ed had taken to Wichita immediately, happy to be out of El Dorado, where people had whispered about him and his father's disgrace behind his back. He had grown into a strong, somewhat stocky young man with a short fuse and a propensity for getting into brawls.

He was also surprisingly light on his feet and had a good sense of rhythm, and this in particular had attracted the notice of Wichita's young ladies. In short, Ed was a terrific dancer. As a teenager, he developed a reputation as a charmer and a "swell." He spent his evenings working at the Palms nightclub, getting paid on the side to teach awkward bachelors how to dance the foxtrot and paso doble.

He was also entangled in the bootlegging business. Although Prohibition ended nationally with the passing of the Twenty-First Amendment in December 1933, it was still enforced in many states, Kansas included. Ed and some of his friends had made the acquaintance of a bootlegger, and they bought from him whatever he could smuggle across the state line from Oklahoma—whiskey, gin, or simply moonshine. Ed drank as his sister had when she was a teenager; he drank to forget his father and to avoid thinking about his future.

Meanwhile, there was scarcely a society family in town that wasn't familiar with the Ramseys. This was partly because Nelle had become quite a prominent businesswoman, having shifted her attention from beauty par-

lors to the new industries of cosmetology and dermatology. Despite her lack of a formal medical education, she taught herself about the newest technologies in these fields, just as she had done in the 1920s with Marcel waves. In the early 1930s, after the governor appointed her to the post of president of the Kansas State Board of Cosmetology, she began lecturing widely.

But the other reason the Ramseys were known around town was because Nadine had fallen in love again—this time with flying.

Throughout the first half of the 1930s, while Wichita was dragging its feet to finish the municipal airport, aviation fever was still running high. The site of the incomplete airport—the hangar and skeleton of the administration building—was something of a curiosity to Wichitans, a cheap place to hang out. Even though passengers were inconvenienced by the hangar's woefully inadequate facilities, air traffic still moved heavily through the city. Many locals fell into the habit of milling around near the runway fields, hoping to catch a glimpse of a movie star or maybe even Charles Lindbergh.

In *Prairie Runways* Susan Thompson explains: "In the dark days of the Depression, a trip to the airport offered free entertainment and a chance to escape the city's summer heat. Families laid out blankets and slept on the cool grass; the airport had been built on one of the highest points in Sedgwick County, and people flocked there for the same reason the buffalo had over the centuries—to enjoy the area's cooling breezes."[6]

Perhaps it was lying in that very grass, watching the comings and goings of men in silk scarves, the takeoffs and landings of silver birds, that Nadine first became enamored with the idea of actually climbing into a plane herself and joining that elite, winged fraternity. Then again, maybe the desire had been in her all along. Flying appealed to Nadine's passionate and reckless nature.

Especially in those early days, flying attracted a certain kind of personality, one exemplified by men like Walter Beech. Pilots were natural thrillseekers, people who rushed to live on the edge. They had to be; flying was extremely perilous and highly unpredictable. Farney notes: "The airplanes of [the 1920s] resembled box kites: sticks braced with wire and covered with fabric. Their engines seized up. Their fuel lines clogged. Parts blew off in mid-flight. Pilots, flying by the seat of their pants, got lost, were blown off course, came to grief when they miscalculated their takeoff or landing

speeds. They took hair-raising chances."[7] Indeed, Clyde Cessna crashed more than a dozen times as he was teaching himself to fly. However, to someone like Nadine, the incredible risk associated with flying was far from a deterrent; it was, in fact, a draw.

On the other hand, Nadine's deep longing to fly presented her with a unique problem faced by many women of her time: there were things women simply didn't do. This was especially true of flying. Women pilots weren't completely unheard of, but they made up only a tiny fraction of licensed pilots nationwide.[8]

Fortunately for Nadine, one of these rare birds had already set for her a high-flying example. Louise McPhetridge Thaden was a local celebrity, an Arkansas-born aviatrix with strong ties to the Wichita area after earning her pilot's license in 1927 and joining Travel Air. Born in 1905, she was six years older than Nadine, and she was a friend of Amelia Earhart. In 1928 she set a world record for the women's altitude mark in the skies over San Francisco. A year later, she set the women's endurance record. In both endeavors, she was sponsored and supported by Travel Air—in other words, by Walter and Olive Ann Beech.

Olive Ann believed passionately that women were more than capable as pilots, and it had been her idea to sponsor Thaden, although Walter liked Louise too. In her memoir *High, Wide, and Frightened*, Thaden recounts several interactions in which Walter Beech joked with and teased her and jovially called her "fella."[9]

Nadine had the same kind of ready-for-anything personality as Louise and knew the Beeches, too, through Nelle. Having made up her mind to fly, she set about finding an instructor who was willing to teach girls and, of course, getting access to a plane. Although the Wichita Municipal Airport remained disorganized and unfinished, aspiring pilots were still learning to fly there. Private businesses weren't hindered at all by a lack of city funding. Beech Aircraft was thriving, and Nadine headed over there to see if the Beeches would lend her a wing.

Nadine didn't expect to fly for free, however. Flying in the 1930s was an expensive hobby, which is why many of the first and most famous aviators came from upper-middle- or upper-class families. (Earhart's grandfather, for example, was a bank president and a federal judge. Lindbergh's father was a congressman.) By now, thanks to Nelle's success, the Ramseys were not

Nadine beside the Velie Monocoupe after soloing, Wichita, ca. 1936

as financially strained as they had been in the late 1920s, but Nadine knew there wouldn't be money to spare—or, as Nelle would probably deem it, waste—on flying lessons. If she wanted to fly, Nadine realized, she would have to pay for it herself. Luckily, she had a job. Since 1932 she had been working as a secretary for the Kansas State Cosmetologists Association and in 1934, at twenty-three, had earned a secretarial and bookkeeping certificate from the American Business College, where Olive Ann Beech had also studied.

One of Nadine's responsibilities at the state's cosmetology association was assisting in the promotion of that organization's yearly conventions, and she was also the editor and advertising manager of its official publication. Unfortunately, this job meant that, in a way, she was also working for Nelle, who, Nadine knew, would strongly disapprove of flying lessons. But as she did at other times in her life, Nadine simply went ahead and did what she wanted. Ed confirms in his memoir: "Unlike me, Nadine was driven

by a purposefulness that pointed her energies and propelled her ambition. Every evening after work she slipped secretly down to the little airfield at the Beechcraft factory to take flying lessons. It was her passion, and so unorthodox in the Kansas of that day that she swore me not to tell Mother for fear of scandal."[10]

Of course, Nelle was bound to find out eventually. News of a pretty red-haired girl pilot could hardly be kept secret in a town like Wichita, and by the time Nadine was ready to solo—after only six and a half hours of instruction—reporters had caught wind of it. By then, in March 1936, Nadine had switched over to lessons at Cessna airfield and was learning from a twenty-seven-year-old Oklahoman named Bill Vacin. She took off in a Velie Monocoupe, soloed and landed magnificently, and climbed out onto the runway. Delighted by the calls of a photographer from the *Wichita Beacon*, she posed, windswept and grinning, beside the plane.[11]

Nadine knew that Nelle would see the photo in the paper, but she was too elated to care. She was flying; that was all that mattered. She was free.

In the mid-1930s, the American press was in the midst of an unbridled love affair with "firsts." The Depression, then approaching its one-decade mark, had left families, particularly in the middle of the country, hungry for a sense of national pride. Starving citizens in the Dust Bowl, like many of the Ramseys' former neighbors in El Dorado, were driven westward or struggled through devastating drought.

Working-class people clung to news articles about the triumphs of early national pioneers in every arena. In 1931 Jane Addams became the first American woman to win the Nobel Peace Prize for her work in Chicago's slums. At the 1936 Summer Olympic Games in Berlin, African American athlete Jesse Owens sprinted and leaped his way to four gold medals—a singular American victory that dominated headlines worldwide. And in 1937 Walt Disney revolutionized the entertainment industry with the release of *Snow White and the Seven Dwarfs*, his spellbinding first feature-length animated film.

Firsts in the still-new field of aviation, however, were among the country's most celebrated, thanks to the nation's ongoing aviation fever. Of course, Charles Lindbergh's many firsts, most notably his transatlantic flight a decade earlier, had changed aviation forever, and his book about it sold half a

million copies in the first half of the 1930s. Louise Thaden's firsts and the air records she seemed to stack up like poker chips were less widely known but still received a substantial amount of attention.

In addition to the first women's altitude and endurance records she had set in the late 1920s, Thaden had gone on to win the first Women's Air Derby, or "Powder Puff Derby," in 1929, then set a new endurance record in 1932 and a new speed record in 1936. In September of that year, while Nadine was busy studying and completing her fifty hours of flying for her pilot's license at the Beech and Cessna airfields, Thaden and her copilot Blanche Noyes became some of the first women to participate in the prestigious Bendix Transcontinental Speed Race, which had been open only to male pilots until that year.

Walter and Olive Ann Beech sponsored Thaden and Noyes in the race, providing them with a Staggerwing C17R for the cross-country speed dash. The two women were thrilled to compete with the men, but they didn't think they'd win, especially because they were competing against several other formidable women pilots, including their friends Amelia Earhart and her copilot, another record-breaking aviatrix named Helen Richey.

However, amazingly, Thaden and Noyes set a new East-to-West-Coast speed record—fourteen hours and fifty-four minutes—becoming the first women pilots not only to cross the finish line but also to win the overall race. Thaden received the Harmon trophy and was crowned the most "outstanding woman pilot in 1936." It was an aviation first for the record books and the press, which called her the "world's leading woman flier."[12]

Then again, not all firsts were as triumphant; some were unspeakably tragic. Lindbergh's fame proved to be a double-edged sword in 1932, when his toddler son was kidnapped from the family's home and later found murdered. Major newspapers exploited the family's horror for months, calling the kidnapping and killing "the crime of the century" and splashing Lindbergh's grief across their front pages in large type. Lindbergh and his family eventually fled to Europe to escape the attention.

Then, in 1937, Amelia Earhart, along with her copilot Fred Noonan, vanished while attempting another first: what would have been the longest flight to circle the globe, twenty-nine thousand miles at its equator. Louise Thaden mourned the loss of her friend, but to reporters a heartbreaking first was just as good as an uplifting one. Earhart's disappearance made her

the subject of a frenzied search, sold record numbers of papers, and eventually became one of the most discussed and studied unsolved mysteries in history.

Thus, when Nadine received her limited commercial pilot's license in April 1937, some local Kansas papers speculated that she had become the first licensed woman pilot in Wichita and even, some said, in the state. A first was a first, in terms of headlines, even if it actually wasn't or couldn't be proved. Moreover, while technically it was true that Nadine was the first Wichita woman to get her commercial pilot's license, she was hardly the city's only aviatrix at the time. Following the Bendix race, Thaden herself accepted a job from Walter and Olive Ann Beech and moved back to Wichita to work for Beech Aircraft.

It was true, however, that as a woman flier Nadine was in very sparse company. She definitely was the first woman admitted into the Wichita chapter of the National Aeronautic Association, becoming the chapter's secretary-treasurer and participating in regional air shows as a stunt pilot. In these breathtaking shows, she often flew an open-cockpit biplane, following in the tradition of daredevil barnstormers of the previous decade. She performed harrowing maneuvers, like loop-the-loops and barrel rolls, much to the delight of her viewers, especially young children.

Victor Murdock, the *Wichita Eagle*'s managing editor, observed:

A six-year-old of this generation who would be cold to a spring buggy, who would flatly refuse to enthuse over a new automobile model, instantly will grow glamorous over an airplane—any airplane. The tots learn to tell the make of a plane by the cut of its rudder before the kindergarten gets the alphabet to them. As a dashboard identified a buggy to grandfather and a hood labeled a motor car to father, so the tail-feathers tell the plane's name to grandson.[13]

Nadine was especially delighted to perform for Wichita's flocks of enthusiastic young airplane fans. She traveled around the state too, joining the All-Kansas Air Tours as a special representative of the *Wichita Beacon*. All in all, she was truly happy.

Although at first Nelle had been upset upon learning that her daughter was becoming a pilot, she soon managed to make her peace with it. Perhaps

she thought Nadine was going through a phase and might someday choose a different profession, but Nelle also recognized her daughter's pioneering spirit—she was a Ramsey, after all—and eventually grew proud of her achievements.

Ed was another story. While Nadine had found her passion in flying, Ed had become more and more aimless. He continued drinking and courting Wichita's young women, and Nelle worried about him immensely. Nadine was now a trailblazing woman in a growing, cutting-edge industry. Ed had no plans. Nelle wasn't the only one worried about Ed; many of her friends in Wichita society, including Walter Beech, were also concerned about his future. In fact, Walter had a suggestion for Nelle: Ed could be sent to the Oklahoma Military Academy, a school with a grand cavalry tradition. Nelle immediately saw the appeal of Walter's idea and approached Ed with it.

In his memoir, Ed wrote, "It was a calculated gesture, for [my mother] knew I was interested in martial things. . . . I loved horses, she knew this also." Ed had always loved horses. He and Nadine had learned to ride when they were young, and growing up Ed looked forward to his visits to the Ramsey and Cozad farms in Illinois, not only because they reunited him with family, but also because they gave him the opportunity to ride: "Riding was for me a release, a chance to merge my energies with the power of the horse, a challenge to master both the animal and myself. . . . Riding was a risk that I relished and the kind of freedom that my restless nature craved. Now mother was offering me both what I wanted and needed: horses and discipline."[14]

What planes were to Nadine, so horses were to Ed. Ed thought about the offer for only a short time, then accepted. In the summer of 1934, he left to attend the Oklahoma Military Academy in Claremore, Oklahoma. Relieved that his future was in good hands, Nelle turned her attention back to her own business. She had been promoted from president of the Kansas State Board of Cosmetology to president of the National Cosmetologists Association. Since she and Nadine were both frequently traveling and Ed was now away at school, she decided to move out of their little home and into the heart of downtown Wichita. In the mid-1930s, she rented a trim, stylish suite in the Hotel Lassen and opened a clinic, which she operated in two rooms adjoining her apartment.

At the time, the Hotel Lassen was the premier hotel in downtown Wichita—a large, lovely eleven-story building erected in 1918 on the corner of Market and First Streets. Named for prominent Wichita flour miller and hotelier Henry Lassen, the hotel was a striking combination of modern commercial and second renaissance revival styles, featuring two-story terracotta Corinthian pillars around its base and ornamented windows.

When it was built, the Lassen was the tallest building in Wichita and the largest hotel in Kansas. It was known as Kansas's Finest Hotel, a moniker that the hotel used for the call letters of its own radio station in the 1930s. Some of the many celebrities that passed through it during this time included William Jennings Bryan, John Philip Sousa, Sergei Rachmaninoff, Knute Rockne, Jack Dempsey, Will Rogers, Rudolph Valentino, Al Jolson, and of course Charles Lindbergh and Amelia Earhart. Nelle's clinic, therefore, was in an area of bustling and upscale traffic, attracting locals and visitors alike.[15]

Having reached the end of what she could teach herself about dermatology, Nelle hired the famous Hungarian cosmetologist Ludvic Aeros and his associate and brought them to Wichita to lecture on dermatology. With their help, she launched the Ramsey Dermatology Clinic, providing the latest technology in facials and other beauty treatments to the wealthiest Wichitans and hotel guests. Her clients stayed at the Lassen for the duration of their treatments, which typically lasted from ten to fourteen days. Nelle built her business—and her home—right in the heart of a Wichita at last beginning to pull itself out of the Depression.

The Wichita Municipal Airport's journey to completion was long and arduous. After construction on the airport had stalled during the financial quagmire of the early 1930s, the city lobbied the federal government for grants, trying to get a piece of President Franklin D. Roosevelt's New Deal in 1933. City leaders also continued to wrestle over budgets, blueprints, and contractors, but they eventually managed to cobble together the funding to restart construction on the airport's administration building.

Even while it was being built, however, the airport's needs were changing. Air traffic through Wichita was growing exponentially. When the administration building—complete with a multipaneled decorative frieze commemorating Charles Lindbergh's transatlantic flight—at last opened

Hotel Lassen, Wichita, 1935 (Wichita-Sedgwick County Historical Museum)

on March 30, 1935, plans were already underway to build a new hangar and put in some proper runways for the larger passenger flights now coming through the city, replacing the prairie grass landing strips that now dotted the landscape. City leaders, desperately and creatively looking for ways to keep building, argued that the US military should pay to help expand the

Nelle's studio portrait, which helped to publicize her dermatology clinic at the Hotel Lassen, mid-1930s

Aerial view, Wichita Municipal Airport, ca. 1945 (Kansas Aviation Museum)

airport because of its vital location—for mail delivery, protection against invasion, interstate commerce, and use by the flying public. The federal government agreed, and the Wichita Municipal Airport was ready for updates.

Meanwhile, having received her pilot's license, Nadine began to wonder how she could help to clear the runway for others with the same goal. Not everyone could learn to fly as she had—by researching at the public library and flying airplanes around, courtesy of her mother's friends at local aircraft companies. With the Wichita Municipal Airport at last functioning, she decided to help organize classes for aspiring fliers. She approached her fellow NAA members with the idea, and in January 1938 the Wichita chapter opened an aviation ground school at the municipal airport.

As secretary of the school, Nadine arranged the curriculum: aerodynamics, theory of flight, airplane engines, navigation and meteorology, parachutes, and aerobatics. Along with applying her aviation knowledge and skills, she also could exercise her fun-loving spirit as chair of the school's dance committee, organizing dances twice a year at such prestigious venues as Wichita's 400 Club.[16] Naturally, most of the school's early students were young men, but the NAA trained a teenager named Mary Chance.

Chance was a native Wichitan who had fallen in love with flying in 1935 after being taken on an airplane ride by Clyde Cessna. Right away, she started saving her babysitting money for flying lessons. In her autobiography, *A Lifetime of Chances*, she wrote,

> As a young girl, long before I ever thought about becoming a pilot, I had a recurring dream. In this dream, I would either be walking or roller-skating on the sidewalk. Then I would flap my arms and fly about six feet off the ground. I remember how much fun this seemed to be, and then I would wake up to find it was only a dream. But the dream became reality.[17]

Upon passing her ground school courses, Chance soloed on December 27, 1938, the day after her nineteenth birthday. Just as Nadine had followed Louise Thaden into the air, Mary Chance (later Mary Chance VanScyoc) followed Nadine, eventually becoming the nation's first female civilian air traffic controller.

After successfully launching the NAA ground school, Nadine eagerly looked for new and challenging opportunities to fly. Then, in May 1938, National Air Mail Week came along.

PART II

EARNING HER WINGS

On Monday, May 16, 1938, the skies over Wichita were crowded with heavy, mottled clouds that sent rain splattering onto the city's runways and its bustling downtown streets. Nadine Ramsey paused beneath the marquee of the Orpheum Theater to survey the hurrying throngs of shoppers and businessmen jostling like ducks beneath their umbrellas. She caught a snippet of someone's conversation— "air mail"—then darted back into the crush of people, heading north, dodging puddles in her high heels.

National Air Mail Week, in celebration of the airmail's twentieth anniversary, was something of a marketing stunt, Nadine thought, and everyone knew it. But the stunt seemed to be working. People speculated excitedly about the upcoming week's events, and schoolchildren eagerly scribbled letters to their faraway friends and relatives. Even Nelle was sending something—a package to Nadine's Aunt Winnie and cousin Barbara in Illinois. Special flights had been scheduled across the country all week from May 15 to May 21, and in most places the weather was cooperating. But in Kansas, along the route between Wichita and Wellington, where Nadine planned to fly on Thursday, the skies were grim.

As she hurried up the white limestone steps of the imposing US Post Office and Courthouse, Nadine wondered if she should have stopped at the Hotel Lassen for a coffee and to see Nelle, who worked and lived there too. Oh well, it was only two blocks south; she could stop in afterward.

Heaving open the heavy courthouse doors, she stepped inside, shook off her coat, and paused a moment to stare at the newly finished murals in the lobby. Both depicted the mail's history on the prairie, but Nadine preferred the more cheerful mural on the lobby's western wall: a wide, colorful quilt of Kansas farmland, with columns of sunflowers and corn in the foreground, surrounded by farmers and postal workers in overalls. Her eye was drawn in particular to two children standing by a mailbox—maybe a brother and sister—both their faces tipped toward the sky at the clear implication of an airplane flying over, the girl clutching a packet of letters, the boy waving one hand at an imaginary pilot. Nadine smiled faintly, patted her hair, and clacked on by.

Minutes later, she found herself standing face-to-face with Wichita Postmaster J. B. Riddle. Riddle was a former politician, a slender, efficient man who in 1919 had become the youngest postmaster to take that office. He walked Nadine through the solemn Oath of Mail Messengers, which would make her an official carrier of the US mail. "Repeat after me," he told her. Nadine nodded, raising her right hand, and repeated the oath in response to Riddle's prompts. Then, after signing the necessary paperwork, she adjusted her hat, touched up her lipstick, and headed back down through the rain to the Hotel Lassen to get that coffee after all.

Later that night, unbeknownst to Nadine, Riddle spoke with a local newspaper reporter, who asked him whether or not he had enough pilots for the big air mail event on Thursday, May 19. Riddle explained that he had been swearing in extra pilots, and he mentioned Nadine.

"A girl! Flying the air mail!" the reporter exclaimed, scribbling furiously. "Say, do you think she could be the first?"

Riddle considered a moment. "I don't know," he said frankly. "But that'd certainly be an honor."

"I'll say," the reporter mused, tapping a pencil on his open notepad. "One of our very own Wichita gals—the first woman to fly the mail."

CHAPTER 3

AT HOME IN THE SKY

Since its inception in May 1918, the US Air Mail had played a huge role in aviation's progress. In the airmail's first decade, the Post Office Department established a lighted night airmail route between Chicago and Cheyenne, Wyoming—one of its chief contributions to the field. In 1920, as a necessity for this route, the first radio stations were installed at seventeen airfields, an incredible leap forward in aeronautical communications.

The lighted airway also created nearly ninety new landing fields across the Midwest and western states and more than five hundred new electric and gas beacons to assist pilots with navigation at night and in bad weather. The Collier Trophy, which honored the most important contributions to the development of aeronautics, was awarded to the US Air Mail Service in 1922 for its outstanding safety record, and again in 1923 for demonstrating the practicability of night flying.[1]

In 1926 Congress passed the Air Commerce Act, which essentially transferred the responsibility of the airmail from the Post Office Department to the Department of Commerce. Now the airmail would be carried by private contractors, and all the airfields built by the Post Office Department would be transferred to their local municipalities. The Department of Commerce began accepting bids from contractors in the summer of 1927, and from that point on, airmail contracts substantially contributed to the growth of commercial aviation. This was largely because in the 1920s, it was simply more lucrative to fly packages than it was to fly people.

As Susan Thompson explains in *Prairie Runways*, "A carrier received $1,003 for 150 pounds of mail, but only $200 for a passenger weighing the same. . . . Contract Air Mail (CAM) operators mailed bricks, spare parts, and even telephone books. The postage might be $15, but they got paid twice that for hauling this merchandise. Someone joked that with all the spare parts sent on Varney Air Lines, a western US operator, an entire plane could have been built."[2] In May 1934, after a scandal in which President Roosevelt tried and failed to hand the airmail operation over to the US Army, Wichita's airmail route from Chicago to Dallas was awarded to Braniff Airways.

By 1938 the US Air Mail had routes serving every state and thirty-seven countries internationally, yet Contract Air Mail had been hit hard, as every industry had, by the Depression. In an effort to promote mail service and to recover from the disastrous 1934 scandal, Postmaster General James Farley established a National Air Mail Week (NAMW) to be held in early May, commemorating the airmail's twentieth anniversary.

The goal of NAMW's organizers was for every citizen to send or receive a letter by airmail during the week of May 15–21. A national essay contest, "Wings Across America," was held for high school students. Local postmasters promoted "the wonderful network of air lines operating day and night throughout the country, and the speed and economy with which letters and parcels may be dispatched over immense distances."[3] A new six-cent stamp debuted on Saturday, May 14, and individual cities throughout the nation were invited to create unique "cachets"—special commemorative designs and slogans to be printed on envelopes. Many were colorful tributes to their hometowns; El Dorado's cachet, for example, featured two stacked scarlet rings, or a Figure 8, containing a plane soaring over a farmhouse and an oil derrick nestled among rolling hills.

As NAMW approached, Nadine became aware that more pilots might be needed to fly the mail, especially on Thursday, May 19, when most of the large celebrations would be held. It seemed that Wichita Postmaster J. B. Riddle estimated that Kansans were responding a bit too enthusiastically to the anniversary commemoration. He was expecting at least thirty pounds of mail from each of the forty-seven larger Kansas cities and three pounds from each of nearly three hundred other small towns across the state.

With this record-high poundage, Riddle was short of pilots—and he wasn't the only one. Postmasters from all corners of the country asked local pilots to volunteer to fly special routes, mostly to service tiny towns that usually weren't reached by the airmail. Dozens of pilots nationwide, including Nadine and Marcellus M. Murdock, the publisher of the *Wichita Eagle*, were sworn in early that week to fly the mail. Many more were sworn in that busy Thursday morning for only twenty-four hours.

Nadine was asked to fly south from Wichita to Wellington, Kansas, and back, a distance of about only seventy miles round trip. Eager to report a historic first, the *Wichita Eagle* printed the headline "Wichita Aviatrix May Become First Woman to Fly U.S. Mail," calling her "one of the city's best

pilots" and quoting Postmaster Riddle, who speculated that if Nadine did indeed fly on Thursday, "it would give Wichita the honor of having what I believe is the first woman to fly the mail."[4]

The day after she was sworn in, on Tuesday, May 17, Nadine headed down to Wellington, a town of about seven thousand, to check out its landing field. Known as the Wheat Capital of the World, Wellington's NAMW blue cachet featured a bag of flour standing on a hill beside two large bushels of wheat.

Like most towns its size, Wellington didn't have regular airmail service or a proper airport; planes that visited the town for exhibitions or stunt flying landed on a parcel of land called Sykes' Field, just west of the main hub. After the rain all week, the field was now soggy. Nadine had a sinking feeling; she knew the ground would be much too rough and muddy for the twin-engine yellow Taylor Cub she was set to fly. Fortunately, the solution was close at hand—right across the street, in fact—at the Wellington golf course and its well-groomed fairways.

On Thursday, May 19, the weather finally cleared, and a headstrong sun climbed into the late spring Wichita sky. Just before noon, Nadine, clad in jodhpurs and a sweater vest, strapped herself into the yellow Cub with a fifteen-pound bag of mail postmarked for Wellington and took off. The sky's expanse was blue, infinite, and beautiful; the flight was a twenty-minute dream. As she approached the Wellington golf course, she could see that a huge crowd had gathered, and they cheered as she came in for a landing.

Nadine climbed out of the plane, smiling and waving at everyone, especially the many small children. The Wellington High School band played as the sheriff's patrol, assisted by local Boy Scouts, held back the throngs. Nelle had driven down for the occasion, and she hurried, beaming, to greet Nadine, followed by the city's mayor and postmaster, who gallantly handed Nadine a bouquet of flowers in return for the bag of mail—only a tiny fraction of the more than sixteen million letters delivered that week. After NAMW, public interest in the mail and commercial aviation surged, and a feeling of optimism imbued towns like Wellington, which still struggled in the midst of the Depression. After posing for a photo, Nadine flew back to Wichita and into journalism history.

Nadine, we know now, was *not* the first woman to fly the airmail, and neither were the other women who flew during National Air Mail Week.

Nadine and Nelle with National Air Mail Week executives in Wellington, Kansas, May 1938

Decades earlier, in 1915, an aviatrix named Marjorie Stinson had earned that distinction when she flew a route from Seguin to San Antonio, Texas. However, news of her flight—a first for women airmail pilots—was lost in the chaotic media storm surrounding World War I. By the time NAMW rolled around, the press still believed there was a title to be claimed but lacked the resources to assign it properly.

Following its first speculative story, the evening edition of the *Wichita Eagle* published a correction, calling Nadine one of "the first two" women airmail pilots and admitting that Charlotte Frye of Griffin, Georgia, also flew a route on May 19 from Atlanta to Griffin in a Beechcraft. Additionally, two Pennsylvanian pilots—Teresa James and Phyllis Burchfield—carried the mail for NAMW, as did Louise Thaden's Bendix race copilot, Blanche Noyes, in Massachusetts.[5]

There may have been more. At the time, none of these women or their local papers had any way of knowing that the others existed, which accounts for much of the speculative and false reporting of women's aviation firsts,

including those of National Air Mail Week. Women pilots were still so rare, making up just 3.5 percent of licensed pilots nationwide.[6]

While Nadine was zooming around in the skies over Kansas, Ed was thriving at the Oklahoma Military Academy. Known as the West Point of the Midwest, the academy was known for strict discipline and grand tradition. Freed from the distractions that had mired him in Wichita, Ed was transformed by the school's emphasis on honor and loyalty. But it didn't happen overnight. Ed's first year as an underclassman was marked by loneliness and conflict, and he butted heads particularly with a senior bully named Victor Whitelaw, who singled him out for torture at every opportunity. Once Whitelaw even taunted him about his sister pilot.

Ed recounted the scene in his memoir:

Whitelaw eased himself around behind me. 'I understand your sister's a flier,' he said slowly. I felt myself beginning to tremble. He leaned closer to my ear. I could hear the malicious sneer in his voice. "How about it, Ramsey . . . you think she'd take me up for a ride?"

I pressed my lips together, trying to master my anger.

"Well, Ramsey?" Whitelaw said.

"No, sir," I answered quietly.

"Oh, and why not?"

I looked him in the eyes. "Because you're a goddamn son of a bitch, sir."

For this insult, Ed was beaten up by a group of Whitelaw's friends and other upperclassmen. In response, he neither reported them to the school authorities nor backed down. Instead, he found a dead rattlesnake and got his revenge by hiding it in Whitelaw's bed. Whitelaw was horrified, defeated, and gave up bullying Ed. Ed's fellow underclassmen began to respect him as a leader—a trend that continued as he got older.[7]

At the Oklahoma Military Academy, which was primarily a cavalry school, Ed was also trained as an officer and properly learned to ride. He began to internalize the cavalry's traditions and values; to him, the cavalry meant leadership and pride. He also became obsessed with polo. Though at first Ed thought that the sport was snobbish, "the plaything of the idle rich,"

he quickly realized that it embodied all the values he was learning to cherish. He wrote, "The ostensible reason for schooling us in the sport was to sharpen our equestrian skills, improve our teamwork, and hone our spirit of competition. But inescapably the game was also an outlet for our pure unbridled verve. For me polo was the perfect blend of my native recklessness and the discipline I was acquiring. . . . Polo became my passion."

As it happened, Ed was also naturally talented at polo. When he graduated from the Oklahoma Military Academy in 1937, he enrolled at the University of Oklahoma to study law. He admitted, "The law was largely incidental. OU had a polo team."[8]

In 1939 Nadine concluded that she had hit a glass ceiling in Wichita and moved to California. For Nelle, this was a heartfelt blow; even when she disagreed with her daughter and worried about her, Nelle had never had to get along without Nadine nearby. Still, she understood ambition and loaned Nadine some money to help her get established on the West Coast. Nadine rented a small house a block from the Pacific Ocean in Manhattan Beach, on the outskirts of Los Angeles.

Like Wichita, Southern California had made a name for itself in the aviation industry. Douglas Aircraft Company was founded in Santa Monica in 1921 and achieved notoriety in 1924, when a team of army pilots circumnavigated the globe by air in Douglas airplanes. Throughout the twenties and thirties, Douglas worked closely with the US military and developed planes for the navy and the Army Air Forces as well as commercial airlines.

One of Douglas's new airplanes was the groundbreaking twin-engine Douglas Commercial 3, or DC-3. Nicknamed the Gooney Bird by pilots, the DC-3 was a fast, reliable commercial plane capable of carrying twenty-one passengers on flights longer than ever before, including cross-country and international runs. In fact, the DC-3 finally made it possible for major commercial airlines to give up flying the airmail and make money primarily carrying passengers. Trans World Airlines, Delta, American, and United ordered entire fleets of the DC-3.

Many of these planes were manufactured in El Segundo, just a stone's throw from Nadine's little bungalow. In July 1939 she got a job at Douglas and became the secretary to the sales and service manager of the El Segundo plant. She also continued flying. In early 1940 she bought a plane and be-

Cadet Ed Ramsey, Oklahoma Military Academy, 1936

gan offering flight training at what was then called Mines Field (later the Los Angeles International Airport, or LAX). At the time, most commercial flights flew in and out of Union Airport (later Burbank Airport) in Burbank or Grand Central Airport in Glendale, both north of downtown Los Angeles.

Like Douglas Aircraft, Mines Field was near Nadine's house. While flight training there, she accepted an offer as secretary at the Aero Acceptance Corporation, an aircraft financing company at the airport. There she continued to offer flight instruction on her own plane as part of her secretarial duties. But before long Nadine was ready for a new challenge. In June 1940 she was offered the dealership for Taylorcraft, maker of one of the country's most popular light planes. She began demonstration flying, soaring over Los Angeles with prospective customers in and out of all the Southern California airports.

Inevitably, as in Wichita, it was impossible for a vivacious, Titian-haired woman pilot to go unnoticed, especially one known as such a "hot flier." Nadine attended parties and hobnobbed with some of the era's most glamorous movie stars, including singer and B-movie star Roger Pryor, who was working on his twenty-fifth movie at Universal and Columbia Studios. Among her friends she also counted Laraine Day, a shy, soft-spoken Mormon actress at MGM who got her big break that year in *Calling Dr. Kildare*, starring with Lionel Barrymore and Lana Turner. She also befriended an unassuming actor and horseback rider about her own age named Dick Simmons, who in the 1950s would eventually become the biggest star of them all: the titular character of the popular syndicated TV show *Sergeant Preston of the Yukon*.

All in all, Nadine's move to California brought her everything she'd dreamed. At twenty-nine, she spent her days wearing slacks, goggles, and bright red lipstick while zooming around in slick, speedy planes, and her evenings in glittering gowns, sipping cocktails at fashionable clubs. In 1940 Nadine was flying high.

In early fall Nadine's fortune changed. She was approached by a woman named Gertrude Snow from San Diego, who wanted to surprise her husband, retired Marine Corps captain James E. Snow, by buying him a plane. Gertrude was about fifty and had little knowledge of flying herself, but Nadine was always happy to entertain a potential customer.

Stunt and racing pilot Nadine with her plane, a sport trainer she nicknamed "my pet,"
Manhattan Beach, California. Newspaper clipping, ca. 1930s

Snow suggested that they chat over lunch at the historic Warner Springs Resort on Highway 79, near her home in Lake Henshaw. Founded in 1884, the resort was a popular getaway location for Southern Californians, an old western-style ranch that offered cottages, horseback riding, golf, and hot springs. Nadine agreed, and the two women met for a meal in the resort's

lounge on a clear, beautiful day, September 2. They talked awhile, and afterward Nadine took her new client up in the small two-passenger plane to show her what it could do.

Snow was enraptured and impressed as Nadine flew them northwest toward the mountains, then banked south, making a wide circle. When she saw her house, she pointed it out to Nadine and asked Nadine to buzz it, to give her husband, James, who was working in the yard, a surprise. Nadine loved a challenge and a good prank; she grinned and swooped in low over the house, capturing Mr. Snow's attention. "Go around again!" Gertrude shouted, laughing, so Nadine obligingly brought the plane in for a second pass.

The crash happened instantaneously. A downdraft seized the little plane and shoved it into the upper branches of a tall oak tree, crumpling the aircraft before it fell to the ground. Nadine had had no time to react. Both women's legs were crushed and mangled, but Nadine was so dazed, she didn't even cry.

James Snow rushed to the downed plane and, with remarkable presence of mind, cut the ignition wires to prevent it from catching fire. It was the shock of his life when he saw Gertrude in the wreckage; he'd had no idea she was flying that day.

Nadine and Gertrude were rushed to the hospital in the nearby town of Julian, then Nadine was transferred at the request of her friends, including Laraine Day and Dick Simmons, to a hospital in Los Angeles. There, the doctors wanted to remove one of Nadine's severely damaged legs, but Nadine, moaning and thrashing, insisted that she would rather die if she could never fly again. Still, the doctors were skeptical that her leg could be saved. One of her friends, claiming to speak for the Ramsey family, definitively refused to let the doctors amputate. Then another friend called Nelle, and Nelle called Ed.

Upon hearing that Nadine was hurt, Ed walked out on his classes at OU, borrowed Nelle's aging yellow Chrysler, and drove to California. When he arrived, he learned that the doctors had managed to save Nadine's leg but that she might never walk again. Her back was broken, as were most of her ribs, and she had several concussions; in a full leg cast from ankle to hip, she would need care for months. Ed officially dropped out of law school and moved into her bungalow to help take care of her as she recovered.

Nadine recovering under Ed's care at her home in Manhattan Beach, 1940–1941

It was a trying time for the siblings. Nadine's injuries at first tortured her with constant pain and left her bed-ridden. Ed, still a bachelor, was unused to cooking and cleaning, and Nadine hated to be dependent on anyone. The wearying, rocky road to recovery made the brother and sister fight viciously.

Still, they had been through hard times before. Ed later wrote:

> Through the difficult days with Father, we had developed the habit of supporting each other. And through all our battles we had emerged victorious, not just from pride, but from spite as well, for neither of us wanted to be the first to surrender. It was a strength born of a deep hurt that we had suffered together, expressed in a determination to preserve each other against the odds. Neither of us would let the other go down, but in the process we spared each other nothing in the way of anger and stubbornness.[9]

Ed told Nadine he would get her back into a plane, even if he had to drag her by the hair.

By Christmas, just four months after the accident, Nadine was walking again. By the end of January 1941, she was ready to fly. Far from being shaken and scarred by the crash, she was eager to get back into a plane above all else. On a cloudy February morning, Ed drove her to an airfield on the coast where she had arranged to fly a little Monocoupe. Despite a small cast that hobbled her leg, with Ed's help she fit herself into the cockpit, then taxied onto the runway and took off into the wind. Ed smiled, watching the plane climb into the misty air. Once again, Nadine was free.

Gertrude Snow was not as lucky. After the crash, she was moved, in critical condition, to Mercy Hospital in San Diego, where one of her legs was amputated. Both her arms were broken. Two days after the crash, government inspectors visited the oak tree hit by Nadine's plane and examined the wreckage. They determined first that without James Snow's quick thinking to cut the ignition wires, the plane certainly would have caught fire and burned both women before they could have been rescued, and second, that Nadine's unawareness of the downdraft was at fault for the crash.

The Snows weren't satisfied by this assessment. In the fall of 1941, Gertrude sued Nadine, accusing her of drinking on the day of the crash. Some papers ran with the story, including the *San Francisco Union*, which headlined a one-column item, "Sued Aviatrix Denies Drinking." Nadine, called upon to testify in the civil case, asserted that although she did have lunch with her client in the Warner Springs Lounge, she hadn't taken a drink. She also maintained that the crash had been caused by the downdraft that had forced the plane into the tree. Gertrude insisted that she and Nadine had both had at least one drink, and several other witnesses reported that the women had spent "considerable time" in the lounge, but none of them was able to testify as to exactly how many drinks were ordered. In the end, the judge awarded Gertrude more than twenty-eight thousand dollars in damages; she sued two airplane companies as well.[10]

Nadine surely felt pity for Gertrude; she had lost a leg and, like Nadine, had been through months of grueling, painful recovery. Nadine also must have understood Gertrude's desire to blame someone, anyone, for the tragedy. But the civil case was ugly and utterly humiliating. While it was happening, Nadine didn't want to talk about it—not even to Ed or Nelle. After it was over, she hardly ever mentioned it again.

CHAPTER 4

AT WAR

Meanwhile, the world was already at war. In early September 1939, Adolf Hitler and the German army invaded Poland; Britain and France declared war on Germany in return. Fierce fighting followed, leading to France's surrender in June 1940. In September, while Nadine and Ed fought the battle of Nadine's recovery, Italy and Japan signed the Tripartite Pact and joined Germany, forming the Axis Powers—an act that would inevitably pull almost the entire world into its second, global bloody war.

In the United States, President Franklin D. Roosevelt desperately tried to support the Allied war effort in Europe without fully drawing the United States into the conflict. In the fall of 1940, Congress passed the Lend-Lease Act, committing US aid and equipment to Britain and its allies. In the summer of 1941, the United States established an oil and gas embargo, cutting off all exports of these valuable commodities to Japan. These acts were frantic measures to preserve American isolationism, to keep the country, still recovering from the Depression, out of a war that would surely change everything about the American way of life.

Nevertheless, the US military had known for years that it had better prepare for war. In particular, the army realized that, like World War I, this new war would be fought in the air and had created an aerial component of its forces, the Army Air Corps (AAC), in 1926. If drawn into this new war, the United States would need more pilots. In June 1939 the government established the Civilian Pilot Training Program, which trained pilots at colleges and universities throughout the nation. The program was organized into seventy-two-hour ground school classes and thirty-five- to fifty-hour flight classes of ten students per class—nine men and, if one wanted to sign up, one woman. Young women nationwide eagerly rushed to get the few available spots; for many of them, CPTP provided the rare opportunity to learn to fly. Along with thousands of other college students, they expanded the country's pilot pool dramatically.

After the 1940 Tripartite Pact, Congress passed the Selective Training and Service Act, requiring the all men ages eighteen to twenty-five to regis-

ter for the draft. In peacetime, this meant that only nine hundred thousand men could be drafted, but plenty of young men were eager to enlist voluntarily. Ed was one of them.

Once Nadine returned to demonstrating planes, Ed had no strong desire to return to Kansas. Instead, he joined the army. He was commissioned as a second lieutenant in the Eleventh Cavalry Regiment near San Diego. The age of the cavalry, though, was drawing to an end. After World War I, men on horseback simply couldn't compete with motor vehicles or tanks. Though the army ordered most cavalry units to give up their horses and train on other equipment, Ed was determined to keep riding as long as he could.

In April 1941 he volunteered for transfer to the Twenty-Sixth Cavalry, Philippine Scouts, one of the army's few remaining mounted regiments. At the time, he was thinking only of his own happiness—the Twenty-Sixth, the "country club of the Army," had a polo team. He didn't even know exactly where the Philippine islands were. When he mentioned this as a joke to the officer processing his transfer, the man didn't smile. "They're damn near Japan," he said pointedly in return.[1] After saying goodbye to Nelle and Nadine, Ed shipped out in the summer of 1941, just after his twenty-fourth birthday. He was stationed at Fort Stotsenburg on Luzon, the Philippines' largest island and home of its capital, Manila.

Ed wasn't disappointed by the Twenty-Sixth regiment; it was indeed a relic of the grand old cavalry age. As General Douglas MacArthur had been placed in command of the Philippine army's undertrained forces, cavalry troops typically consisted of American officers in charge of Filipino privates. The officers, Ed included, trained their units strictly, running drills and practicing maneuvers with the enlisted Filipino men, all the while surrounded by Luzon's exotic beauty.

Ed found the work intense but rewarding. In the evenings, the officers changed into pristine, white, high-collared uniforms and danced the night away with enchanting Filipinas in the officers club. Ed quickly gained a reputation not only as one of the stars of the Twenty-Sixth's polo team but also as one of its best dancers, becoming again, in some ways, the swell he had been in Wichita.

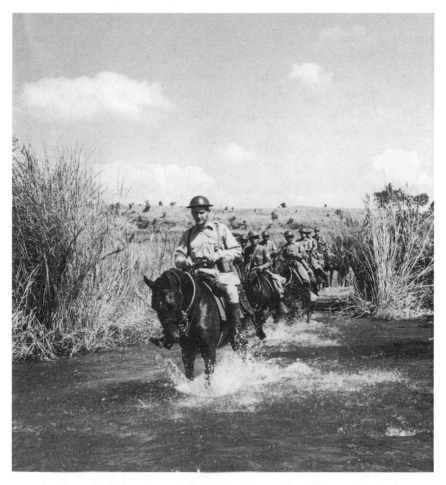

Captain John Wheeler leading American and Filipino soldiers of the Twenty-Sixth Cavalry Regiment (Philippine Scouts) in Luzon, Philippines, just before war with Japan, 1941 (The LIFE Picture Collection/Getty Images)

On December 7, 1941, about ten hours before dawn in Hawaii, Ed rode with his team in a polo match against the Manila Polo Club, a hard-fought game the Americans ultimately couldn't win. They didn't care. The men of the Twenty-Sixth Cavalry believed they were invincible. That evening, the officers club hosted one of its most lavish and raucous parties yet.

Then the world changed overnight. When Ed awoke the next morning, more than two thousand American sailors had died in Hawaii, and the United States was at war. The Japanese bombed Clark Airfield at Fort Stotsenburg that very day, December 8, obliterating most of its planes and crippling the American forces on Luzon. In command of his small unit, G Troop, Ed was hastily sent to a bay on Luzon's northern shore. His assignment there was to watch for the inevitable Japanese invasion.

Nadine was in the air over Long Beach, demonstrating a plane to a potential buyer, when news of the attack on Pearl Harbor came in on the radio. She was ordered down, as all civilian planes on the West Coast were being grounded immediately. Nadine felt sick with fear; she knew what was happening. The United States was going to war, so Ed was at war too. After landing at the first opportunity, Nadine's buyer declared that he would take the plane. She sold it to him in a daze of worry, then, realizing she was stranded at Long Beach Airport, hitched a ride back to Culver City, where her car was parked.

On Luzon US forces were in trouble from the start. Without sufficient air cover, the American and Philippine armies were mercilessly strafed and bombed by Japanese planes. After Pearl Harbor the US Navy simply had few resources to defend the islands against Japanese ships. A Japanese force of about forty-three thousand invaded at Lingayen Gulf on December 22, 1941. The Americans were disorganized and unable to offer any serious resistance, and within two days General MacArthur implemented a plan to withdraw all the US and Philippine troops onto the Bataan Peninsula.

To delay the Japanese while the Americans retreated, MacArthur sent forward, among other troops, the Twenty-Sixth Cavalry. Ed was fighting at the front. By New Year's, Japanese General Masaharu Homma had realized what MacArthur had in mind, but every Japanese attempt to cut off the Americans' retreat into Bataan was repulsed.

MacArthur's delaying tactics were vital but costly. In early January 1942, a series of small battles fought at the front lines near Layac devastated the cavalry. The Twenty-Sixth was now reduced to only 450 men. Ed's soldiers and their horses fell before the onslaught of Japanese artillery, and the American troops began to suffer from hunger and inadequate supplies.

At one point, Ed's G Troop was cut off from the main body of the Twenty-

Sixth and was forced to forge through the jungle for days, trying to find its way back without being captured. Luckily, the men met villagers who provided food and guidance; it was as though the whole of the Philippines was resisting the Japanese forces. At last, hungry and exhausted, they rejoined their regiment, where they heard the happy news that MacArthur's retreat had been successful. Bataan had become a bastion, a peninsula of about four hundred square miles now sheltering more than a hundred thousand troops and civilians.

After a brief rest, G Troop, one of the last still on horseback, was ordered to patrol a road winding along Bataan's west coast between towns Olongapo to the north and Mauban to the south. Along this road was only one small village, Morong, a tiny cluster of huts and one stone building, a Catholic church. On January 16, though his men were again ordered to the rear for a rest, Ed, already familiar with the jungle terrain, volunteered to assist Captain John Wheeler's E Troop with reconnaissance in the area. No sooner had he spoken up than he was recognized by General Jonathan Wainwright, who had been the referee of the December 7 polo match at Fort Stotsenburg. Wainwright ordered Ed and Captain Wheeler to ride immediately up to Morong and attempt to occupy the village until a larger division of the Philippine army could properly secure it. Wearily, Ed and Wheeler obeyed and mounted up.

From the east, Ed's platoon led the way into Morong, across the single footbridge over a narrow river that ran along the north side of the village. All was quiet; the village seemed deserted. Ed had sent two point men forward to investigate when suddenly an explosion and a burst of gunfire sounded from the north. An advance guard of Japanese infantrymen in brown uniforms plunged across the river into Morong. Ed's reaction was pure instinct; if the Americans and Filipinos were to have any chance, he had to break up that line of infantrymen, and only a charge could do that. Almost instinctively, he brought up his arm and yelled, "Charge!" The men of E Troop kicked their horses and flung themselves forward, galloping, bent over the horses' necks, yelling and firing from the saddles. Only a few Japanese soldiers returned fire; most fled in confusion, stumbling back across the river or running for the swamps.

Once through the line, Ed and his men dismounted and pulled out their rifles, picking off fleeing soldiers, then returned to the village to try to clean

out soldiers who were hiding in huts. Soon the Japanese were lobbing mortar shells into the town; explosions sent men and horses scattering in all directions. At last, Captain Wheeler's platoons rode in to reinforce Ed's, and together they were able to hold off the Japanese forces until late afternoon, when the First Regular Division of the Philippine Army came up to secure the village.

Ed was reeling. At first, he didn't realize he'd been wounded; a piece of shrapnel had punctured his left knee. Wheeler had been hit too. Ed was ordered to the rear, and his commanding officer made sure he went this time. Volunteer or not, there wouldn't be any more dangerous missions for Ed until he received some medical treatment and long-overdue rest. For his actions at the battle that day, Ed would receive the Silver Star Medal.

Though he had no way to know it at the time, Lieutenant Edwin Price Ramsey had just led the last horse-mounted cavalry charge in US Army history.[2]

Although the CPTP had created thousands of young new aviators across the United States, the country still didn't have enough pilots. Now that America was officially at war, the army was training young men for combat flying as quickly as possible, but there were plenty of flying jobs that didn't involve combat. As US factories produced sleek new military aircraft, those planes had to be moved wherever they were needed, which changed as the war progressed: first, trainer aircraft were redirected to flight schools and training bases; in 1943 and later, fighter planes and bombers were relocated to modification sites where they were upgraded with improved weaponry, bigger fuel tanks, and enhanced communications technology; and finally, fighters and bombers were sent from embarkation points overseas. One of the army's greatest needs was for pilots to ferry these planes from one place to another safely and efficiently. Who could it get to do those jobs?

After the Lend-Lease Act of 1941, the AAC, under the command of General Henry "Hap" Arnold, had formed the Air Corps Ferrying Command (ACFC), with Colonel Robert Olds in charge. It was the ACFC's specific job to move aircraft domestically and overseas to "lend" to Britain. Most of the pilots who served in the ACFC, some of whom were specifically trained only to ferry aircraft, were civilians. After all, theoretically, anybody who could fly could do the job.

Just a few months later, in June 1941, the AAC became the AAF, and General Arnold continued as commanding general. Now a division of the AAF, the ACFC was placed under the command of General Harold George (General Olds's prevailing health problems had prevented him from remaining in command). When the United States entered the war in late 1941, General George faced the new, enormous challenge of ferrying planes in wartime with a shortage of pilots. Britain's version of the Ferrying Command, the Air Transport Auxiliary (ATA), faced a similar dilemma.

Women pilots, of course, were the answer.

One woman to propose a solution to the ferry pilot shortage was a celebrity aviatrix named Jacqueline Cochran. Born Bessie Lee Pittman in 1906, Cochran, known as Jackie, was a ruthlessly ambitious beauty who had begun her uphill climb to fame from poverty in northern Florida. At age ten she walked barefoot into the local hair salon and begged for a job. By twenty-six, she was one of the best hairdressers in New York City.

Cochran was blond and fiercely independent, the kind of woman who knew how to impress and intimidate, who walked avenues to power in alligator heels. While making the social rounds among New York's elite, she met businessman and Hollywood mogul Floyd Bostwick Odlum, the CEO of RKO Pictures and then one of the ten wealthiest men in the world. Odlum helped Cochran launch a line of cosmetics, and he married her in 1936.

Becoming the younger wife of a millionaire (she was thirty and he was forty-four) would have been enough to shove Cochran into the limelight, but the southern-born social mountaineer wasn't content to be simply a rich cover girl. She had her sights set on more permanent fame. Jackie Cochran was after firsts.

Cochran had learned to fly in the early 1930s in New York. As with Louise Thaden and Amelia Earhart, the press loved her and gladly used her exploits and her beautiful face to sell papers. In return, Cochran thrived on the attention. She won the Bendix Transcontinental Speed Race in 1938, two years after Thaden, and she set new speed and altitude records in 1940. Every year between 1938 and 1941, the Women's National Aviation Association gave her the outstanding woman pilot award. The press called her the Speed Queen and the best female pilot in the United States.[3]

On September 28, 1939, Cochran wrote to First Lady Eleanor Roosevelt,

Jacqueline "Jackie" Cochran, ca. 1943 (Courtesy WASP Archive, Texas Woman's University, Denton, TX)

proposing that women pilots be trained to ferry military aircraft. During the 1930s Roosevelt had developed a friendship with Amelia Earhart and had obtained a student permit to fly, which she never pursued. On April 4, 1938, she had presented Cochran the Harmon trophy for "the most distinguished achievement of the year by an aviatrix." The First Lady's interest in flying, combined with her support for women's rights and Cochran's personal relationship with the Roosevelts, paved the way for Cochran to work directly with General Arnold and the AAF to advocate using women pilots during wartime.[4]

As the United States hadn't yet entered the war, the pilot shortage wasn't dire enough for General Arnold to agree to Cochran's suggestion. However, in Britain, the ATA, which was already recruiting civilian women, jumped at Cochran's idea. With the war drawing nearer, she decided to round up some of the country's best women pilots and take them to England to work for the ATA. One of the names on her list was Nadine Ramsey.

In January 1942 Nelle and Nadine were both extremely worried about Ed. His last letter to Nelle from Luzon had arrived in Wichita on November 20, 1941, and there had been no word since. Nonetheless, every day the news reminded them of the grim situation on Bataan: American troops there were starving, suffering from tropical diseases, and facing inevitable defeat. Nadine and Nelle's best hope was that Ed would survive the siege and eventually be taken alive as a prisoner of war. It wasn't much to hope for. Nadine gave up the lease on her bungalow, closed her aircraft dealership, and flew home to Wichita to be with Nelle. The two women, strong and not typically prone to panic, tried to comfort each other and carry on.

Then Jackie Cochran called. Nadine knew who she was, of course; nearly everyone, and especially every woman pilot, knew of Cochran and her magnetic personality and rich, persuasive voice. Cochran asked Nadine to go to England to ferry bombers for the ATA, but Nadine hesitated. She desperately wanted to support the war effort, but there was something about Cochran's celebrity that rubbed her the wrong way. Besides, as Nadine began wondering, shouldn't American women be ferrying American planes? She thanked Cochran and asked for time to think it over.

On March 2 *Life* magazine ran an article written by Captain John Wheeler, who, like Ed, had been awarded the Silver Star along with the Distinguished

Service Cross for his part in the action at Morong. In it, Wheeler described the battle, with full coverage of Ed's courageous charge.[5] When the issue landed in Nelle and Nadine's hands, relief swept over them, and their hearts swelled with pride. Ed was alive, or recently had been, and, like Captain Wheeler, was surely a decorated hero now. Moreover, receiving the news from a magazine and not official army correspondence felt sensational and ironic.

The *Wichita Beacon* ran a two-column story accompanied by a photograph of Nadine and Nelle reading their copy of *Life* with loving, serious expressions. It also mentioned that Nadine had been approached about ferrying planes in England but quoted her as saying, "I haven't made up my mind yet whether or not to go."[6]

In the end, Nadine turned down Cochran's offer. Of course, her decision was hardly due to a lack of patriotism. As the granddaughter of pioneer homesteaders and raised in America's heartland, Nadine, like many Americans, took to heart President Roosevelt's call issued from the Oval Office on December 9, 1941: "Every citizen, in every walk of life, shares this same responsibility. The lives of our soldiers and sailors—the whole future of this Nation—depend upon the manner in which each and every one of us fulfills his obligation to our country."[7]

Nadine was ready to fulfill her obligation, but she didn't want to go to England to do it. She simply was confident that, sooner or later, her own country would give women the chance to ferry aircraft and that she would be one of them.

On April 10, 1942, a month after *Life's* good news, the American troops on Bataan formally surrendered. Though Japanese General Homma had anticipated he would be able to take Bataan in a matter of days, the US and Philippine troops fought harder than he expected, and the drawn-out siege lasted four months. The Japanese also were weakened by malnutrition and ravaged by disease, including malaria, dysentery, and beriberi.

By the time of the surrender, the entirety of the American forces had been placed under the command of General Wainwright, the polo referee who had sent Ed to Morong. General MacArthur, against his own wishes, had retreated to Australia, ordered there by President Roosevelt. "I came out of Bataan," he said famously, "and I shall return." Corregidor, a well-

defended island south of Bataan, held out for a month longer but ultimately surrendered on May 6, 1942.

In the United States, the fall of the Philippines was devastating. In the wake of the surrender, thousands of American soldiers were declared dead or missing in action. On May 19 the War Department informed Nelle that Ed was missing in action on Bataan. When she received the letter, she and Nadine crashed into the depths of anxiety and grief. Now there would be no *Life* issue offering news of Ed; there would likely be no news at all for years to come. But if there was the tiniest sliver of hope that Ed was alive on Luzon and hadn't been captured, Nadine knew he would keep fighting.

In his last letter to Nadine, postmarked March 4, 1942, before the fall of Bataan, Ed had described his life in the Philippines, "the jungle, mountains, and how tough it was to run out of cigarets." Nadine told a reporter from a local newspaper that these descriptions left her feeling optimistic about his chances for survival. In addition, the article explained, "Miss Ramsey said since her brother's morale appeared so strong, and at the time of his letter he was enjoying such good health, she sincerely believes he is alive, somewhere, somehow."[8] Now for the first time, Nadine began to have doubts. But she would not simply sit around and wait for news—good or bad. There was still a war on.

In the spring of 1942, Nadine joined the Civil Air Patrol in Wichita. CAP had been founded in December 1941 under the Office of Civilian Defense. Its mission was to use civilian fliers for home defense and disaster relief in the event of a national emergency. Remarkably, CAP was opened to both men and women, and the patrol eventually also welcomed youth ages fifteen to seventeen into its cadet program. Nationally, CAP volunteers did any jobs they could to support the war effort, including spotting Nazi U-boats in the Atlantic and stopping their attacks. CAP members—by the war's end some two hundred thousand strong, forty thousand of them women—also patrolled the country's borders by air, towed targets for military trainees on antiaircraft weapons, detected forest fires, ran search-and-rescue missions, provided disaster relief and emergency transport of people and parts, and conducted orientation flights for future pilots.

Nadine was assigned squadron commander, first lieutenant, of an all-female group of about thirty aspiring young pilots. She helped train them

in required CAP courses and, using a leased airplane, took them on cross-country maneuvers. In late 1942 CAP transferred her to Douglas, Arizona, to complete a flight instructor's course conducted by the government—one of only about fifty women to perform war service training instruction during the war.

PART III
IN FLIGHT

At the sound of reveille, Nadine threw off her thin cotton sheets, careful to keep them from falling in the dirt. The air was already humid and filled with the electric whine of insects; it was going to be another sweltering day with no rain. Yesterday's heat had melted into one of those brutal Texas summer nights that made it impossible to sleep indoors, so Nadine and her roommates, or baymates, had been allowed to drag their cots outside to sleep under a pearlescent half-dollar moon set against the brilliant swath of the Milky Way. A good night for night flying, she had thought, though neither she nor anyone else had been sent up. Meanwhile, they risked the darkness of night when the ground became rife with Sweetwater's ever-present tarantulas, scorpions, and rattlesnakes. But Nadine had learned to tuck her sheets in tightly around her body when sleeping under the stars, and that usually kept the critters out.

"Ramsey!" A voice called, and Nadine looked over to see her best friend Jo comically struggling to wrestle her cot back into the bay where they lived. She jumped up, grinning, and hurried to help the petite blond trainee, Helen Jo Severson, from Billings, South Dakota. Nadine and Jo had arrived at Sweetwater on the same day and because their names were close alphabetically had been assigned to the same bay. They had taken to each other immediately; Jo was sweet, stubborn, and deeply good-hearted. Nadine found it funny that Jo and some of the others looked up to her, though she was always glad to give flying advice if anybody wanted it.

At thirty-one, Nadine was the oldest woman in her bay, one of the most experienced trainees on the base, and because she'd been married, however briefly, to her high school sweetheart, she was thought of as "worldly." Jo was twenty-four and married too; her husband, Rob, was a captain, fighting in the skies over Europe. She missed him terribly and talked about him daily. Nadine and Jo hauled their cots into the long barracks, where Nadine noticed with annoyance that, although she had just swept it yesterday, the floor was already covered with dust. Sweetwater was hotter than Hades, as dirty as the Dust Bowl, and windy to boot. One of the girls had joked that when a windstorm and a thunderstorm happened at the same time, it was actually capable of raining mud.

First up was flight instruction, so Nadine and Jo quickly changed, pulling on their "zoot suits"—standard-issue army coveralls—and pausing to tediously roll up the trailing sleeves and ankle cuffs. Nadine darted into the bathroom, where at least eight other women crowded around two sinks, frantically brushing their teeth. A couple looked hungover; some daubed on makeup and pulled rollers out of their hair. Nadine studied her own reflection; her hazel eyes were merry and her cheeks sunburned pink.

Once ready, she joined the formation outside under the direction of her squadron commander, Marianne Beard. As she waited for the last few trainees to hurry and take their places, Nadine thought about her brother Ed, wondering where he was, if he was alive, if she would ever see him again. She imagined him thinking of her and Nelle and of home. All this thinking was useless, she concluded, reminding herself that she was exactly where she needed to be and that Ed would be proud of her.

CHAPTER 5
A BUNCH OF GALS

Another aviatrix to suggest a resolution to America's ferry pilot shortage was Nancy Harkness Love. Born on Valentine's Day 1914, Love was a practical, iron-willed natural leader. At age sixteen, she had announced to her family that she was going to quit school to become a pilot. Her parents, at the time living far north on Michigan's Upper Peninsula, instead struck a deal with her: she could learn to fly if she stayed in school. As a teen, she started flying lessons and was sent first to a prep school in Boston, then to Vassar College in New York. There she became known in the local press as the "Flying Freshman" and earned her commercial pilot's license in 1932, at only eighteen years old.

Forced to quit school during the Depression, Nancy, like Nadine and many other young women pilots, got a job demonstrating flying and selling airplanes. In 1934 she went to work for Robert M. Love at Inter City Aviation in Boston, where she demonstrated aircraft built by the local manufacturer, WACO. An office romance blossomed, and Bob and Nancy were married on January 11, 1936.

The press loved the story of Nancy and Bob's romance, and the Boston papers called her the "Flying Bride." Nancy, however, was the polar opposite of Jacqueline Cochran. An intensely private person, she hated attention. She was drawn to flying purely for the challenge of it. In fact, she was a careful, deliberate pilot, not a daredevil. Nancy didn't enjoy races, and she didn't care about records. She just loved to fly.

With war looming on the horizon, Love saw as plainly as Cochran had the need for women pilots. In 1940 she wrote to Colonel Robert Olds, then of the AAC, saying she knew of some fifty highly capable women pilots who were well qualified and could be mobilized quickly to ferry military planes. But Love's suggestion, like Cochran's, was discarded.

When the United States entered the war in 1941, Bob Love was already in the reserve; placed on active duty as a major, he became the deputy chief of staff for the ACFC in Washington, DC. Nancy worked for the ACFC as

well, in Baltimore. As it was easier to get gasoline for an airplane than for an automobile, she flew to work every day.

Working at the ACFC brought Bob into close proximity with Colonel William H. Tunner, who had heard about Love's commuting by plane. Tunner was impressed by Love and by her suggestion that the ACFC hire women ferry pilots. Together they drew up a plan for a women's pilot program and submitted it to General Harold George in the summer of 1942, just as he was reorganizing the ACFC as the ATC. George approved the plan and sent it on to General Arnold.

In early September 1942, even as Jackie Cochran was helping the last of her ferry recruits get settled in England, Nancy Love was named the commander of the country's first group of female military ferry pilots, the Women's Auxiliary Ferrying Squadron (WAFS).

Love had particular ideas about the kind of women she wanted to recruit. Her program was not designed to train women how to fly; she wanted aviatrixes who were already experts and could be quickly approved to fly, or checked out in, military aircraft. She set high qualification standards for her first group of WAFS: the female pilots had to have at least a high school education, five hundred flying hours, a commercial license, a two-hundred-horsepower rating, and recent cross-country flying experience. The army added one requirement of its own: although male pilots at the time could be between the ages of nineteen and forty-five, female pilots had to be between twenty-one and thirty-five. This restriction was set because male pilots refused to "babysit female minors" and because they were afraid that menopause would make older women pilots "irrational."[1]

Love knew the restriction was nonsense—it disqualified some accomplished women pilots, like Louise Thaden and Blanche Noyes—but the army stood firm. She assembled a list of eighty-three women pilots around the country who met all the qualifications and sent telegrams asking them to join the WAFS.

At thirty-one and with plenty of experience, Nadine Ramsey would have been a prime candidate for the WAFS. And, since she was on Jackie Cochran's radar, it's likely she was on Nancy Love's too. However, in September 1942, when Love sent the telegrams, Nadine was in transition; she had just moved from Wichita back to California and then to Arizona as an instructor for CAP. If she had received a telegram inviting her to join a

Nancy Harkness Love, founder of the Women's Auxiliary Ferrying Squadron, Newcastle Army Air Base, Wilmington, Delaware, ca. 1943 (Courtesy WASP Archive, Texas Woman's University, Denton, TX)

new women's squadron to ferry aircraft for the United States, she certainly would have hurried to answer the call.

Of the eighty-three women Love contacted, about two dozen responded, and others heard of the program by word of mouth. Highly qualified female pilots started trickling in to Wilmington, Delaware, one by one, to apply for the program throughout the fall of 1942.

On October 22, after a thirty-day orientation period, the first six WAFS to qualify made their initial ferrying trip, delivering six single-engine L-4B liaison planes from the Piper factory at Lock Haven, Pennsylvania, to Mitchel Field on Long Island. The number of WAFS pilots would top out at twenty-eight on January 23, 1943.

These women—the Originals or Waffies, as they were nicknamed—were an eclectic group. They spanned the age range the army allowed. In their personalities, some were practical and deliberate, like Love; some were flashy, like Cochran. Some were feminine, and some were tomboys. Some were modest and conservative; others were fun loving and loved to cut loose. Like Nadine, most had been called the only or first women fliers in their hometowns. At least two had flown the airmail on the same day as Nadine.

The Originals first assembled at the spare accommodations of New Castle Army Air Base in Wilmington, Delaware. They came from all over the country. One of the women joked that their accents were so varied it was as though they all spoke different languages. For all their variety, the WAFS had two things in common: they all loved flying, and they all had answered the call to serve their country. As a March 1944 ATC bulletin confirmed, "They were the first [organized group of] women to be used in military flying in this country."[2]

At first all the WAFS were absorbed into the ATC's Second Ferrying Group at New Castle, but by December it was obvious that women ferry pilots were needed on a national scale. Nancy Love divided the WAFS into four groups and stationed them at ATC bases that she felt could suitably accommodate them and where the base commanders would accept them: Long Beach, California; Romulus, Michigan; Dallas, Texas; and of course, Wilmington, Delaware.

Throughout the winter of 1942–1943, the Originals were dispatched nationwide to ferry liaison aircraft as well as basic trainers (BTs), including the

Florene Miller, flight instructor with the Civilian Pilot Training Program and one of the first WAFS pilots, instructing cadets in ground school, 1941 (Courtesy WASP Archive, Texas Woman's University, Denton, TX)

WAFS pilot Barbara Erickson (left) and Betty Takaberry at Long Beach Airforce Base, ca. 1942 (Courtesy WASP Archive, Texas Woman's University, Denton, TX)

BT-13, primary trainers (PTs) PT-17, PT-19, PT-26, and more. They also were authorized to transition into advanced trainers (ATs).

The first WAFS were keenly aware that they were part of an experiment to prove that women pilots could match the skills and abilities of male pilots. As Original Cornelia Fort wrote, "Because there were and are so many disbelievers in women pilots, especially in their place in the army, officials wanted the best possible qualifications to go with the first experimental group. All of us realized what a spot we were in. We had to deliver the goods or else. Or else there wouldn't ever be another chance for women pilots in any part of the service."[3]

The WAFS of World War II started small—twenty-eight women flying trainer planes—but a change was already coming that would bring over a thousand more women into the fight.

In early fall of 1942, the WAFS' training and ferry work served as the backdrop for a frantic bureaucratic scene unfolding in Washington, DC, where Jackie Cochran was throwing her star-quality weight around. On September 10, when Nancy Love was publicly named the head of the army's new women ferry pilots organization, Cochran completely lost her cool. She was shocked and offended; she assumed that she had been promised command of a women's squadron if it were to be formed. Cochran had gone all the way to England because her ambition to direct a group of female ferry pilots had been stymied stateside. Now she saw the creation of the WAFS as a great injustice and a broken promise. On September 11 she flew to Washington and indignantly demanded an explanation from General Arnold.

Cochran put Arnold between a rock and a very hard place. She had clout; she was a personal friend of President and Mrs. Roosevelt; she had a wealthy, influential husband; and she had a reputation in the press and with the public as the Speed Queen. In his meeting with Cochran, Arnold deflected, blaming George, Tunner, and the ATC for going ahead with the women's ferry program without his approval. Cochran accepted his explanation, but it didn't calm her down: the fact remained that the WAFS had already been established and announced with Love in charge.

Now Arnold had to give Cochran something too, so he issued an order that the women's pilot project should be revised, leaving General George and Cochran to work out the details. Cochran responded by proposing a

program that would train women pilots with less experience to fly military aircraft. George settled for that compromise, naming Cochran the director of a new program: the Women's Flying Training Detachment (WFTD). The program was hastily announced on September 15, 1942, less than a week after the WAFS announcement. Cochran worked fast.

She wasn't the only one in a hurry. In 1942 the war wasn't going well, particularly in the Pacific. There was a true desperation to all this political maneuvering; American soldiers were dying every day.

Both the WAFS program and the newly formed WFTD were established without congressional approval, which would have slowed the process considerably. This meant that, like male ferrying pilots, women ferry pilots were hired as civilians. However, the women Cochran recruited were told that they would be commissioned into the AAF. Both she and Love assumed that Congress would approve the women's militarization eventually, so they moved ahead with their programs. In the meantime, there was plenty of ferrying to do.

On paper the goal of the WTFD was to train five hundred women pilots for ferrying duty with the ATC by no later than December 30, 1943. Because Cochran was planning to train them, the requirements for joining the WFTD were considerably less stringent than those required for Love's WAFS.

At first, WFTD applicants needed 200 flying hours, but after assembling the first class, Cochran—knowing that there were not enough women pilots with 200 hours—dropped the hours to qualify to 100, then to 75 for the third class and finally 35 for the fourth class and after.

Colonel Tunner soon saw that because of an increase in accidents, some of the women pilots from the training program would never have the skills to ferry aircraft. Ferrying demanded a certain level of skill. He asked Cochran that they be assigned instead to non-ferrying duty.

With WFTD training set to take approximately four months, the program was established at Howard Hughes Field in Houston, Texas. When the first class of twenty-nine women arrived in November 1942, nothing was ready for them. If the WAFS housing in New Castle wasn't luxurious, the quarters in Houston were nonexistent.

Cochran named a brisk, resourceful Texas housewife named Leni "Dedie" Deaton as the WFTD's chief establishment officer and placed her

in charge of figuring out where the first class, 43-1—so designated for the year of graduation and class number—would live. Deaton helped this first group, known as the Guinea Pigs, though they called themselves Woofteddies, settle in at hotels, boarding houses, and tourist motels all over town. Because most of the trainees didn't have the means to establish themselves in five-star accommodations, they lived in shared housing, usually low quality and sometimes infested with cockroaches and rats.

The trainees also had to arrange their own transportation to and from the Houston airport every day. They took classes in an old shack at the end of the field, requiring a half-mile walk from the terminal just to eat poor-quality food or use the single restroom designated for women. At first they didn't even have military planes to train on. Primary trainers like those ferried by the WAFS arrived only in January 1943, forcing WFTD leadership to expand the program from four to six months. All in all, morale in Houston was low, but the women were flying. For them, that alone made up for a multitude of sins.

By the time the second class of trainees reported for duty on December 13, 1942, it was already obvious that the Houston facilities would not support the rapidly expanding program. With fifty-one members in class 43-2, Cochran and the WFTD leadership began looking for a bigger base with sufficient accommodations and space. Cochran was openly recruiting; she placed advertisements for women pilots in newspapers and magazines and conducted many of the entrance interviews herself.

Although the vast majority of the early WFTD graduates had a lot of experience—the average number of flying hours of class 43-1, for example, was 315—some of the recruits had barely the minimum seventy-five hours. Many of the women had learned to fly with the CPTP at their colleges and universities, and many, like Nadine, had flown for CAP. Like the WAFS, WFTD trainees poured in from all over the country, bringing with them their own unique backgrounds and forming a colorful tapestry of personalities. In January 1943 fifty-five more women reported to Houston for training in class 43-3, and the program continued to grow.

Jackie Cochran had not forgotten about Nadine. In early 1943 Nadine was working as a CAP instructor in Douglas, Arizona, when she received a letter from Cochran's office in Fort Worth, informing her of the WFTD's forma-

tion. Nadine had turned down Cochran's invitation to ferry planes in England partly because she didn't care for the woman's celebrity, but mostly because she had wanted to ferry aircraft for the United States.

By this point, Nadine also had heard about Nancy Love's WAFS, which was already ferrying aircraft for the ATC. However, Cochran had asked General Arnold to prevent the WAFS from any further recruiting, so Nancy's program was no longer accepting pilots. The WFTD's early graduates would serve with ferrying groups around the country and would fly exciting new military planes. Nadine was itching to get behind the throttle of one of those planes, and fervent patriotism demanded her response.

On February 9, 1943, with Ed never far from her mind, Nadine wrote back to Cochran requesting more information about the WFTD, particularly the most immediate steps she would need to take to join up. She also discussed her qualifications and her ultimate goals: "I have over seven hundred hours, a Commercial license, have completed the oral and written for Flight Instructor's Rating. I am extremely anxious to avail myself of any additional training and knowledge pertaining to flying, and am anxious to know if the Flying Training Command offers this opportunity. I am particularly anxious to acquire an Instrument and multi-engine rating—would this be possible in the course you offer?"[4]

A quick response from Cochran's office answered Nadine's questions and encouraged her to apply for the program. She was required to provide some character references for her application, and one of the people she asked was family friend and lawyer Claire V. Eberhard, who had represented Nadine in the civil case Gertrude Snow had brought against her. He wrote: "I consider this person to be the very highest type of American citizen. I am well acquainted with her mother, who is also the finest type. I also know her brother, who is missing in action on Bataan. They are all fine people." To the question about whether Nadine was a loyal citizen of the United States, Eberhard responded in firm script, "Yes, extremely so."[5]

Nadine, with her breadth of piloting experience, was quickly accepted into the WFTD. This was the organization that would become the Women Airforce Service Pilots, claiming the title of a particularly historic first: the first women to fly US military aircraft. In all, more than twenty-five thousand women applied. Of those, only 1,830 were admitted. Nadine was set to report in March 1943 as a member of class 43-5.

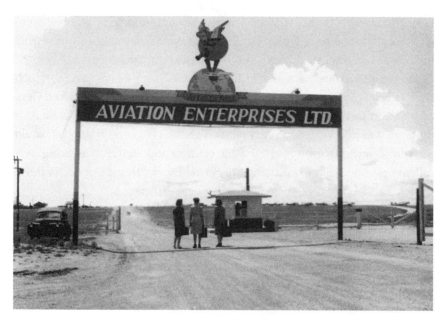

Arriving at Avenger Field, Sweetwater, Texas, date unknown (Courtesy US Air Force)

Meanwhile, the WFTD was relocating. Jackie Cochran and Dedie Deaton found a better, more practical place for the program: Avenger Field in Sweetwater, Texas. Sweetwater was a small town—population ten thousand—more than four hundred miles northwest of Houston and forty miles west of Abilene, the closest really "big" city. It had been founded along the Texas and Pacific Railroad line in the mid-1800s. Before the Depression the area had experienced a small oil boom, but by the 1940s its primary industries were cotton and cattle.[6]

At the time it was selected as the new WASP home, Avenger Field was the home of an army basic training base, the 318th Training Squadron, which could accommodate up to five hundred cadets. There the ATC also ran a refresher course, where experienced male pilots could fly BTs and then move up to twin-engine planes before beginning active service overseas.

The facilities at Avenger Field were compact and well suited to the WFTD, and Sweetwater was considered a nice community. But it wasn't perfect. Sweetwater was known as the Rattlesnake Capital of the World, and the wide, rolling plains of Texas endured all kinds of weather, including

tornado-force winds, thunderstorms, and even snow. It could be over a hundred degrees in the summer and below freezing in winter. Sweetwater was windy, dusty, and remote, but it was a lot better than Houston. It would do.

For the WFTD trainees, the move to Sweetwater meant better organization, facilities, and food. Some locals, however, feared the influx of women pilots and the one hundred planes they would bring from Houston. One citizens' group worried about planes crashing in their little town.

Recalling the move to Avenger Field, Mildred "Micky" Axton (class 43-7), a new trainee, remembered the excitement on the ground: "Everybody in Sweetwater packed a picnic that day and went out to the airfield along the road, and all the men were making bets on how many of the girls would crash, how many would get lost, and all this. And they said they were just flabbergasted when every one of the girls flying one hundred planes came in and landed, no problem." Jean Landis (class 43-4), who became a good friend of Nadine's, recalled, "As we flew our planes into Avenger Field, the Army cadets moved out. The base was almost transformed over night from a bunch of guys to a bunch of gals."[7]

The move to Sweetwater was conducted in stages, since the original classes in Houston were already in the middle of training. In February the male pilot program was relocated, and Avenger Field became an all-female pilot training ground. By the middle of that month, half of the incoming class 43-4 went straight to Sweetwater, while the other half reported to Houston and were sent to Sweetwater in April. Class 43-3, which had reported to Houston originally, was transferred to Sweetwater in May. Nadine's class, 43-5, would be the first to report entirely to Sweetwater.

On a bright windy day in March, Nadine packed her bags and, with heartbeat racing, headed to Sweetwater, arriving with 124 other trainees at Avenger Field on March 23, 1943.

CHAPTER 6

AVENGER FIELD

Life at Avenger Field for the trainees was dramatically different than it had been for the earlier classes. In Houston the program was still experimental and "finding its wings." The women weren't living all in one place, so they couldn't be constantly supervised. In Sweetwater the trainees were all housed together on the base, where they were assigned alphabetically to large rooms called bays, each with six plain cots surrounding a central desk area and lockers ranging along each wall. Each bay typically housed six women, but class 43-5 was particularly overcrowded, and some bays contained eight or even nine. Every two bays adjoined a bathroom with two sinks, two toilets, and two showers—which at first didn't even have partitions or curtains—all to be shared by at least twelve women.

One of Sweetwater's biggest advantages was its remoteness; unlike in Houston, there were few social opportunities to distract the trainees. In fact, Avenger Field became a popular spot for "forced" landings during the women's first few weeks; male pilots conveniently invented problems with their planes so they could set down at Sweetwater to get a look at or even a date with a WFTD trainee. However, Jackie Cochran believed the WFTD women needed to maintain a spotless reputation, so she quickly closed Avenger Field to outside traffic. Surrounded by high cyclone fences on all sides, the base became known as "Cochran's Convent."

The WFTD program was a period of intense training designed to turn inexperienced young fliers into highly capable and versatile pilots. There were classes in meteorology, navigation, and Morse code. The women spent hours in the Link Trainer—a small, stuffy wooden box used to simulate instrument flying. In the air, they accumulated 115 hours of flying instruction: 25 hours in liaison aircraft, 75 in commercial aircraft, and 15 in basic and advanced trainers of the kind the WAFS pilots were already ferrying. Periodically, they were put through check rides, or "army checks," on planes they were supposed to have mastered.

Army checks were universally dreaded and often resulted in cadets "washing out"—failing the program—and being sent home. WFTD train-

WASP living quarters at Avenger Field, ca. 1943 (Courtesy WASP Archive, Texas Woman's University, Denton, TX)

ees were put on a strict, army-inspired demerit system and could wash out if they received too many demerits. Military inspections were meticulous and conducted like clockwork. While the women stood at attention, inspectors with white gloves searched the bays for dust—and dust could get into anything in Sweetwater. Trainees could receive demerits for dirty bays, for their shoes or towels being out of place, or for behavioral problems.

In a letter to a former trainee, Nadine's friend Irma "Babe" Story (class 43-6) wrote:

> Our demerit system—Z!!@% The girls are getting demerits for everything—name in wrong place on laundry—associating with instructors in canteen, and associating to [establishment officer] Miss Bristol means sitting next to them because there aren't any more seats—and a bunch of other silly stuff. We have to wear name tags all the time while on the post. Pinned mine on my dorsal fin the other night when I went to sleep

(sleep on my tummy), but I went to sleep before bed check, so I don't know what Bristol thought. Can't find a way to wear it in the shower though—any suggestions? Ah! Yes, J. Cochran's kindergarten.[1]

Often, the women weren't even told when a classmate had washed out; they simply returned to their bay to find the trainee gone and her mattress rolled up. Dedie Deaton ran a tight ship.

Nadine and her classmates were now living the lives of all army cadets in training: they arose at dawn to reveille, marched everywhere, reported for mess and classes, and were trained and drilled relentlessly. Like the WAFS, they were expected to train in calisthenics and marching in formation— again, under the assumption that they would eventually be militarized. Not allowed to speak while marching—and they marched nearly everywhere— the trainees creatively devised songs about their training experiences, usually set to the tunes of popular music. Despite the Cochran's Convent moniker, they were young and vivacious, and some of their lyrics were funny and crude. Again and again, women pilots proved they could cuss with the best of the men.

During training the women wore their "zoot suit" coveralls. But because the suits were designed for men, the trainees were forced to belt the suits tightly and roll up their sleeves and ankle cuffs. While that solution worked for taller women, it was a challenge for petite trainees (Nadine was only five-foot-four and about 125 pounds), who felt like they were swimming in their zoot suits. The trainees were also required to restrain their long hair; at first they wore hairnets, then turbans, and eventually flight caps.

The planes weren't designed for women, either. Some of the shorter trainees had to add stacks of cushions to the pilot seats. Moreover, on the longer cross-country flights, the women couldn't relieve themselves. The planes were outfitted with a "relief tube" for male pilots, but that wasn't a practical solution for female pilots, though some of the more desperate female pilots did try it. Instead, they simply stopped eating or drinking for several hours before a long flight. Many ground crews knew female pilots would need to hurry to the nearest facilities as soon as their wheels touched down.

Socially, Nadine and her fellow trainees amused themselves on the weekends by sunbathing or swimming at the Sweetwater town pool. At night, they were allowed to go into Sweetwater to the movies or just out on the

town, provided they were back by midnight bed checks. One of Nadine's 43-5 classmates, Dawn Rochow, founded a little second-story club called the Avengerette Club for the trainees in Sweetwater .

The women also published their own newspaper, the *Fifinella Gazette*, named after the female gremlin Fifinella from Roald Dahl's *The Gremlins*. Dahl had written the book early in the war as a morale booster for the men of Britain's Royal Air Force. Illustrated by Walt Disney, it blamed the pilots' in-flight problems on the eponymous tiny mischievous creatures, and held cute little Fifinella in particular responsible for fog, missing runways, and lost maps. When creating their newspaper, members of Houston's class 43-1 asked Disney to design an insignia for them. Disney bedecked the character Fifinella with wings and flying goggles, and the WFTD's mascot was born.

As she had been in high school, outgoing Nadine was popular. Her baymates and other classmates called her Ramsey and quickly became her friends, and she developed a reputation as everyone's helpful older sister. Although most of the WFTD women were in their twenties, some were as young as eighteen (Jackie Cochran had lowered the age requirement in mid-1943). Nadine turned thirty-two that August during her training at Sweetwater. She also had much more experience than most of her classmates; after all, she'd been flying for half a decade.

Nadine was fearless and well suited to the rigorous life of a WFTD trainee. In a letter home, her best friend Helen Jo Severson mentioned her reputation as a highly experienced, tough pilot, one eager for challenges and unlikely to back down even in dangerous situations. In another letter, Irma "Babe" Story wrote: "W-5 started on XC [cross-country] this morning and they all turned back because of the weather except [Edna] Modisette. She went thru rain and clouds, but she made it—that do it or else attitude! Everybody got a bang out of it because even Ramsey came back."[2]

A month after Nadine's arrival at Sweetwater, the WFTD's first class of female ferry pilots, the Guinea Pigs of class 43-1, graduated on April 24, 1943, in Houston. It was the only graduation held at the WFTD's first home. In the weeks leading up to the ceremony, Dedie Deaton realized there were no wings for the new graduates to receive, and she was worried that Cochran, who was ill at the time, wouldn't be able to address the problem. Along with the airfield's commanding officer Major Walter W. Farmer and Lieutenant

*Nadine (second from right) with fellow WASP trainees at Avenger Field, 1943
(Courtesy WASP Archive, Texas Woman's University, Denton, TX)*

Alfred Fleishman, the WFTD's tactical officer, special services officer, and physical education director, she devised a plan to ensure that the women would graduate with their wings.

First, she contacted Cochran's husband, millionaire Floyd Odlum, who agreed to pay for the design and production of the new wings. Next, Fleishman bought twenty-three sets of silver AAF Sweetheart wings with a traditional shield shape in the center. Finally, a local jeweler engraved the wings with Deaton and Fleishman's design. The first seven classes all received wings of the same design, each bearing the class designation. Beginning with class 43-8, the earlier shield was replaced with a diamond one, representing the shield carried by Athena, the Greek goddess of war and wisdom.

By 43-1's graduation, Cochran had recovered enough to attend the event, and she pinned the wings on the first twenty-three graduates of her program. Dressed in khaki pants and white blouses, the women received their wings, beaming with pride.

The forty-three women of class 43-2 graduated on May 28, 1943, at Avenger Field. Class 43-3, another forty-three women, graduated on July 3.

All graduates of the first three WFTD classes joined Nancy Love's WAFS, fly-ing for the ATC at one of the four ferrying bases in Long Beach, Dallas, Ro-mulus, or Wilmington. However, twenty-five graduates from the third class were quickly transferred to North Carolina to learn to tow gunnery targets.

All this time, the original twenty-eight WAFS had been ferrying light trainer aircraft. Typically, their journeys were long and complicated; they delivered planes as quickly and safely as they could but were at the mercy of fickle weather and limited fuel supplies. WAFS almost always had to Remain Over Night (RON) in various cities, and many bases were unable to properly house them. They stayed in hotels, the requisitioned rooms of male officers, and motels of questionable reputation. Once a desperate WAFS pilot even voluntarily slept in a jail cell.

Many male pilots and officers were open-minded enough to give the women the chance to prove themselves. Once a female pilot successfully and safely delivered a plane, she almost always received the respect of the men.

On December 12, 1942, a group of twenty-seven male ferry pilots and six WAFS set out to fly a squadron of open-cockpit PT-17s from Great Falls, Montana, to Jackson, Tennessee. On the day they left, it was zero degrees on the ground and significantly less at five thousand feet. The WAFS pilots wore their leather and wool winter flight gear, but even so the bitterly cold winds were punishing. To make matters worse, the PT-17s had no radios, so navigation over the snow-covered landscape was all but impossible. The WAFS pilots could barely cover a few miles each day and often were ground-ed by the weather entirely. Sometimes they had to stop for days on end, waiting for better flying conditions. By the time they arrived in Jackson, it was New Year's Eve. Upon landing, they were greeted with "Well, did you finally get here?"[3]

As it turned out, the WAFS pilots had beaten all twenty-seven male pi-lots to their destination. Incidents like this became common; no matter the difficulties, women pilots could do the job, usually faster and more safely than the men. As WFTD trainee Dorothy "Dot" Swain Lewis (class 44-5) later said, "Our record stood up. They found that little old ladies could fly. They didn't make mistakes, and they didn't crash the planes, and they didn't jump out."[4]

Of course, the women still faced plenty of chauvinism and harassment. In early 1943 Nancy Love and some of the more ambitious WAFS were eager to train on bigger, heavier planes, especially pursuit (P) or fighter aircraft. In particular, Love wanted to fly the P-51 Mustang, a swift single-engine fighter plane capable of speeds up to 425 miles per hour. In February 1943 she was finally given the chance, handling the graceful, responsive Mustang beautifully. In March another WAFS pilot soloed in a P-47, and Love flew the twin-engine C-47 (a version of the commercial DC-3 aircraft).

Just when it seemed the floodgates were opening for women to fly some of the bigger and more powerful planes, the army took a step back. In March, when Nadine began her WFTD training, army officials reissued an order restricting WAFS pilots to light trainer aircraft. They added further restrictions: women could not fly as copilots with any men other than their instructors, and they could not fly during their menstrual periods, including one day before and two days after.

Of course, the women knew how ridiculous this directive was. Lois Brooks Hailey (class 43-3), recalled: "The medical doctors would say, 'We want you grounded during your period.' Well, nobody would go report to him when their period was, so of course, he couldn't ground us. If we were off on a ferry trip and we had to deliver the airplane by a specified date, we couldn't allow ourselves to be grounded until we got the job done."[5] For the women of the Ferrying Command, the job came first.

Nancy Love strenuously objected to the regressive orders, and she went over Colonel Tunner's head to protest them directly to ATC headquarters. At first Tunner was upset with Love's behavior, but he fundamentally agreed that the women pilots shouldn't be needlessly restricted, especially when they were so crucial to the war effort. In April 1943 Ferry Division Headquarters rescinded all three orders. That spring, two more WAFS pilots flew the Republic P-47 Thunderbolt and the Bell P-39 Airacobra, and Love flew a B-25 bomber. These women brought Nadine one step closer to her dream of flying multiengine planes.

The public had mixed reactions to the women pilots. From the beginning, they were under intense scrutiny. Some newspaper articles painted them as scheming, aggressive women who were out to steal jobs from men. Others raised questions about their morals, since they were zooming

around the country, staying in different cities every night. All pilots, but especially women pilots, were viewed as "fast."[6]

Rita Davoly Webster (class 43-6) recalled: "Back when I first started working, people were not accustomed to women working, and so nurses were considered fast because they knew everything, and hairdressers were considered fast. . . . You meet people and they say, 'Ooh! You were a pilot!' and to themselves they're thinking, 'I bet she was pretty fast.'"[7] Indeed, both Nancy Love and Jackie Cochran went to great lengths to keep their pilots' reputations above reproach.

Sometimes sexism in the media took a completely different form. In early 1943 Hollywood began to wonder how it could capitalize on the fame and glamor of these "lipstick pilots."[8] Universal Pictures decided to make a movie about them, casting Loretta Young as the lead character, based on Nancy Love. The script of this film, *Ladies Courageous* (Universal Pictures, 1944), portrayed them as silly, selfish, and overly emotional. Moreover, the film suggested (not too subtly) that women pilots were far less capable than men. Their portrayal was so negative that some WAFS pilots left the movie theater before the film was over, desperately trying not to be recognized. In short, the movie smeared the WAFS's reputation, and among women ferry pilots, it quickly became known as *Ladies Outrageous*.

One good thing came out of the Hollywood debacle: One of the WAFS Originals, Teresa James, was given the opportunity to ferry a PT-19 (to be used in movie stunts) from the factory in Hagerstown, Maryland, into Burbank, California. Upon landing in Los Angeles, she became an instant celebrity and met a galaxy's worth of movie stars, including Loretta Young, Katharine Hepburn, Spencer Tracy, Marlene Dietrich, Ingrid Bergman, Gary Cooper, and Bob Hope. Outgoing, witty, levelheaded, and a crack pilot, she was the perfect person to help create a more accurate image of the WAFS—even if only among the film's cast and crew.

Despite the negative press, some publications correctly identified the women pilots as heroes risking their lives for their country. One example was WAFS Original Cornelia Fort, who was making headlines for her valor even before she joined Nancy Love's squadron. A tall, aristocratic brunette from a prominent Nashville family, Fort had learned to fly in 1940 at the age of twenty-one.

On December 7, 1941, she was in the sky above Pearl Harbor in Hawaii.

As an instructor with a private flying service, she was aloft with a student in a little Interstate Cadet when she saw a Japanese plane zooming straight toward her. She seized the controls from her student and swerved the Cadet just in time; the Japanese aircraft passed so close, it rattled the plane's windows. Landing as quickly as she could, she and her student climbed out onto the runway, with bullets spraying the ground around them. They were being strafed by the Japanese. They fled the machine-gun fire, running from the plane into the hangar.

West Coast papers lauded Fort's quick thinking and courage, and back in Nashville she was pressed to give interviews and endorsements.[9] She was just grateful that, unlike some of her friends in Hawaii that day, she had survived. When she received Love's telegram about joining the WAFS, she responded immediately, becoming the third woman—after Love and an older and exceedingly experienced pilot named Betty Gillies—officially admitted to the program.

Tragically, Fort's service to her country was short-lived. On March 21, 1943, two days before Nadine reported to Sweetwater, she took off from Long Beach with six male pilots to ferry a batch of BT-13 trainers to Dallas. The pilots flew this route regularly, ferrying BT-13s and BT-15s from their manufacturing point to army training bases in Dallas and in Enid, Oklahoma.

Although the pilots often traveled in groups, they were forbidden from flying in tight formation because it was too risky. In ferrying work, safety was paramount; pilots were instructed to keep their planes at least five hundred feet apart at all times, but male ferry pilots often disregarded the protocol and practiced formation flying anyway. In his biography of Cornelia Fort, Rob Simbeck explains:

A percentage of the men flying these missions were young, inexperienced, and sometimes reckless, and the presence of women could bring out the worst in them. All the WAFS experienced or heard of incidents in which male pilots, showing off or attempting to frighten the women, would play fighter pilot, rolling and weaving near them, buzzing them or coming suddenly alongside, so the women generally kept a wary eye on them. Still, the WAFS, especially as they grew more comfortable in their role, ignored the rule.[10]

WASP Memorial Plaque, Avenger Field, dedicated December 1944 (Courtesy WASP Archive, Texas Woman's University, Denton, TX)

On this particular mission, the men talked Fort into formation flying. Somewhere over Texas, the left wing of her BT was struck by the landing gear of a plane that was flying too close. During the collision, the plane snapped off her left wingtip and likely knocked her unconscious. Her plane veered, rolled, and went into an inverted dive, smashing into the ground nose-first. Fort was killed on impact, the first female pilot to die on active duty in US military history.

Nancy Love was devastated. She and Barbara Jane "B. J." Erickson, another WAFS Original, flew to Nashville for the funeral. Because civilian pilots could not be buried with military honors, Fort's footstone instead was inscribed, "Killed in the Service of her Country." Many years later, a Nashville airport was named in her honor.

After Fort's death, no one was under any illusions about the very real dangers of ferrying military aircraft. In fact, one WTFD trainee, Margaret Sanford Oldenburg (class 43-4), had been killed two weeks earlier in Houston during a training exercise on March 7. On June 3 her classmate Jane Delores Champlin died flying a BT-13 at night, marking the first death at Avenger Field.

Again, because the WFTD program was not officially militarized, the army refused to pay for transport or funeral expenses for the fallen women. Instead, Oldenburg's and Champlin's bodies were sent home on the train, accompanied by a classmate, at Jackie Cochran's expense. Though all the trainees were shaken, they knew these deaths had occurred in the line of duty. One of Champlin's friends, Yvonne "Pat" Pateman, from Nadine's class 43-5, wrote in a letter to a former trainee: "You remember Janie. She was one of the Houston girls. . . . We all felt pretty low about it, but in this flying business, you got to forget those things. There wasn't a one of us who went up in a BT that day that wasn't scared to go up. Once up, we got over the fear."[11]

In July 1943 *Life* magazine sent a small team of interviewers and photographers to Sweetwater. The editors planned to feature a female pilot on the cover and run a story about life on the base. The WFTD trainees had mixed feelings about being thrust into the public eye. Some hated the idea and tried to avoid the magazine staff; others thought it was exciting.

One of Nadine's classmates who lived in an adjacent bay, twenty-three-year-old Shirley Slade, was chosen as the face of the WFTD trainees; her photograph ran on the cover of the magazine's July 19 issue. Wearing braided pigtails adorned with bows, she is seated on the wing of a plane with a far-off look in her eyes. Another photograph in the cover article on the inside pages featured Nadine's classmate Anne McClellan, whose young husband, like Ed, had been declared missing on Bataan. In still another, Nadine's friend Jean Landis (class 43-4) reclined on a bench, using her parachute for a pillow.

Accompanied by many pictures of the women doing calisthenics, studying, and sunbathing on the weekends, the article portrayed the trainees as smart, patriotic young women: "Fly first, then relax is the unwritten law for trainees, most of whom have immediate relatives on active duty with

the Army and Navy. That flying agrees with them anyone can see as Uncle Sam's suntanned girl pilots march along at Avenger Field, lustily singing."[12] For once, the women pilots were getting positive press.

The article was especially right about one thing: the women mostly focused on flying. Toward the end of training, they were sent up for night-flying experience, trips that frequently inspired them to wax eloquent about the drama and beauty of flying in darkness. Nadine's friend and classmate Irma "Babe" Story (class 43-6) wrote:

> The night I soloed, I was up flying in circles in my particular zone. There was no moon, it was as black as the night could ever be. It gave me the feeling of flying around in a cereal bowl. The lights beneath me seemed an infinite distance away and the lights farther away seemed higher, like they were on the rim of the bowl and it was so very black between the rim and the bottom. It gave me a shut-in feeling and at the same time, a free feeling. . . . I can't explain the two feelings together—one my greatest fear and one my greatest joy.[13]

Night flying was clearly a memorable and influential experience for all the pilots. They eventually adopted the motto "We live in the wind and the sand, and our eyes are on the stars."

CHAPTER 7

BECOMING A WASP

The last phases of ferry training included transitioning from BTs to the bigger, heavier advanced trainers. Once they had begun to master these heavier planes, particularly the AT-6, trainees could at last imagine themselves graduating. For Nadine's class 43-5, graduation was scheduled for September 11, 1943. As the summer waned, the women anticipated joining the Waffies and dreamed about where they would be stationed.

In a letter to her family, Nadine's friend and classmate Helen Jo Severson called the AT-6 "a dream of a ship," writing:

> We were given blanks the other day to fill out and our preferences on bases where we would like to be stationed after our training. I chose Long Beach, California, because Ramsey, my best friend here and who has about 1,000 hours in flying, wants to be there and she helps me an awful lot with flying, and I have never been in California and I'd like to see what it is like. Long Beach, too, is the chief ferry base, so I think the opportunities and living conditions out there will be better. Also there are so many big aircraft companies in California, we ought to be given chances to fly larger ships out there. . . . Of course, we shall be transferred, I imagine, from base to base just as much as the men so preference for a base doesn't mean much, I'm afraid.[1]

Her mindset in August was typical of the trainees on base: They were ready to complete their training and begin ferrying.

In another letter, Severson wrote about transitioning into the AT-17 and eagerly made plans to stop at home before her first assignment: "Immediately after graduation I am starting for South Dakota with two girls from Nebraska. They have a car, and as reservations are so impossible to get, I think I would be far more comfortable just going with them. . . . I actually think Mom + Daddy are anxious to have me come home and certainly excited about it. Maybe they think I'm actually amounting to something."[2] Nadine, too, was surely excited about stopping in Wichita to see Nelle.

Nadine beside a BT-13 Vultee Valiant at Avenger Field, 1943

However, tragically, Severson would never begin her first assignment. On August 30, just eleven days before graduation, she was sent up, along with another good friend and classmate Margaret "Peggy" Seip. At some point during the flight, when Severson was practicing instrument flying under the hood, an unexpected structural failure caused the aircraft to crash. Both women and their instructor were killed. Adding to the tragedy, shortly after receiving the news of her death, Severson's young husband, Rob, volunteered for a dangerous mission and was shot down over Germany.

The deaths of Helen Jo Severson and Peggy Seip rocked the entire base; both were loved by all who knew them. Wisconsin-born Seip was a gardener and when she arrived at Avenger Field in March, she had planted a vine of morning glories behind the barracks. By September it covered the back wall of the structure with verdant leaves and white, trumpet-shaped blossoms. Seip's green thumb had also cultivated a flower garden, particularly zinnias; Nadine joined her classmates there the night after Severson's and Seip's deaths to cry and remember their friends.

Nadine sought permission to accompany Severson's body back to South Dakota, but her request was denied, as there was so little time before gradu-

ation. She tried to pack up Severson's things and fought for the assurance that Severson's wings would be sent home to her family. Still, these actions seemed hollow and provided little comfort.

Nadine felt lost after her friend's death. In a letter to Severson's mother, she shared her firm belief that the crash couldn't have been Jo's fault, calling her "a very sensible, capable, and cautious pilot" and expressing her grief at the loss of a very dear friend:

> It has been terribly hard for me to resign myself to losing Jo, as I had grown so very close to her, and couldn't have grieved more over losing an only sister. As you perhaps know, we had been almost inseparable since we first arrived in Sweetwater, and we had such great plans for the future. . . . I have never known anyone like her, so sweet and lovable and infinitely wise for one so young. Jo was loved by everyone. . . . There is just nothing we can say or do to make it seem right that she of all people should be taken, and yet it is so and we must try to believe there was a reason. I shall always think of her, and go on with the work we planned as though she were with me. Just having known her has been an inspiration to me.[3]

Nadine's WFTD yearbook features a poem written by Mary Amanda Bowles (class 43-4) on one of its final pages. It concludes:

> If Death should become one with us
> In that land of space and the wind,
> Our rough wild wind
> Would wind round some of us
> And his touch would engulf
> And possess us and hurl us
> Like juggernauts, down from the upper air,
> Let love of flight and our laughter,
> Like avenging thunder unfurled
> Come tumbling down the heights we claim,
> A challenge to those who come after
> To cast their craft yet with us
> Across the free skies that protect our land
> In War and Peace, for country and with God.[4]

Sept. 19, 1943

Dear Mrs. Anderson

I have tried so many times to write you, but felt so hopelessly at a loss for words to say what is in my heart. I wish I could see and talk to you but as that is impossible at this time I do want you to know I've thought of you all. I felt badly about not being able to accompany the body home, but they would not allow me to do so as it was so near graduation.

It has been terribly hard for me to resign myself to losing "Jo" as I had grown so very close to her, and couldn't have grieved more over losing an only sister. As you perhaps know, we had been almost inseparable since we first arrived in Sweetwater, and we had

First page of Nadine's letter to Mrs. Amy Anderson, Helen Jo Severson's mother, September 19, 1943 (Courtesy WASP Archive, Texas Woman's University, Denton, TX)

Throughout the summer of 1943, as Nadine and her classmates completed their training, the WAFS and WFTD programs experienced shake-ups at the administrative level. On July 5 a notice went out from the War Department officially naming Jackie Cochran the AAF's director of women pilots. The same day, a different announcement named Nancy Love the executive for WAFS on the staff of Colonel Tunner, Ferrying Division, ATC. What did it all mean?

First, it meant that Love had more authority within the ATC than before. She was tasked with designing a "progressive" air training program to help her pilots transition into flying bigger and faster aircraft, including bombers and pursuits. She also wanted to get into those bigger planes; she didn't want to spend the remainder of the war flying a desk. She was wary of the implications of her new title but eager to help her WAFS pilots fly more exciting planes—particularly pursuits—that were essential to the war effort.

The announcements, however, also fueled headlines about a feminine rivalry brewing. Newspapers began to pit the women against each other. As Marianne Verges writes in *On Silver Wings*:

> The newspapers and magazines had a field day with the shake-up in the women pilots' program, playing up the rivalry between Jackie and Nancy. They made Jackie's appointment seem like a victory in an ongoing war. Up until now this war had been undeclared, but from July 5, 1943, onward, the careful guarding of command prerogatives versus the aggressive attempts for headquarters-staff control often overshadowed the accomplishment of the women pilots—and in the long run contributed to their doom.[5]

In other words, by setting the tussle over WAFS and WFTD leadership center stage, the press effectively shoved the heroism of the women pilots out of the spotlight. And, given their already controversial portrayal in the media, that spotlight was crucial.

Finally, the July 5 orders ultimately meant a reorganization of the entire women's pilot program. On August 5, with a formal announcement following on August 20, the WAFS and WFTD program were renamed as one organization—the Women Airforce Service Pilots (WASP)—under the leadership of Jackie Cochran.

For the WAFS Originals, nothing could have felt more sudden or disorienting. As Betty Gillies said, "We went to bed WAFS and woke up the next morning WASPs." For the trainees at Sweetwater, however, the change was exciting; they were sure it meant that militarization was imminent. On August 19, 1943, Irma "Babe" Story (class 43-6) wrote to a former trainee: "Something has been added. We have dog tags now, just like the Army. Incidentally, we will be militarized Oct. or Nov. and wait until you see our new uniforms we are to get. Wow!"[6]

For the women in the air who were already or soon would be ferrying, the bureaucratic orders had very real implications. The most visible change was to their uniforms. All this time, the WAFS had been wearing smart, gray-green gabardine uniforms fitted for them by a tailor in Wilmington. Though they occasionally ran into trouble on ferrying trips if they forgot to pack their skirts (most restaurants wouldn't permit entry to women in slacks), the pilots loved and wore their uniforms with pride.

The new graduates from the first three classes of Cochran's program, on the other hand, were not issued the same gabardine uniforms. Instead, they primarily wore army "pinks"—white blouses and khaki slacks. Cochran, using her new leadership power, determined that all WASP would wear a new uniform, chosen by her. Her decision was surely influenced by General Arnold, who had plans to put the men of the air forces in blue, not green uniforms, to distinguish them from the rest of the army. Cochran hired a Bergdorf Goodman fashion designer to create uniforms incorporating a light wool jacket, slacks, skirt, and a beret—all in a pretty, striking blue known as Santiago blue. The women received their new uniforms in the spring of 1944.

Although the WAFS pilots were reluctant to give up their gabardine grays, the new Santiago blues were stylish and surprisingly practical. No longer would they be mistaken for stewardesses, senior girl scouts, or even plane mechanics or ground crew. The Santiago blues and new sterling silver wings with the diamond shield fixed all that, and most of the newly minted WASPs loved their new uniforms. The downside, as most WASPs saw it, was that they had to pay for certain uniform pieces themselves, since they still hadn't been militarized.[7] Working for the ATC, for example, Nadine received $250 per month, but she had to pay 20 percent of it for room and board, plus as much as $12.50 for a required piece of the new uniform.

Nadine in her WASP Santiago blues, ca. 1944

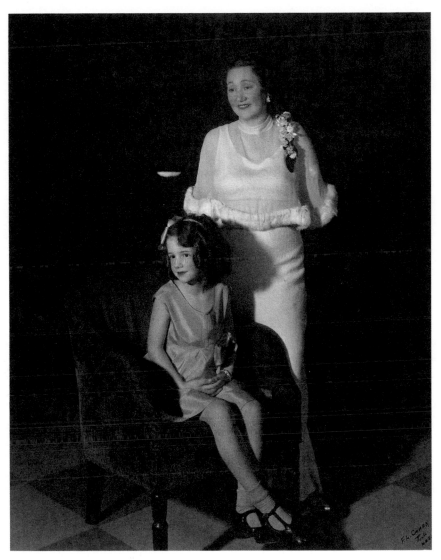

Nelle Ramsey and Nadine Berniece Ramsey (age five), 1916

John Ward Lockwood, Pioneers in Kansas, *1936 (Carol M. Highsmith Archive, Library of Congress, Prints and Photographs Division [LC-DIG-highsm-11465])*

Richard Haines, Kansas Farming, *1936 (Carol M. Highsmith Archive, Library of Congress, Prints and Photographs Division [LC-DIG-highsm-11464])*

Entering Wichita's US Post Office and Courthouse for her 1938 swearing-in as airmail carrier, Nadine would have felt a special affinity for the Kansas settlers and farmers featured in the murals on the lobby walls. Above: Like the Ramsey family, the pioneering men and women of Kansas overcame hardship and obstacles to settle the land. Below: Farm children look to the sky for the mail that will soon reach their rural outpost.

By their clothing and the aircraft they flew, the WASP showed that they had "earned their wings."

Nadine's WASP patch featuring the WASP mascot Fifinella, designed by Disney. This patch was worn on WASP flight jackets.

WASP pilot's badge, worn as a pin, wings with shield center, 318th (Nadine's training squadron), W5 (Nadine's class). Donated by Jill S. McCormick (43-W-5) (Smithsonian National Air and Space Museum [A19760937000])

Dan Kelly, Young and Invincible, *1989 (Courtesy of the artist)*

Nadine was one of only twenty-six WASP qualified to fly the P-38 Lightning, Lockheed's sleek twin-engine pursuit plane. They are represented in Dan Kelly's painting Young and Invincible *by a woman hovering in the sky.*

John Solie, Last Cavalry Charge, *2005 (US Cavalry Association)*

Gil Cohen, WASP Special Delivery, *2013 (Courtesy of the artist)*

The exploits of war heroes Lieutenant Edwin P. Ramsey and Nadine Berniece Ramsey come to life in these works of art. Above: John Solie depicts the last horse cavalry charge, under Lt. Ramsey's command, in US Army history. Below: Gil Cohen's WASP Special Delivery *features a WASP squadron—a redhead among them—viewing a map for ferrying P-38 Lightning fighter planes to airfields across the country.*

Publicity Poster, Never Surrender: The Ed Ramsey Story, *2016 (Courtesy Vanilla Fire Productions)*

(Above and following page) *Outpouring of recognition for Ed Ramsey began in 1990, when his memoir,* Lieutenant Ramsey's War, *was published. Since his death in 2013, Raquel has carried on his legacy with love, devotion, and gratitude to all US military heroes—accepting awards and honors, contributing his memorabilia to museums and archives, and creating commemorative media and events.*

Raquel Ramsey accepts Ed's Congressional Gold Medal from General Oscar Hilman, president, and Marvin Dumlao, vice president, of the Philippine Scouts Heritage Society, San Antonio, Texas, 2018 (Courtesy Philippine Scouts Heritage Society)

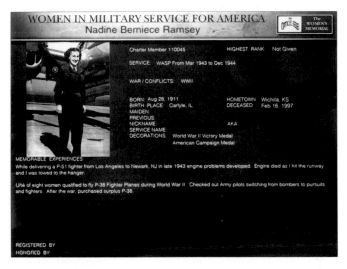

Nadine Berniece Ramsey, database, Women in Military Service for America Memorial (Women's Memorial), Arlington, Virginia, 1997

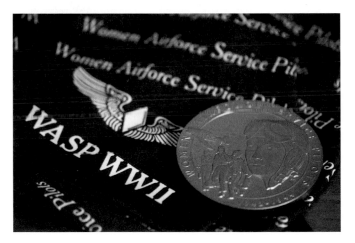

Nadine's Women Airforce Service Pilots Congressional Gold Medal, received March 2010 (Photograph by Amy Baroa)

Though she did not live to attend the opening of the Women's Memorial, Nadine contributed her most memorable WASP experience to its database before her death: "While delivering a P-51 fighter from Los Angeles to Newark, NJ3 engine problems developed. Engine died as I hit the runway and I was towed to the hanger." Nadine's legacy appears in archives and exhibitions across the nation, and her medals are lovingly displayed at Raquel Ramsey's home.

Nadine Berniece Ramsey (1911–1997)

Class 44-7, one of eighteen WASP classes, marching for graduation exercises at Avenger Field (Courtesy WASP Archive, Texas Woman's University, Denton, TX)

For Nadine and the 43-5 trainees, the merger meant that they were the first WFTD class to officially graduate as WASPs. On September 11, 1943, full of bittersweet emotions and without their classmates Helen Jo Severson and Margaret "Peggy" Seip, eighty-five women of class 43-5 graduated from Sweetwater. Jackie Cochran was present to pin on their engraved wings.

Upon graduation, Nadine was assigned to the Fifth Ferrying Group in Dallas, Texas. Fortunately, she was granted leave on the days between graduation on September 11 and the date she was set to report to Love Field, September 24. She returned to Wichita and stayed with Nelle at the Hotel Lassen, where the Ramsey Dermatology Clinic was thriving. Nadine was happy to be back with her mother; now thirty-two, she and Nelle rarely butted heads anymore. They were both fiercely independent yet firmly united by their love of family and all the obstacles they had overcome.

Mother and daughter dined at local restaurants and attended church downtown. Nelle had grown increasingly devout as she got older, Nadine

Building trainer aircraft for the US Army and Navy, Stearman Aircraft Division, Boeing Airplane Company, Wichita, 1944 (Wichita State University Libraries, Special Collections and University Archives)

less so. She said hello to her mother's many friends, including Walter and Olive Ann Beech and Otero (Ote) Beeson, who, Nadine teased, was Nelle's beau. Ote was the son of famed Kansas City Saloon owner Chalkley Beeson, and he had been smitten with Nelle for years, although Nelle insisted they were just friends. In response to her daughter's teasing, Nelle asked Nadine if she was planning on getting married again, but Nadine said she was too busy. Flying now occupied her thoughts completely.

Nadine also picked up any mail that hadn't made it to her at Avenger Field and was treated to letters and news from the Cozad and Ramsey families in Illinois. By now, her favorite cousin, Barbara Branch, had graduated from high school and was attending business school in Centralia, about fifteen miles southwest of Odin. Due to wartime rations, Barbara usually

drove her father's truck into downtown Odin every day and hitched a ride from there with five or six other students to school.

Nadine was surprised by how Wichita, too, seemed almost completely transformed by the war. The Kress Department Store's candy counter, which Nadine remembered as a glittering, sugary wonderland, nowadays sold only dull-looking peanuts and cookies. Shoes now were made of shoddy reclaimed rubber that left black splotches on floors and sidewalks, and filling stations seemed abandoned. Most strikingly, the population was booming, and new construction at the airport and on city streets left traffic in tangled knots. Nationally, a "victory" speed limit of thirty-five miles per hour was instated to save rubber and gas. Sugar, meat, cooking oil, and even shoes were rationed. Nadine saw an Innes Department Store ad advising ladies on which ration stamp to use for the new fall line of shoes.

Not surprisingly, the already high-flying aviation industry witnessed a new explosion of growth. The Wichita Municipal Airport's administration building was almost completely leased by the army, but commercial airlines still used the runways as well. Large new wings were added to the building, and some of the runway lengths were doubled. By 1944 there was a takeoff or landing at the airport every ninety seconds.

In early 1943 the Boeing-Wichita Company (formerly Stearman) built a new plant, hired more than twenty thousand workers, and began manufacturing the four-engine bomber, the B-29 Superfortress. Contractors erected huge new housing developments just to keep up with the city's ballooning population.

Whether in Kansas, Illinois, or anywhere else in America, there was no place the war didn't reach.

PART IV

WASP AT WAR

On September 8, 1944, the DC-3's engines roared in Nadine's ears as it banked slowly, turning one glossy, silver wing over the gunmetal gray Pacific. As a passenger this time, she was free to enjoy the scenery; grinning, she pressed her cheek to the window glass. The sun was sinking into a vast mercury sea, throwing dusky pink rays onto Los Angeles's high rises and the jagged shapes of mountains to the north.

As Signal Hill, crested by its forest of oil derricks, came into view, a necklace of lights appeared along the harbor. A thrill ran along Nadine's spine as the plane pointed its nose toward a crosshatch of runways she recognized instantly as Long Beach Army Air Field. The plane taxied to a stop, and Nadine climbed into the aisle. Stretching her stiff back, she began collecting her things.

A friendly voice broke in, and she turned to see an older man with graying whiskers gazing at her smart Santiago blue uniform. "You're one of them WASPs, huh?" he asked, nodding at the highly polished wings pinned over her heart. "Do you fly the big ones?"

Nadine was glad his expression was kind; the passenger she'd had to bump to get on this flight hadn't been so pleased. "Sometimes," she replied, grinning.

Despite her exhaustion, Nadine climbed off the DC-3 with a new wave of energy. She took a deep breath of fresh, ocean-scented air. On the West Coast, she was—at least geographically—closer to Ed. Nadine thought about her brother as she made her way to the terminal building. She imagined him, alive, marching through a labyrinth of tropical jungle, pressing his way forward through the tangle of vines and darkness, surviving, fighting. This past year in Nadine's life had felt no less confusing—different planes every day, different cities every night, fallen friends, public insults. A war is a war, she thought, no matter where you're fighting it.

Weaving briskly between buildings in the twilight on her way to the Sixth Ferrying Group office, Nadine could hear the roar of a twin-engine pursuit aircraft coming in for a landing. She paused to look up as a P-38 landed on the airfield runway. She was impressed; the landing was textbook perfect.

Nadine continued gazing as the beautiful twin-tailed Lockheed Lightning taxied to a stop and a lean, athletic-looking young woman in a WASP uniform climbed out of the cockpit, removing her headphones and shaking out dark blond curls. She smiled to herself; she was in the right place. Moments later, she set her bag down beside a door labeled "WASP Squadron Operations" and took a deep breath. She knocked. A low, authoritative voice called, "Come in!"

Nadine entered. The big room was a blur of warm light, flight suits on a rack, and cozy couches and armchairs, all dominated by an enormous US map covering the back wall. A slender, black-haired young woman was working on a complicated chart that seemed to track the progress of the WASPs under her command. She immediately stood up and came forward to Nadine, her hand extended.

Nadine's instant impression was one of poise; this was B. J. Erickson, who was running the female ferrying division of the most important base in the country. At twenty-four, she was one of the youngest WASP commanding officers. Just a bit taller than Nadine, she stood erect, looking steady and serious. "Glad to have you," she said, responding to Nadine's introduction. Then she cocked her head, indicating the runway where the Lightning had just landed. Her chocolate eyes twinkled. "How'd you like to fly a P-38?"

CHAPTER 8

FERRY PILOT

In late September 1943 Nadine reported to the ATC's Fifth Ferrying Group, which operated out of Love Field (named after World War I cavalry officer Moss L. Love, no relation to Nancy Love), just north of Dallas. Though it wasn't Long Beach as she had requested, she was luckier than many WFTD graduates. A quarter of class 43-4 had been sent to non-ferrying bases, as had many of Nadine's 43-5 classmates. Nadine had been selected to ferry for the ATC.

With its stringent requirements, the ATC only accepted the most experienced WASPs for ferrying missions. Highly qualified as she was, Nadine was a natural choice to be a ferry pilot. She was now part of an elite corps; before the war's end, only 303 WASPs would qualify as ferry pilots for the ATC.

The Texas-based Fifth Ferrying Group was established in 1941. Love Field, its base, was located near several key aircraft manufacturing plants; it became a major modification site. From there, many of the modified planes were dispatched across the world. In January 1943, five WAFS Originals joined the male ferry pilots at Love Field. Upon their arrival, they began ferrying BT 13s and DT-15s, followed quickly by PT-17s. By the time Nadine and other new WFTD graduates arrived, Dallas WASPs were regularly flying AT-6s, 9s, 11s, and 17s, the latter three models twin-engine aircraft.

Nadine was comfortable at Love Field. The women pilots were housed in barracks right beside the men's, and each woman had her own room—a far cry from the cramped quarters in Sweetwater. She was also fortunate to be joined by quite a few of her 43-5 classmates from Avenger Field, including Anne McClellan and Shirley Slade, who had both been featured in the *Life* article.

Although other base commanders had more critical views of female pilots, in Dallas the WASP were treated as well as the men. According to Ruth Dailey Helm (class 43-2), "The men of the Air Transport Command—the ones we were directly under, the ferry pilots at Dallas—accepted us. They treated us like their sisters. They were not military; they were airline pilots

and older men who had instructed on many different aircraft. . . . We had very little military protocol at Dallas."[1]

WAFS Original Florene Miller, appointed to command the Dallas WASPs by Nancy Love, was a tall, dark-haired Texan only twenty-two years old. Despite her youth, she was wry and resilient, having lost her father and brother in a plane crash on July 4, 1941. At Love Field, she led a group of WFTD graduates and three other Originals, Helen Richards, Dorothy Scott, and Betsy Ferguson.

The WAFS took Dallas by storm. Original Delphine Bohn recalled, "The first Saturday night at the Officers' Club in Dallas, Betsy, the blonde, blue-eyed doll, and Florene, the tall, gorgeous green-eyed brunette, nearly caused a stampede among the men in the Fifth Ferrying Group."[2] Elizabeth Whitlow Smith (class 43-2) remembered playing ping-pong and cards with the men in the officers club in Dallas and said of her commanding officer, "Hardly anybody is as colorful as Florene."[3] Though ten years Miller's senior, Nadine respected her as an excellent pilot and commanding officer. She also got along with Richards, Ferguson, and Scott just fine. Of course, the WASPs were always on the move, so the women rarely spent time together; ferrying aircraft was the priority.

All in all, their schedule was busy and exhausting. Like all new arrivals, Nadine was placed under the guidance of the Originals already stationed there. They needed to learn a few additional skills before they were ready to ferry full-time. They were trained in paperwork, group flying (*not* formation flying), and crosswind landings, and they received more instruction in military organization and courtesy (adding to the expectation that they would be militarized by the end of the year).

Once cleared to ferry, which for some WASPs took as little as three days, ATC pilots were on duty seven days a week.[4] They were fully responsible for an airplane from the moment they officially picked it up, which they called "buying" a plane, to the moment they "sold" it, signing it over at its destination base. When WASPs Remained Over Night on ferrying trips, they were required to send a RON telegram back to their home base, and they had the privilege of using the local officers club.

For many of Nadine's fellow WASP, staying away from base had its own challenges. Lorraine Zillner Rodgers (class 44-2) recalled:

Find a place to stay. That was always something, too, because all of the wives were traveling to meet their husbands someplace and the hotels were full. Many a night in hotel lobbies, those of us who traveled together, would just be on the floor of the lobby with about umpteen other ferry pilots, using our parachutes as our pillow . . . and then up in the morning and out to operations. We'd have to leave when it was dark and get out there and be at the runway ready for takeoff.[5]

Dallas did offer one particular advantage to Nadine: the city was close to family. Nadine's uncle—her mother's brother, Baptist reverend John Cozad—lived in Sulphur Springs, about eighty miles northeast of Dallas. Moreover, the Dallas WASPs were responsible for picking up planes from the Beech, Boeing, and Cessna factories in Wichita, and Nadine flew there often, allowing her to visit Nelle more frequently at the Hotel Lassen. Typically, Nadine and other Dallas pilots would be flown up to Wichita to pick up Stearman PT-17s, Beechcraft AT-7s and AT-10s, and Cessna C-78s, which they would then fly back to Love Field for modification and then on to California for delivery.

After delivering a plane, Nadine, like other ATC pilots, was required to report back to her base as soon as possible, so she was granted War BB or Class 2 status for commercial flights, which meant she could bump civilians or even lower-class military personnel off a flight to get back to her base. If she arrived back to Dallas before 10 p.m., she would be sent back out on another ferrying trip at 8 a.m. the next day.

Dallas WASP Catherine D'Arezzo (class 44-4) recalled flying planes into small towns in central California and sleeping on wooden benches at the train station while waiting to catch the 2 a.m. train back to Los Angeles. "But if you got into Los Angeles and you found a plane, you had top priority for transportation back," she noted. "If you found that the plane was going to get into Dallas before midnight, you were smart enough to take the next plane! If you took the next plane, you could have the day off."[6]

The ferrying WASPs were always on the move. Nadine was highly adaptable and usually didn't mind the busy life of a ferry pilot, but she occasionally suffered from the fatigue that plagued them all. Mostly, she was putting in her time while waiting for her chance to fly more powerful planes. She

Nadine with Nelle during one of many wartime visits to Wichita, ca. 1943

ferried PTs and other trainer aircraft throughout the fall of 1943, but P-51 Mustangs and P-38 Lightnings were also passing through the modification plant in Dallas. Nadine would watch them come and go with envy, eager to get her hands on these exciting aircraft.

By fall 1943 the progressive air training program established by Brigadier General Bill Tunner, who had been promoted in July 1943, and Nancy Love was flourishing. Ferry pilots all over the country were flying bigger and bigger planes, with round-the-clock training and ferrying. When not ferrying, they attended ground school, received under-the-hood instrument time in the Link Trainer, and reported to instrument flying school to prepare themselves to fly more advanced aircraft.

To help categorize what any given pilot was qualified to fly, Tunner developed the Ferrying Division's Pilot Classification System. As the pilots moved up through the system, they were issued cards stating their classification, from Class I (low-powered, single-engine planes, including primary, basic, and advanced trainers) to Class V (four-engine bombers and transports, such as B-29s and C-54s).

One of the special qualifications for Class V certification was the ability to transfer those largest aircraft overseas. Since female pilots were not allowed to ferry aircraft overseas, theoretically the highest class a WASP could reach was Class IV-P (twin-engine, high-performance pursuits, or fighters, such as P-38s). The special P qualification was developed because flying pursuits wasn't actually a necessary step for male pilots, who eventually flew the big four-engine planes. (Nancy Love and a limited number of other women pilots did occasionally fly or copilot Class V planes domestically.)

During the summer and fall of 1943, WASPs regularly ferried planes at the Class I and Class II (twin-engine trainers, such as the AT-9 and AT-17) levels. Some were even flying Class III (twin-engine cargo and transport planes). But in the spring and fall of 1943, due to the needs of the war in Europe, the production of trainer aircraft dropped significantly and the production of pursuit aircraft increased sharply. WASPs were desperately needed to ferry those fighters.

Nadine was eager to learn to fly pursuits. She and other WASPs took advantage of the necessary ground school and instrument training to obtain the necessary certification, the army instrument card or "white card," that would permit them to fly pursuits. Instruction involved hours in the Link Trainer, the early flight simulator she'd trained in at Avenger Field. The "blue box," as it was nicknamed, was a wooden cockpit-sized box with an opaque canopy, situated on bellows that could rotate the box on all three axes. Within the cockpit was, of course, the instrument panel. Inside the Link, pilots experienced a simulation of "flying blind."

Fortunately for Nadine and her fellow Dallas WASPs, there was a Link Trainer right there at Love Field. In fact, the instructor was Flora Miller, Florene Miller's mother. In the fall of 1943, the WAFS pilots at Dallas received instrument training: among them, Dorothy Scott then received her white card on October 8, and WAFS Original Teresa James was sent from Wilmington to Dallas to obtain her instrument rating. Miller received hers, too, later recalling that her mother was especially tough on her. "I probably had the best Link instruction of anyone," she admitted, "because she tried her best to crash and burn me."[7]

Nadine earned her white card in Dallas at the earliest opportunity. The ATC eventually set up a specified instrument training school in Saint Joseph, Missouri, which the women headed for pursuit school attended. Fly-

ing pursuit aircraft required more than an instrument rating, however. After receiving her white card, Nadine was qualified to attend pursuit school, but she would have to wait her turn.

The ATC established its first pursuit school in Palm Springs, California, in December 1943. The course lasted about four weeks, and pilots received instruction and flight experience on four single-engine pursuit aircraft: the P-39, P-40, P-47, and P-51. Nancy Love sent three WAFS Originals from Dallas—Florene Miller, Helen Richards, and Dorothy Scott—there immediately. Original Delphine Bohn replaced Florene Miller as Dallas WASP commander. On December 1, WASPs from all four ATC bases, eight in total, joined thirty-five male pilots in the first class at the Palm Springs pursuit school.

On December 3, Dorothy Scott was flying an AT-6 with her instructor. As they made their final approach to land, a male student pilot in a P-39, who was also on final approach, miscalculated his speed and flew nearly on top of Scott's plane, causing a midair collision that killed all three pilots. After Cornelia Fort, Dorothy Scott was the second of the Originals killed in the line of duty. Helen Richards, Scott's close friend and roommate at pursuit school, was deeply bereaved; all the Dallas WASPs mourned the loss of another excellent, courageous female pilot. Blame for the accident was placed on the tower.

After graduation in January 1944, most of the first class of pilots from Palm Springs pursuit school, including Florene Miller and Helen Richards, were sent to Long Beach to ferry the P-51 Mustang, an aircraft that would soon become known as the Game Changer.

Around this time, Nancy Love, executive of pilots in the ATC, provided the Public Relations Section of Headquarters Ferrying Liaison a summary of accomplishments for the year 1943. Just a few months earlier, on November 12, 1943, the WASP had celebrated its first anniversary at a "big birthday jamboree" in Sweetwater with a "cake that's fit for queens served to the 'queens of the skies," *The Avenger* reported on its front page.[8]

Indeed, Love had a lot to crow about: the memorandum resulting from her summary, "Ferrying WASPs," listed the forty-three types of planes on which the WASPs were qualified, including five pursuit aircraft: P-47, P-51, P-39, P-40, and P-38. When the public relations report was filed, twenty-

Nadine in the cockpit of a P-51A fighter plane, early 1940s

two WASPs held white cards.[9] But the report didn't stop there. Along with details of WASP training and qualifications, it was peppered with anecdotal evidence of the realities of ferrying aircraft:

> There's not any glamor for the women who help ferry the planes from factories to army air bases in the United States and Canada. It's a job to be done and the women perform their tasks under conditions, frequently, which are exhausting and distasteful.
>
> Mrs. Love is especially proud of the manner in which the women are flying the open-air trainers to bases in Canada. These deliveries are made under conditions which are extremely cold. The WASPs have dubbed this route ICICLE LANE.
>
> The WASPs also call attention to the recent accomplishment of a woman pilot who ferried four planes, three pursuits and a cargo ship, in five operating days, flying each plane about 2,000 miles. . . . In

increasing numbers women ferry pilots are being checked out on heavier types of aircraft.[10]

In 1944 additional accomplishments could be added to Love's list as more pursuit-trained WASPs entered the pool of men and women ferry pilots who qualified to fly them. The entry of the WASP into pursuit ferrying would help the United States change the course of the war, in both the European and Pacific theaters. These swift, highly maneuverable fighter planes were primarily designed to accompany and protect heavy bombers deep into enemy territory. However, up to this point, no pursuit aircraft had the fuel capacity to fly to and from enemy targets alongside heavy bomber aircraft.

In December 1943 British engineers figured out a way to modify the P-51, adding six hundred miles to its range. The P-51 Mustang became the only plane with the ability to perform the crucial task of accompanying bombers deep into Germany and on bombing missions to obliterate the Nazis' fuel supplies in Romania. As most P-51s were manufactured in Long Beach, the pilots of the Sixth Ferrying Group ferried them cross-country to Newark, where they were loaded onto ships and sent to England. P-51s were manufactured in Grand Prairie, Texas, near Dallas, as well; they, too, were ferried to Newark by the Fifth Ferrying Group pilots. In April 1944 the P-51D model was equipped with a new engine, expanding its range still further and making the Mustang truly a game changer.

Although WASPs couldn't fly pursuit aircraft overseas, every woman ferrying pursuits in the United States freed a man for combat abroad. Ferrying pursuits, particularly the P-51, became the singular priority of the now thirty-five Ferrying Command WASPs qualified to fly them, and still more women pilots were desperately needed to move high-priority pursuits across the country.

In all, seven classes graduated from pursuit school through March 1944. Subsequently, the ATC reassigned the base at Palm Springs to the Twenty-First Ferrying Group, and the pursuit school was relocated to Brownsville, at the southernmost tip of Texas, right where the Gulf of Mexico meets the US-Mexico border.

General Tunner was anxious to send every woman who wanted to fly fighters to pursuit school, and Nadine was ready to go. Armed with her white

card, she was in the first group of WASPs to train in Brownsville, just as the weather began heating up in April. She was ecstatic, not only because her adventurous spirit longed to fly the fastest, most powerful aircraft available, but also because she knew that pursuits were absolutely crucial to the war effort. Learning to fly them, she knew, was the most valuable way she could help her country.

Then again, as Dorothy Scott's experience had shown, pursuit school could be extremely dangerous. Pilots in training had to take a blindfold test in each aircraft cockpit, pointing to all the instruments and controls before ever taking off. The Bell P-39 Airacobra, in particular, had a reputation as a pilot killer; male pilots called it a flying coffin, and at least fifteen male pilots from the Romulus base had already died ferrying P-39s. Nadine's friend Jean Landis (class 43-4), who attended pursuit school at Brownsville in June, recalled the first day the new students were sent up in one. "We were scared to death—the guys, too, not just us gals," she said. "One of the guys started to sing 'When the roll is called up yonder, I'll be there.' We all chimed in."[11]

Fortunately, there were no fatal accidents in Nadine's class, although 37 percent of all pilots sent to pursuit school ultimately washed out. Nadine passed the arduous course with flying colors, graduating with fourteen other women on May 1, 1944. She became one of only 134 WASP pilots qualified to ferry pursuits.

Following graduation from pursuit school, Nadine was granted fifteen days' leave and once again traveled to Wichita to be with Nelle. Always happy to brag about a local heroine, one Wichita paper ran her photo on the occasion of her visit, featuring a smiling Nadine in uniform under the headline "Pilots Pursuit Plane."[12] She was just thankful, at last, to rest at home.

Together, mother and daughter celebrated Ed's twenty-seventh birthday on May 9 and prayed they would hear news of him soon. They missed him and were profoundly worried. In addition, Nelle's friend Ote Beeson had died unexpectedly in January of that year, and she took it hard. Even all of Nadine's accomplishments couldn't erase their feelings of loss and foreboding.

In late spring 1944, as Nadine began ferrying P-51s regularly from Dallas to Newark, Jackie Cochran once again was stirring the pot in Washington, DC. The debate over militarization of the WASP program was reaching a boiling point. The program needed to be militarized; that much was clear.

Already, more than twenty WASPs had been killed in training and active service, and their families were incensed at the lack of formal recognition for their sacrifices.

Since the military wouldn't even pay for the bodies to be sent home, often other WASPs would take up a collection among themselves to help cover the cost. Friends and relatives could not drape an American flag on their caskets, nor were their grieving parents permitted to display a gold service star in their windows. At a time when Americans needed to pull together and honor their fallen, the WASPs who had given their lives for their country were not properly recognized.

At the same time, there was another practical reason for WASP militarization: their work was a critical component of the AAF's machine. As such, they deserved military insurance, pensions, and eventually veteran status and benefits.

The first, most obvious way to militarize the WASPs was to absorb them into the Women's Army Corps (WAC). Established in May 1942, the WAC was militarized in July 1943 under the leadership of its first director, Colonel Oveta Culp Hobby. General Tunner and Nancy Love thought that, with some stipulations, female pilots might be successfully integrated into the WAC. Cochran, however, disagreed. She wanted to incorporate the WASP program directly into the AAF, with herself as director of her own division and on the same level as Colonel Hobby.

While General Arnold went along with what Cochran wanted, from December 1942 through early 1944, General Tunner tried multiple times to reach terms on WASP militarization via the WAC. His efforts were to no avail.

Unfortunately for the WASP, by the summer of 1944, the war was in a completely different place; it seemed that the Allied Powers surely would be victorious. More and more male pilots were surviving their missions, and there was no longer a pressing need to continue training men to fly in combat.

Earlier that year, General Arnold had drastically cut back on the AAF's pilot training program. In January he ended it entirely, putting hundreds of male pilots and flight instructors out of work. These men immediately feared they would be drafted and began looking desperately for any way to keep flying stateside. They and their family members wrote angry letters to

their congressmen, demanding that men should be given priority for any flying jobs available.

The press once again got involved, publishing articles on the potential WASP militarization. Some major newspapers took the side of the WASPs, but many others trashed them, falling back on old stereotypes of the women as scheming, aggressive, or loose. By spring, author Sarah Byrn Rickman notes in *WASP of the Ferry Command*, "WASP ferry pilots out delivering aircraft around the country began to notice the change in attitude towards them, and it often was manifested by abusive language and incidents. A backlash of public opinion against women had begun in wartime America."[13] While this backlash certainly wasn't exclusive to the WASP—affecting women in many industries—these women pilots suffered uniquely because of it.

On February 17, 1944, HR 4219, an amended bill drafted by Congressman John Costello of California to propose WASP militarization, was submitted to Congress. But rather than bring the bill to a vote immediately, Congress instead formed the House Committee on Post Office and Civil Service under Georgia Congressman Robert J. Ramspeck to investigate the WASP program, pushing the vote to June. Once more, the WASPs were forced to wait on the question of militarization and once more, they were not idle. For the WASPs of the Ferrying Command, there was still plenty of ferrying to do.

Confident that Congress would pass the Costello Bill in June, Jackie Cochran and General Arnold were anxious to get the WASPs ready for their new commissions. On April 19 the ATC sent a group of WASPs for training as prospective officers to the School of Applied Tactics—also known as Officer Training School (OTS)—in Orlando, Florida. The four-week course offered instruction in military discipline, military courtesy, and army organization.

The women in this first group were selected by their length of service. Not surprisingly, many were WAFS Originals. Nancy Love was included, as were the squadron commanders from all four ferrying bases. They were glad to be back together after being sent to their various assignments.

In contrast to the four ferrying bases, the OTS's accommodations were almost luxurious. In *The Originals*, Rickman writes: "Maids kept the barracks, did [the trainees'] laundry, and polished their shoes. The women had never

been treated so well. Consequently, the WAFS—who hadn't had much in the way of leave time over the course of twenty months of active service and busy ferrying schedules—and their fellow WASPs set out, in their off time, to enjoy themselves on Florida's beaches, in the warm Florida sunshine."[14]

Unfortunately, the timing couldn't have been worse. With the eyes of the public, the press, and the Ramspeck Committee on the WASP program, it seemed presumptuous to send women who hadn't even yet officially been militarized to Officer Training School. Cochran, in particular, came under fire for sending her best pilots to Orlando at a time when they were sorely needed; the absence of advanced WASPs in the middle of 1944 put a significant strain on the Ferrying Division.

After months of investigation, including a visit to OTS, the Ramspeck Committee announced its findings. The date was June 5, the day before D-Day, which marked the beginning of the end of the war in Europe. The committee asserted that training women fliers from scratch at Sweetwater was too expensive. According to the committee, this had nothing to do with the pilots' gender; the problem was their inexperience. By lowering the hours the women needed to enter training, Cochran had also lowered the number of cumulative hours the graduates brought to the job. Many arrived at the ATC bases not adequately prepared for the demanding jobs ferry pilots were asked to perform. The committee also made recommendations: qualified WASPs should continue to work, but their salaries should be adjusted in accordance with their experience and responsibilities. Also, provision should be made for them to obtain insurance and hospitalization. Finally, on June 21, 1944, the Costello Bill, introduced to Congress as HB 4269, came to a vote in the House of Representatives. It failed by nineteen votes. That failure on Capitol Hill would lead to the end of the WASP program.

Already by the end of 1943, the number of available male pilots had increased, and the men were given priority for flying jobs. Consequently, fewer WASP graduates were assigned to ferrying bases. WASPs who were already flying and serving in other capacities were allowed to stay on in active civilian service, but the training facility in Sweetwater would be shut down as soon as all the present classes graduated. The last WFTD class, 44-10, had begun training at Avenger Field in mid-June 1944, just one week before the vote in Congress. Its sixty-eight graduates ultimately were on active duty from December 8 through December 19, 1944—only twelve days.

On August 2 Nadine arrived at OTS in Orlando. Though she enjoyed her time there as a much-needed break, she began to be plagued by vicious headaches, which she assumed were related to the concussion she suffered in her 1940 crash. Her neck and back muscles also felt increasingly stiff. Never one to complain about physical discomfort, she simply tried to rest as much as possible and get back to the job. She graduated from OTS at the end of August with an overall grade of 91 percent.

Why were WASPs still being sent to OTS if they weren't going to be militarized? Though the Costello Bill was dead, the debate over the WASP still raged in the court of public opinion. While Nadine was in Orlando, a leading columnist for the *Washington Times-Herald*, Drew Pearson, visited OTS to see the WASP officers' training up close. On August 6 he wrote a brutal assessment of the program and of Jackie Cochran, painting her as a vain, power-hungry schemer and the WASP program as nothing more than her pet project.[15]

Cochran responded with a desperate, defensive eleven-page report detailing the history of the WASP project and its achievements, as well as her role in them. She asked for "simple justice" for herself and the WASP pilots.[16] Then, in a last-ditch effort, she sent the report to General Arnold and to newspapers on the same day. Her riposte had the tenor of an ultimatum: either militarize the WASP once and for all or disband the program. It was the wrong move. General Arnold took the ultimatum seriously and in the fall decided to end the WASP program.

On October 8, 1944, the 1,102 WASPs received the news that all women pilots would be sent home on December 20. There was now no future for them. To the WASPs of the Ferrying Division, deactivation seemed especially cruel and illogical because there were still more planes to deliver, especially pursuits.

By the time the women heard about their disbandment, the WASP ferry pilots were responsible for delivering three-fifths of all pursuit aircraft within the United States.[17] Their situation was maddening and unfair, but Nadine and her comrades resolved to keep serving and flying until their very last day.

CHAPTER 9

IN PURSUIT

In late summer 1944, it became obvious to General Tunner and Nancy Love that Long Beach, California, was the base most critically in need of more pursuit pilots. There were now virtually no trainers coming into Long Beach. Instead, P-51s were still manufactured there daily, as were bigger twin-engine pursuits such as the P-38. In the "Great Transfer" of August 1944, Tunner released 126 ferry pilots from the Ferrying Command and transferred them back to Training Command—specifically, those who had no desire to ferry pursuits, had washed out of pursuit school, or had insufficient qualifications, experience, or time to transition into pursuits.

For her part, Nadine once again requested a transfer to Long Beach to fly pursuits with the Sixth Ferrying Group. This time, her request was granted. She was thrilled to learn she would report to Long Beach in early September. Finally, she was headed west.

Nadine was eager to return to Long Beach, which had made a name for itself among pilots and aircraft manufacturers. In fact, the story of Long Beach was strikingly similar to that of Wichita: in the twenties and thirties, Long Beach's population swelled, thanks to the discovery of oil in the area and the expansion of the aviation industry. In 1938, just as in Wichita, the city utilized funds from the national Works Progress Administration to extensively update its municipal airport, Daugherty Field (named after local aviator Earl Daugherty). Over the next few years, the airport added new runways and a $150,000 administration building.

Then, in 1940, Donald Douglas began looking for land he could buy to expand the Douglas Aircraft Company—the same manufacturer Nadine had worked for in El Segundo before her 1940 crash. Los Angeles and Santa Monica were already becoming crowded and overpriced, but Douglas saw an opportunity in Long Beach. He purchased more than one hundred acres of open farmland right beside Daugherty Field and put in an enormous new aircraft manufacturing plant. By the time war broke out at the end of 1941, Long Beach was recovering well from the Depression and was home to a

Nadine in her WASP uniform, ca. 1944

population of about 164,000, a large percentage of them happily employed in either commercial shipping or aviation.

After the Japanese attack on Pearl Harbor on December 7, the city suddenly found itself thrust onto the front lines of the war effort. Other Pacific port cities, including Honolulu and San Diego, faced similar responsibilities and abrupt changes. Literally overnight, the US Navy, Army, and Coast Guard took over operations at Long Beach Harbor, and the navy requisitioned nearby Terminal Island to construct a new shipyard, an expanded airfield, and facilities for ship repair and military training—all of which became Roosevelt Base.

Unfortunately, for the purpose of building the base, the military forcibly removed all civilian communities from Terminal Island, most of them immigrant families from Japan, Greece, Yugoslavia, and Portugal, as well as neighborhoods of Japanese American citizens. A booklet released by the Historical Society of Long Beach, *A Big Change for Long Beach*, describes how quickly the lives of these residents were upended:

> By the evening of December 7, 1941, Los Angeles and Long Beach police officers, FBI agents, and military units fanned out across the island, arresting community members identified by federal authorities as threats. Over the next few days, U.S. military police continued to visit Terminal Island neighborhoods, ordering people to leave, in some cases in less than twenty-four hours. Houses were abandoned and the community was closed down. The FBI cited the war emergency as the reason for such actions, a rationale reinforced by the Los Angeles County Board of Supervisors when it voted unanimously to support the removal of Japanese aliens from the county.[1]

In all, more than 3,000 Japanese Americans and Japanese nationals from the greater Long Beach area were arrested and sent to guarded camps throughout Southern California for the duration of the war. (They were among the nearly 120,000 civilians of Japanese descent, most of them American citizens, to be imprisoned in isolated locations away from the Pacific Coast.) The entire community of Terminal Island was destroyed. Citizens and their families were driven out, and 50,000 sailors and workers moved in.

Similarly, the army essentially took over operations at Daugherty Field, renaming it Long Beach Army Air Field and quickly leasing more land in the adjacent area to build the ATC's Ferrying Division headquarters. The navy, which had been using Daugherty Field as a Naval Reserve Aviation Base, moved its operations to a new airfield in Los Alamitos six miles inland.

To accommodate the Ferrying Command, the AAF built a vast, $1.25 million base, including flight operations and personnel sections, engineering and maintenance buildings, mess halls and commissaries, a hospital, a training school, and barracks. The Sixth Ferrying Group was established there in 1941 and welcomed WAFS and WAC in early 1943. Soon it became the army's largest ferrying group, with more than a thousand male and female pilots ferrying planes all over the country and the Pacific. The group was understandably proud of its important role in the war effort; above the pilot's loft on the base hung a sign that read, "Through these portals pass the finest pilots on earth."

All the while, Douglas Aircraft's Long Beach factory was rapidly rolling thousands of new military aircraft off its assembly lines. By 1943 it employed nearly forty thousand workers, more than half of them women—the now-famous Rosie the Riveters of the war. Operating twenty-four hours a day, the plant employed so many parents with young children that the company provided onsite childcare facilities. Other aircraft factories in the area followed suit. Eventually, more than twenty-four thousand children were cared for at the Douglas plant and others.

Nationally, the Douglas factory ranked first in total airframe weight produced, its output totaling 171 million pounds. In all, it built nearly 9,500 military planes during the war, all of which would be delivered by the Sixth Ferrying Group.[2]

The WASPs of the Sixth Ferrying Group were under the command of WAFS Original B. J. Erickson. Seattle-born Erickson was a reserved, dark-haired young woman who was accomplished well beyond her twenty-four years. She began flying at nineteen and put herself through her junior and half of her senior year at the University of Washington by working as a flight instructor.

After Pearl Harbor, when all airports on the West Coast were shut down,

C-47s produced by Douglas Aircraft Company's plant adjacent to the Long Beach Army Air Field (background), 1940s (Courtesy Long Beach Airport Archives)

Erickson worked on the Boeing assembly line in Seattle to pay for her final semester of college. She helped build the B-17, the famous Flying Fortress, then took a job teaching flying in eastern Washington, where civilian flying was still permitted. She taught until Nancy Love recruited her for the WAFS in early fall 1942. Love quickly recognized Erickson's natural leadership abilities and placed her in charge of the crucial Long Beach WASP ferrying group when it was formed in January 1943.

Erickson was younger than virtually all the women pilots under her command, but she quickly gained their respect as a strict and fair commander. She was one of only a few women qualified to fly the B-17 Flying Fortress, and she transitioned into pursuits on her own as opportunity arose, without attending pursuit school. She was also a member of the first OTS class at Orlando.

In the summer of 1943, Erickson distinguished herself further when she

Frances Green, Margaret "Peg" Kirschner, Ann Waldner, and Blanche Osborn leaving "Pistol Packin' Mama," their B-17 Flying Fortress, during pursuit school training, Lockbourne, Ohio, 1944 (Courtesy U.S. Air Force)

completed four cross-country ferrying trips in record time. She flew a P-51 Mustang from Long Beach to Evansville, Indiana, then checked out in and ferried a P-47 Thunderbolt from Evansville to San Pedro, California. After reporting back to base in Long Beach, she picked up a C-47 cargo plane and ferried it to Fort Wayne, Indiana. Finally, she flew another P-47 from Evansville back to Long Beach. In total, she covered more than eight thousand miles in nine days.

Erickson didn't think such a feat was particularly impressive, but Jackie Cochran disagreed, seeing Erickson's record deliveries as a snapshot of all the WASPs' achievements. As a result, Erickson was nominated for and awarded the Air Medal, the only WASP to receive the honor. Created by President Roosevelt in 1942, the medal was given to any pilot—male or female—for "meritorious achievement" in flight. She received it from General Arnold in March 1944 at a WASP graduation in Sweetwater, in a display

of pomp that frankly embarrassed her. Later, she recalled, "Any one of the WAFS could have done the same under similar circumstances. We had the feeling during the war that no matter what it was, we could do it and we knew we could. I didn't accept [the Air Medal] for what I did, but because it represented what the women pilots were doing every day."[3]

Nadine quickly grew to love and respect her strong, self-assured Long Beach commander.

B. J. Erickson was the third woman to transition into the P-38, the Lockheed Lightning. Manufactured in Southern California in Burbank, about thirty miles north of Long Beach, the twin-tailed, twin-engine plane with high horsepower wasn't among the aircraft that the WASPs were trained to fly at pursuit school. Although it didn't have the range of a P-51, the Lightning served as the country's primary long-range fighter throughout 1943. Moreover, it was relatively quiet and highly maneuverable, ideal for night fighting, reconnaissance, and dive-bombing against the Japanese.

On December 1, 1943, Nancy Love went to Long Beach to check out in the P-38, clearing the way for other WASPs to qualify to fly it as well. Not all pursuit-qualified WASPs were interested in the Lightning: since they hadn't learned to fly it at pursuit school, it required additional training, and it was harder to fly.

The Lightning's twin engines rotated in different directions, which, when operating together at full strength, helped to offset the aircraft's powerful torque. However, if there was a loss of power in one engine, the P-38 would roll. In his book *The Few*, Larry Bledsoe explains:

> To be checked out in a P-38, the pilot had to demonstrate they could handle an engine-out situation. . . . The procedure for the P-38 is to first add opposite rudder to stop the roll, reduce the power on the good engine, feather and shut down the bad engine, crank in trim to reduce the need for rudder while slowly increasing power in the good engine. All the while keeping airspeed well above stall speed.[4]

In other words, the P-38 required expert handling and was a real challenge, even for a savvy pursuit pilot.

One incident exemplifies the risks of flying the Lightning. In early spring

1944, just as Nadine was headed for pursuit school in Brownsville, twenty-four-year-old Evelyn Sharp was on the last leg of a cross-country P-38 delivery from California. A WAFS Original stationed first at New Castle, then at Long Beach, Sharp had flown more than three thousand hours, delivered eighteen different kinds of military aircraft, and transitioned into pursuits on her own, as B. J. Erickson had, without training at pursuit school. She completed transition into the P-38 in March.

On April 2, during a ferrying assignment, Sharp had RONed in Harrisburg, Pennsylvania. The next morning, April 3, she climbed into her P-38 Lightning and took off, but at about seven hundred feet, her left engine began smoking and stopped. Sharp was in trouble: dead ahead were radio towers and Beacon Hill, which she didn't have enough power to clear, and to the right lay downtown Harrisburg, where a crash could prove fatal for civilians. Heroically, she made the decision not to follow procedure and turned left into the dead engine. The plane narrowly missed the towers on Beacon Hill, caught the tops of some trees, and hit the ground in a flat pancake position. The P-38 was barely damaged, but Sharp's neck was broken when she was thrown into the plane's canopy; she died before anyone could reach her.

As Sharp's commander, Erickson bore her loss heavily. Because Erickson was on the other side of the country in Long Beach, Nancy Love asked Nancy Batson, an Original in Wilmington, to accompany Sharp's body home to Ord, Nebraska. At the funeral, a man asked Batson if he could drape an American flag on Sharp's casket. Of course, the WASP wasn't military, so the gesture of draping a flag over the coffin wasn't officially allowed. But Batson knew what was right and she didn't hesitate. "Of course you can," she answered. Later, the city of Ord named its airport after Sharp.

Historian Deborah G. Douglas explains the impact of the government's policy: "When a woman died, the other women felt betrayed that the government was incapable of expressing condolence through some formal gesture of recognition to the survivors. . . . In being treated and trained as equals with men, they had come to expect, at the least, equal recognition in the form of comparable death benefits."[5]

Evelyn Sharp was the third and final WAFS Original killed in the line of duty, but WASPs all over the country were putting their lives on the line daily—and they weren't just ferrying. New recruits at Sweetwater risked accidents during training, while other WASPs flight-tested repaired aircraft,

moved war-weary decommissioned aircraft, and towed targets for live aerial and ground antiaircraft fire. The women logged thousands of miles, flying every kind of aircraft the army asked them to pilot. Before the end of the war, thirty-eight of them had made the ultimate sacrifice.

In spite of the many accidents associated with the P-38, Nadine wasn't afraid of what the German Luftwaffe called the Forked-Tail Devil. Many of her peers in the Fifth Ferrying Group at Dallas had already flown the Lightning from the modification center at Love Field to the embarkation point at Newark. After transferring to Long Beach, she finally got her chance to check out in the Lightning; she fell in love with it instantly.

At Long Beach, Major Jack London, who was dating B. J. Erickson, ran the training department, and Erickson named Iris Cummings Critchell (class 43-2) as WASP squadron training officer. Critchell was blond, lean, and athletic; before the war, she swam for the United States in the 1936 Summer Olympic Games in Berlin. She was the fifth woman to check out in the P-38, and she oversaw Nadine's transition into the Lightning, as she did other women pursuit pilots in the Sixth Ferrying Group who wanted to fly it.

Critchell recalls meeting Nadine during this time: "I saw her as a serious, well-grounded pilot who wanted to do her job and do it thoroughly and well. . . . I remember with pleasure the warm, deeply dedicated spirit, which I saw in Nadine even during her first days at Long Beach. Clearly she loved to fly and was very pleased to have the honor of flying those planes for the Ferry Command."[6]

For Nadine, the complexities of flying the P-38 were part of its appeal. She loved a challenge, and the Lightning's finicky nature assured her that there would never be a dull moment flying it. As Critchell observed, "Though I had no trouble with the P-38, they were a lot trickier and much more critical in loss of one engine. It is a glorious, exciting airplane to fly, but quite complex in systems. If they all work, you are OK!"[7] To Nadine, high risk meant high reward.

WAFS Original Betty Gillies, the second woman to fly the P-38, described her first trip out of Long Beach in the Lightning: "The sun was coming up and the sun was very golden, and when it hit my silver wings out here it was the most beautiful thing I've ever seen. I wanted to pull something and stop right there because here were these two mountains and there was the sun coming right up through the pass. . . . Ah, it was a picture I'll never forget."[8]

Main terminal, Long Beach Municipal Airport, 1940s (Courtesy Long Beach Airport Archives)

Nadine (standing, far left), and B. J. Erickson (standing, far right), with fellow WASP ferrying pilots, Sixth Ferrying Group, Long Beach Army Air Field, 1944 (Courtesy Long Beach Airport Archives)

The magic of the P-38 captured Nadine's imagination. After transitioning into it, she became a certified Class IV-P pilot—the highest WASP classification—and ultimately one of only twenty-six WASPs who flew it.

Fall 1944 was a bittersweet time for the WASPs of the Ferrying Command. Following D-Day in June, the Allies swept into France, liberating Paris from the Germans on August 25. Meanwhile, in the Pacific, General Douglas MacArthur kept his promise to return to the Philippines when he led American forces in an amphibious invasion of the island of Leyte in October. Fierce fighting would continue in both theaters for months, but Americans everywhere began to hope that the end of the war was in sight.

For the WASP pilots, ferrying continued as usual, with both triumphs and heartbreaking tragedies. In September, one of Nadine's 43-5 classmates, Alice Lovejoy, died after a mid-air collision at pursuit school in Brownsville, Texas. Then, during Thanksgiving week, another highly qualified pursuit pilot Nadine had known at Sweetwater, Hazel Ying Lee (class 43-4), was killed in a P-63 accident. One of only two Chinese American WASPs, Lee had already survived several harrowing incidents, including one in which she was forced to land in a field and then nearly shot by a farmer who mistook her for a Japanese invader. However, on November 23 a midair collision at Great Falls, Montana, set her plane on fire and she was badly burned. She died two days later.

Now that it was clear the WASP program would not be militarized, deaths like Lovejoy's and Lee's took on an even deeper element of tragedy. And with that came a deeper need for the WASPs to connect with one another. But what would happen once they were deactivated?

A group of WASPs stationed at Maxwell Air Force Base in Montgomery, Alabama, had an answer. As the year 1944 neared an end, they formed the Order of Fifinella, named after the WASP's little gremlin mascot, as a resource for keeping in touch with one another, spreading information about employment opportunities, influencing potential legislation, and organizing gatherings and reunions—primarily through the organization's newsletter.

In its issue published on December 20—deactivation day—the organization explained a key philosophy for moving forward: "The Council recog-

nizes the value of bringing our strength to the whole of women pilots, but feels that the maintenance of our identity as the only group of ex-Women's Air Force Pilots in America is vital to the fulfillment of the professional and organization purpose of the 'Order of Fifinella."[9]

Word about the Order of Fifinella spread quickly, and most of the female pilots wanted in. By deactivation day, three hundred WASPs were members. By the end of the war, the number had jumped to seven hundred—about 60 percent of all former WASPs. The order elected its own officers and chose representatives from every class that had graduated from Sweetwater.

During their final months of service, WASP pilots were often assigned to transport aging aircraft, designated Class 26. These "war wearies" were damaged or simply old aircraft that needed to be moved, but because they were less reliable than the factory-new planes, the pilots were wary. In *Women in Pursuit*, Kay Gott explains, "War-weary airplanes sometimes fell apart as they were being flown to depots. At the end of 1944 to ferry a war-weary airplane was very 'chancy,' not highly regarded by any ferry pilot as a desirable job." WAFS Original Teresa James concurred: "Flying war-weary junk airplanes gave me more than a few gray hairs."[10]

Original Betty Gillies had a close call flying a war-weary P-38 out of Harrisburg—the same airport where Evelyn Sharp had died flying that same aircraft. However, Gillies took off in the opposite direction, so when one engine quit on takeoff, she was able to maneuver the plane safely back in for a landing. Jill McCormick, one of Nadine's 43-5 classmates, barely escaped with her life when a war-weary A-24 she was ferrying to a reclamation site in Reading, Pennsylvania, burst into flames. Amazingly, she managed to extinguish the fire by diving toward the waters of the Baltimore harbor and pulling up at the last second, dousing the plane.

In Long Beach, Nadine continued flying pursuits as frequently as she could. In late October, she was sent on a routine P-51 delivery from Long Beach to Newark, New Jersey. The P-51D Mustang could make it cross-country in about ten hours total from coast to coast. Ferrying Command pilots making the 2,500-mile trip from Long Beach stopped twice for fuel, in Albuquerque or El Paso, and again in Ohio or Indiana.

On this delivery, Nadine was just approaching Newark when the Mus-

tang's powerful Merlin engine began sputtering. With no idea what was wrong, she hastily radioed the tower in Newark to tell them she was in trouble. She knew it would mean disaster if the Mustang's engine died and she couldn't restart it.

Desperately, she descended in a downwind turn to slow the aircraft and lowered the landing gear. The engine struggled once again, then suddenly cut out completely. Heart pounding, she continued her approach. Setting the Mustang down first on its front wheels, then onto the single "taildragger" wheel in the back, she struggled to keep the bucking P-51 between the runway lines. Then she braked to a stop in eerie silence. The Mustang had to be towed to the hangar, but they had made it. When it came to flying, even "routine" assignments weren't always routine.

Amid all these adventures and misadventures, December came too soon. For Nancy Love's Originals, who hadn't gone through training at Sweetwater, deactivation was especially confusing, and some blamed Jackie Cochran for their disbandment. All along, they had simply wanted to fly for their country. In fact, they hadn't asked for anything more: to become WASPs, or wear Santiago blue, or be militarized. They had just wanted to fly because they were needed.

Other WASPs who had been WFTD trainees felt differently, especially about Cochran and the opportunity she had provided. Nadine's 43-5 classmate and friend Dawn Rochow Seymour later said of her: "Fascinating woman. Absolutely fascinating woman. In two short years, maybe two and a half years, she was able to accomplish more for women than anyone I know, and opened doors. She didn't really open the door. She opened the transom. We jumped in the transom. And then when that closed, military aviation closed to women, you see, for many years. Many years."[11]

Nadine's Long Beach commander, B. J. Erickson, offered a more nuanced view:

Our group was just an absolute melting pot of different types of people. And every one of them is going to have a different view of what these three years were. It depends a lot on when they came in, why they came in, and where they were stationed. I talk to some of the girls in the later classes who think Cochran gave them the world. Well, she did in a way; they never would have flown without her and that opportunity. But the

very pattern of what was done with that whole program is what put us out of business.[12]

Some WASP pilots, including the women of Nadine's Sixth Ferrying Group, offered to keep flying for one dollar per year, but their proposal was turned down. "To 20 former WASPs in Long Beach who thus volunteered," one California newspaper reported, "General Arnold explained on behalf of President Roosevelt and Secretary of War Stimson: 'Your offer to serve is appreciated but must advise that available combat returnees and others in the pilot pool meet all current requirements and do not occasion retention of women pilots.'"[13] The explanation could not have been well received. As Erickson told the *Los Angeles Times*, "Some of our girls gave their lives. All we ask is nothing more than to do a job."[14]

In early December 1944, the Battle of the Bulge began in Europe, making pursuit aircraft even more critical overseas. During their final week before deactivation, WASP pilots steadily delivered P-61s and P-47s to the Newark airbase, from which they were then shipped across the Atlantic for combat.

On their last day, December 20, Nadine and the WASP of the Long Beach Sixth Ferrying Group attended a farewell dinner at the base. "It was really nice to have everybody come in and say we're sorry you're leaving, and you did a good job, and thanks for everything but good-bye you know," Commanding Officer B. J. Erickson later recalled. Then the WASPs of the Sixth Ferrying Group were forced to walk away, leaving planes stranded on the runway without anyone to deliver them. "It was very sad because there really wasn't any reason for it, and we were so badly needed. . . . I saw all those airplanes . . . P-51s and P-38s sitting in the middle of the airport that morning," she said. "I thought, you know, what a mistake this is."[15]

For the WASPs, deactivation felt like the end of the world. WAFS Original Teresa James wrote: "I remember it like it was yesterday when I walked out of that gate. . . . Something died right there. After flying around for twenty-seven months with the women like you were sisters, flying around the country and then coming back and chatting about it—just like a big family, and then all of a sudden you lose that. How could we go home to people who didn't understand?"[16]

The leadership of the Ferrying Command, at least, knew what it was los-

Nadine (first row, far right) with fellow pilots and friends of the Sixth Ferrying Group at the WASP's final banquet, Long Beach, December 1944 (Courtesy Long Beach Airport Archives)

ing. General George dictated a letter praising the WASP ferry pilots, to be delivered to each of the women on the day of the program's deactivation: "It is my desire to especially commend the Air Transport Command WASPS for their performance of the difficult and dangerous missions which they so successfully have completed over the period of their assignment to the Air Transport Command."[17]

General Tunner sent his own letter to Ferrying Command leadership, writing: "It was these [Ferrying Division] WASPS who progressed in their training to the point where they could be depended upon to deliver safely and swiftly the heavy two and four-engine bombers and the fast pursuit ships, including P-51s, P-38s and others. In the delivery of pursuit aircraft particularly the WASPS excelled." He concluded, "To each of these women goes my personal commendation and my warmest good wishes."[18]

On a more personal note, General Arnold wrote to each WASP, foreshadowing their future impact: "It is on the record that women can fly as well as

men. We will not again look upon a woman's flying organization as experimental."[19]

On December 21, 1944, the nine-hundred-plus WASPs still on active duty woke up, in the eyes of the world, as "normal" women again. In all, they had flown more than sixty million miles in every type of military aircraft available at a better safety record than the men.[20] Nadine had personally flown fifteen different types of aircraft and logged nearly six hundred hours, including more than one hundred hours delivering P-51s alone. Like many WASPs, she had paid her own way to join up, and she paid her own way home. The women boarded buses, trains, and planes to return to lives they would never be able to view the same way, back to families that could probably never understand all they had done.

The WASPs had done everything that was asked of them to help win the war. They had given their time, their skills, and for some, their lives. In the words of General Tunner, "They have accomplished far more than the safe and efficient delivery of hundreds of vitally needed aircraft; they have proven beyond all doubt that in times of national emergency, America can give its women the most challenging assignments with complete confidence."[21]

It would be decades before they were thanked.

PART V
LUCKY

Nadine raised one hand to shield her eyes against the Arizona sunlight glinting off nearly six square miles of parked military airplanes. This was Storage Depot No. 41, according to the newly formed War Assets Administration, but Nadine was used to calling it Kingman Army Air Field. More than 5,500 retired army trainer, fighter, and bomber planes languished on the tarmac.

She lifted her chin as a hot wind whipped auburn curls and a curtain of sand across her face. Silver fields of handsome old war birds resting among sagebrush and cactus stretched almost to the horizon. She thought it was sad; many of these planes, which had served the United States so faithfully, would never fly again. But, she thought, following the young man who had been assigned to guide her, there is at least one that will be back in the sky today.

"There's the Swoose!" Nadine's guide shouted as they walked. He pointed to a battered B-17. "Barely made it out of Manila in '42!"

Nadine paused, taking several steps closer to the hulking, four-engine bomber. She could see the funny half-swan, half-goose cartoon bird painted on the fuselage. She smiled, her eyes now drifting from the nose to the distinctive shark fin tail. It was war-weary all right.

Walking closer still, she laid one hand against the B-17's warm metal side. "What's going to happen to it?" she asked.

The young man grinned. "They were gonna smelt it down for the aluminum, but Colonel Kurtz wouldn't have it. He bought her for $350 last week. Says he's gonna turn her into a memorial in Los Angeles."

Nadine nodded. That seemed right.

Remembering himself, the young man hitched up his pants and started off. "Let's get you to your Lightning, ma'am."

Nadine had already spotted the twin-tails of the Lockheed Lightnings up ahead. She hurried on, overtaking the guide in her eagerness to see the pursuit plane she had come to purchase. "Most of these are nearly new," he explained, now double-stepping to keep up with her. "The one you want's flown only twenty-two hours. So you really are getting a bargain." As they arrived at the field, he paused

and looked at Nadine, cocking his head to one side. "You sure you know how to fly one of these?"

Nadine hardly heard him; she stopped and stood gazing. The P-38 sitting before her was a dream: an L model, nearly forty feet long with a wingspan of fifty-two feet, capable of streaking across the sky at four hundred miles an hour. She scrambled up to look into the cockpit, then circled the plane on the ground, inspecting its wide silver wings. As far as she could tell, the ship was in perfect shape. Nadine could almost sense the Lightning's anticipation. It didn't belong here; it yearned to be flying again.

"These things cost over a hundred grand to make, you know!" The young man hollered at her from under the plane's belly. "But we're selling 'em cheap—just $1,250!"

"I know," Nadine replied, stepping back to give the Lightning a final, satisfied look. "I'll take it."

Within the hour, she was buckling herself into the cockpit, starting the P-38's dual Allison 1,475-horsepower engines. She could hardly believe it was hers. Her purchase had created quite a stir, and at least a dozen War Assets Administration employees were watching her curiously from the edge of the runway. She knew word would spread about this; there would probably be reporters waiting for her by the time she landed in Long Beach, eager to get a headline, something like, "First Woman to Own P-38."

Nadine took a deep breath as she taxied, pumping the hydraulic brakes, waiting for clearance for takeoff. The Lightning's engines rumbled with their distinctive galloping sound, a deep pulsing that went straight to Nadine's heart. Flexing her palms against the yoke, she thought of the mystical bond her brother Ed had often described between a cavalryman and his horse. She had never understood it until now, but this plane already seemed like it knew her.

Nadine received clearance, let off the brakes, and felt herself pushed deep into the seat as the horizon rushed to meet her at 120 miles per hour. Her heart was pounding as she lifted off in the miraculous, ten-ton machine that felt lighter than air. Climbing into the infinite blue expanse of Arizona desert sky, she savored each moment as the P-38 responded to her slightest touch. They were heading west.

Lucky, she thought, cresting a ridge of dusty purple mountains far below. I'll call you Lucky.

CHAPTER 10

ON THE WING

After the WASP program disbanded in December 1944, the army made it clear that it would not allow female pilots to ferry planes, but virtually all of the women wanted to continue flying. As the *Long Beach Independent Press-Telegram* reported, "Almost unanimously after Dec. 20, 1944, when Ferrying Division WASPS at Long Beach, Palm Springs, Dallas, Texas; Detroit, Mich., and Wilmington, Del., are deactivated, the women will start looking around for jobs that will keep them on the wing."[1]

And search they did. With the help of job postings in the *WASP Newsletter*, they explored numerous civil service positions in the aviation field, such as Link Trainer instructors and operators, aircraft inspectors, aircraft accident analysts, control tower operators, dispatchers, air-ground communicators, instrument ground school instructors, air evacuation nurses, and secretaries "preferably with an aeronautical background." Some aircraft manufacturers welcomed applications for field and service mechanics or flight inspectors.[2]

The hunt for purposeful work—sometimes unsuccessful—took them to workplaces they might never have considered: gas stations; cab companies; department stores; and educational institutions. Of more relevance to flying were US Weather Bureau field stations; aviation companies (twenty-four were located in Alaska alone); and the agricultural, forestry, energy, fishing, and industries that required aviation work in crop dusting, hunting animal pests, and fish-spotting.[3]

Nancy Lee Baker (class 43-4), who took a job as a flight instructor for black student pilots in Waco, Texas, made an unexpected discovery: "I had the whole school because nobody else would teach them. . . . I was their ground instructor. I was their transportation in and out of town. I had an open jeep. . . . They all worked during the day, so I'd pick them up at different hours and bring them out to fly and then I'd fly them. I was their only teacher, and your only teacher is god, you know, for anything like that." As new airports sprung up across the country, Baker's classmate Mary Bowles

had the distinct opportunity of running one of them—the Palm Springs Airport—with the help of five other WASPs.[4]

As might be expected, some WASPs acquired an entrepreneurial spirit, like M. Allaire Bennett (class 43-7), who bought a jukebox route in Los Angeles.[5] Nevertheless, the era's gender norms prevailed. Some of the women applied to commercial airlines but were instead offered work as flight attendants—a particularly distasteful idea. They felt insulted by the suggestion they should ride in the back, serving cocktails and coddling passengers, when they could be flying the plane just as well or better than the male pilots in the cockpit. Others accepted work with the American Red Cross while war still waged in Europe. They took jobs as staff assistants, hospital staff aides, and hospital recreation workers or overseas as secretaries or in the foreign club program, where they could provide "a home away from home" to soldiers "in their precious hours of leave from the battle-front, or a refreshing drink when they return from a hazardous mission, or just a smile and an American 'hi-ya.'"[6]

A few were lucky enough to get jobs ferrying new and surplus planes from storage to sales points, civilian airports, and other locations, including overseas, and even to branch out into flying other aircraft, such as helicopters. Some with commercial Civil Aeronautics Administration licenses were eligible to ferry light planes, while those who could afford it took college courses in aviation or attended resident flight schools. But most simply went home to be with their families and tried to find other work.[7]

WASPs who had been putting off getting married during wartime now got hitched and settled down to the rhythms of domestic life. As historian Katherine Sharp Landdeck reported, "Nearly one hundred of the women were married in the first year after the WASP ended. Babies often quickly followed."[8] Peggy Parker Eccles (class 44-4) had given up on her dream to go back to medical school: "I didn't have enough money to go, for one thing, and I wasn't going to ask Dad for it. And we didn't have the GI Bill like all the boys did. And so, my hands were tied. So I got married and raised a family."[9] Those who were already mothers and had left their children with relatives while serving their country now tried to make the disorienting transition from zooming around in cutting-edge aircraft to cleaning up after their husbands and raising their children—and facing the prospect of never getting back into those planes.

For most WASPs, acclimating to a postwar life was a difficult task. WAFS Original and former Long Beach WASP commanding officer B. J. Erickson recalled her listlessness. "I had to do something, so I tried to go back to where I'd worked in college which is at Marshall Fields selling sportswear. That lasted about a week. . . . Finally I got to the point where my mother and dad said, "Just go back to California. You're not any good here. You're absolutely useless. You're unhappy. Just go back to California."[10]

From her surveys of former WASPs, Landdeck found that the word most of the pilots used to describe their emotions upon disbandment was "heartbroken." Some had more extreme feelings. Faith Buchner Richards (class 43-4) felt that she was "a very bad person. I didn't like anything or anybody. I guess the resentment was the fact that the war was still going on and there was still work to be done.'" Nadine's 43-5 classmate Violet Thurn Cowden wanted to "just die for a while. It was just horrible. I went home and I didn't know what to do."[11]

In a letter to a fellow WASP, Nina "Cappy" Morrison (class 44-10) likened her emotional state to that of her hometown:

This town is so dead—or maybe it's me. Mother says it's me. She can't figure out what's wrong with me—says I have a one track mind and it's on airplanes—reckon that's about rages. She and Pop want me to forget about airplanes and flying—settle down to something conventional *and* be happy. So far I haven't been able to see it—maybe I will if I stay here long enough. . . . I'm all mixed up. . . . Don't know which way to turn.[12]

Those who read the February 1946 issue of the *WASP Newsletter* might have recognized their own predicament in a column penned by Mardo Crane (class 44-1) called "Just between Us." In it Crane offered a remedy to disillusionment suggested by a fellow WASP:

Most of us were a pretty sad bunch after our deactivation. We had, and still are having, a terrific time getting readjusted. In fact we got so darn tired having people tell us that after a while we'd get adjusted—after while. . . . I . . . had my own little three-point program: First: Keep busy. Second: Keep flying—at least once a week, even if I had to pawn the family jewels! Third: Keep being glad I had the wonderful training and

experiences I had as a WASP, instead of being sorry I wasn't still flying those beautiful airplanes.[13]

Perhaps her advice was well heeded: by October 1945, not one job posting appeared in the *WASP Newsletter*.[14] The WASPs were on their own.

Whereas once the WASPs had been indispensable to their country's well-being and even survival, now they were expected to embrace roles as women in postwar society. Like the approximately four hundred thousand women who had been told that it was their patriotic duty to do the work US servicemen had done before the war, the WASPs were now informed that it was their patriotic duty not to—to give up their jobs to the returning male veterans. In hindsight, Landdeck explains, "their gender, not their skills as pilots, both got the WASP their jobs for the AAF and caused their disbandment."[15]

For now, most WASP held onto a sense of gratitude and appreciation for their wartime roles. Dorothea Johnson Moorman (class 43-4) explained this prevailing attitude: "It was a fabulous, fabulous experience. And there are 1,078 stories there for people. Everybody had a different mission, but it was all for the same thing. You flew because this was your contribution to this horrible war." It was this prevailing attitude that kept the WASPs from openly expressing their disappointment and despair. As historian Katherine S. Gray has noted: "When the military unceremoniously disbanded their organization, [the WASPs] expressed their pain and anger among themselves and not toward organized authorities."[16]

Nadine felt the same sense of shock as the others upon learning that she would be deactivated. She was one of the Long Beach WASPs who had offered to keep ferrying for a dollar. But unlike many others, she was in a unique position. At thirty-three, she wasn't married, and she didn't have children. She could travel, especially back home to Wichita, where she and Nelle could hope together for news of Ed, still missing in the Philippines. After the Long Beach WASPs' final farewell on December 20, Nadine returned to Wichita to spend Christmas with family and friends.

Mother and daughter were now closer than ever, coping with Ed's disappearance in their own ways. Just as Nadine had followed her path as a ferry pilot, Nelle, too, had kept herself busy. In addition to her cosmetology business, she was now the secretary of the Philippine Society of Kansas, a soci-

ety for the close relatives of soldiers, sailors, and marines who were listed as prisoners of war or missing in action in the Philippines. The group had more than one hundred members.

She was also in touch with several other mothers and relatives around the country whose sons or brothers were missing on Bataan. Quite a few had reached out to her in letters after Captain John Wheeler's 1942 *Life* magazine article, which had featured Ed and painted a picture of life on the front lines on Luzon. Though Nelle had no more information than other parents, she tried her best to keep up correspondence with all the worried and bereaved family members in her position.

Moreover, she organized and participated in wartime fundraising events, leading committees that hosted dinners and social activities. A poem by Edgar A. Guest published in the *Wichita Beacon* captured her philosophy during this time, so much so that she clipped it out and saved it. Titled "How to Stay Young," the poem offered, "Well, I'll tell you the way: refuse to think old tho the temples are gray. Keep going to meetings; keep going to shows, keep working at something and keep on your toes!"[17] Although Nelle missed and worried about Ed constantly, she battled her anxiety with action.

In early January 1945, Nadine flew straight back to Long Beach. Now a licensed pilot for almost a decade, and with nearly as much experience as an instructor, she knew she still could be useful to the Sixth Ferrying Group. Civilian Personnel and Training Officer Major John C. Martin agreed; he hired her as an instructor in preflight training.

After the war, aviation instructors were in high demand. Commercial and defense aviation companies were growing and more and more pilots were needed. By accepting the job, Nadine was technically being demoted, and she agreed to take a significant pay cut, from the $3,000 she had been making as a WASP to $2,000 annually (from nearly $43,000 down to $28,600 in 2020 dollars). Still, she knew she was fortunate just to be working for the ATC and directly helping the war effort. She rented a room in a newly built four-bedroom house on Hanbury Street, about a mile and a half from the base. She was glad to be teaching again. Her students were primarily battle-tested combat pilots who had already been decorated for valor. They had been flying bombers and now needed to transition into pursuits.

As a WASP Nadine had learned the hard way that pursuits posed unique

Preflight instructor Nadine (standing, far left), B. J. Erickson (standing, far right), and Civil Air Patrol cadets at Long Beach Army Air Field, March 1945 (Courtesy Long Beach Airport Archives)

challenges. As a Class IV-P pilot, she was qualified to help the men transition into single- and twin-engine pursuits, including the P-38. Given the risks of flying the Lightning, she handled the pilots in her charge with a nononsense attitude, quizzing them relentlessly on the ground before sending them up and testing their knowledge on everything from fuels and hydraulics to possible emergencies.

Despite the deactivation of the WASP, some reporters were still interested in the "lipstick pilots," and they found it notable that the Sixth Ferrying Group had employed a female flight instructor. An article in the *Los Angeles Times* described Nadine as a teacher, calling her "an attractive redheaded girl" who put pilots through their checkouts "accompanied by frequent demands, such as: 'What would you do if your left engine quit on takeoff? What if your canopy came loose just as you were preparing to lift her off the runway? What if something damaged your propellers at the critical takeoff stage?'" More impressively, the article noted, Nadine was "the

only woman in the United States to be classed as an instructor in transition with the routine duty of instructing male pilots in the flying of the army's fighting planes."[18]

Nadine's superiors were pleased with her results and filed reports on her work as "excellent." As WASP historian Sarah Rickman notes, "Nadine, with her ties to CAP and earlier instruction while active with them . . . is probably the only WASP who instructed on pursuits after the war."[19]

An atmosphere of excitement was building in Long Beach and across the world as the end of the war approached. Allied forces advanced across both the European and Pacific theaters, compelling the Axis Powers to strike out in desperation and, eventually, to surrender.

In Europe, after Germany's defeat at the Battle of the Bulge in December 1944, the Soviet army forged toward Berlin from the east, even as American and British forces crossed the Rhine and moved on the city from the west. In the Pacific, combined American and Australian forces attacked Japanese installations at Lingayen Gulf in the Philippines on January 6, 1945. After three days of fighting, the Allies cleared the way for an amphibious invasion designed to retake the islands, which had remained under Japanese control since the United States' surrender in early 1942. On January 9, Allied forces, including those already in the Philippines, launched the Battle of Luzon, code-named S-Day, and invaded the Luzon island group.

Of course, the Ramsey family paid special attention to any news regarding the battle, praying that soldiers in the campaign might at last discover what had happened to Ed. On January 11, the *New York Times* quoted General MacArthur's assessment of the invasion as "a complete success" and reported that Allied troops were pressing inland for a drive to Manila.[20] Nelle and Nadine hoped that if they were going to hear word about Ed, it would be soon.

In the meantime, Allied forces fought a hard battle for the soul of the Philippines. American and Filipino troops stormed Manila in early February, and the ensuing month-long struggle devastated the city. Virtually all major city structures were obliterated. Nearly eighteen thousand soldiers and more than a hundred thousand Filipino civilians were killed, making it the bloodiest battle in the Pacific Theater. The Japanese did not go quietly, but MacArthur and the Allied troops eventually emerged victorious.

In March the Allies took control of the island group's most strategic locations; they would continue their military campaign in the Philippines until the Japanese surrendered in the fall. But for Ed, the war seemed far from over. His life and the lives of his men were a daily struggle for survival. Confronting his possible demise, on April 7, 1945, Ed began a letter to Nelle and Nadine from "Somewhere in the Philippines": "I hope you will always remember that the courage I have had to keep going was gained from thinking of you and remembering that your bravery and courage in giving me all the benefits of life and love would be poorly repaid and I would be unworthy of you if I failed to carry on to the last with equal courage. For this reason I have refused to surrender." Attaching his will, Ed—now a major—sealed his letter on May 4 and left it with a priest in Manila for safekeeping until the end of the war.[21]

That spring the Red Cross intervened on Ed's behalf to locate his family, and Nelle finally learned that her son was alive.[22] He had been fighting in the jungle for the past three years and had risen through the ranks of the guerrilla army to become commander of more than forty thousand American and Filipino guerrilla soldiers.

Nadine and Nelle were nearly hysterical with relief. Although Ed would remain in the Philippines a while longer, the army released Colonel Amado N. Bautista, one of the Philippine Scouts who had served at Ed's side. During Bautista's stay at the US Army Command and General Staff College at Fort Leavenworth, Kansas, he received permission to visit Nelle at the Hotel Lassen in Wichita to share Ed's story with her and the local newspapers.

The news of a hometown hero spread rapidly. On June 5 the *Wichita Beacon* ran a three-column article headlined "Wichitan Hero in Luzon as Leader of Guerillas." The story featured a photo of Bautista beside a beaming Nelle at the Hotel Lassen with photographs of Ed and his guerrilla forces that Bautista had brought to show her, along with a letter from Ed explaining them. The visit was the first time Nelle had heard about Ed's exploits during the three years he was officially missing in action.[23]

Ed's story was a tale of intense struggle. Caught behind enemy lines, he lived in constant peril. During the fall of Bataan in 1942, he and a small group of soldiers were separated from the main body of American troops; thus, they were never officially ordered to surrender. Ed and another cav-

Nelle with Colonel Amado N. Bautista learning about Ed's three years as a guerrilla commander, Wichita, May 1945

alryman, Alabama-born Colonel Joe Barker, considered trying to escape to Australia, but after hearing about the horrific treatment of the American and Filipino prisoners at the hands of the Japanese—including the now-infamous Bataan Death March—they decided to stay. They felt an intense loyalty to their fallen friends and to the people of the Philippines, which had been a US protectorate since the end of the Spanish-American War in 1898.

Determined to carry on the war behind enemy lines, they joined the Philippine guerrilla army, which was being organized under orders from General MacArthur by American Colonel Claude Thorpe. Thorpe divided the Luzon guerrillas into four regions, placing Barker in command of the East Central Luzon Guerrilla Area Force, with Ed as his deputy. From that point on, Ed and Barker were hunted relentlessly by the Japanese military police, the notoriously ruthless Kempeitai. Barker was captured in early 1943 and

Thorpe soon after; they were interned at Fort Santiago prison, convicted of being guerrillas, and executed in Manila in October 1943.

Ed took Barker's place. He was now the most wanted man on the Japanese death list. Colonel Bautista described Ed's reputation to the *Wichita Beacon*: "Against great odds, because of a lack of every kind of necessity but with great resourcefulness and courage and much aid from the natives, his activities grew until he became the scourge of the Japanese, the greatest sore spot in their dominion of Luzon."[24]

As the commander of a growing army, Ed's primary responsibility was the collection of information, particularly regarding Japanese troop positions and movements. He shifted his guerrilla base around Luzon several times and eventually established a secret camp on a high hill known as Balabag, less than twenty miles from Manila. From there, he and his men could observe the harbor and Japanese ship movements. Amazingly and at great cost, he managed to obtain a radio, broadcasting information from his spy network to US forces and General MacArthur.

Ed also masterminded several daring sabotage missions. On July 15, 1944, his spy network planted dozens of improvised explosives—all time-delayed and set to detonate at midnight—at key Japanese sites in Manila. That night, from his camp at Balabag, Ed watched in satisfaction as his guerrillas struck a significant blow against the Japanese army, decimating its fuel-oil depot and railroad yard, as well as sending a ten-thousand-ton tanker ship to the bottom of the sea.

All the while, he battled dysentery, malaria, and hunger. Bautista told Nelle that her son would sometimes describe her delicious home cooking to his men in the jungle, helping them imagine they were eating more than plain rice, frequently their only meals for days on end. He struggled with malnutrition, losing at least forty-five pounds. At one point, he was so weak he could no longer carry a .45 pistol on his hip and instead carried a smaller .38 in a shoulder holster. He and his troops were often ill clad and barefoot.

In December 1944, as the WASPs faced deactivation, Ed came through a particularly debilitating bout of dysentery. While still recovering, he suffered an attack of appendicitis. At this time, the Kempeitai was closing in, and Ed knew that he and his men would surely be captured if they left Balabag to take him to a hospital. He would have to have emergency surgery in the camp, under extreme conditions, or he could die. Ultimately, a trusted doc-

tor from Manila removed his appendix on a crude operating table in the camp hospital shack, without anesthesia and only a jug of rum to dull his senses. Miraculously, he survived. Soon after, in January 1945, he was nearly captured when the Kempeitai raided his camp at Balabag. Many of his soldiers were killed or captured in the raid. Still weak, Ed escaped with some of his men, who faithfully carried him into the jungle, away from the Japanese.

In early February, soon after MacArthur's return to the Philippines, Ed officially rejoined the war, determined to keep fighting. As the *Beacon* reported: "When the American invasion forces met the guerrilla forces, high ranking army officers were amazed at the training and efficiency of the guerrillas trained under the command of 'Bud.' They requested that he discontinue actual combat and train an additional 20,000 Filipino natives. He himself stated that he wants to stay there until they 'straighten things out.'"[25] After all Ed had been through, he wanted to see the liberation of the Filipino people, his friends, with his own eyes.

After the *Beacon* article, Nelle wrote to the Ramsey and Cozad families to share the good news, and other newspapers throughout the Midwest picked up the story of Ed's incredible tale of survival and heroism. He was alive, but it was clear that his struggles were far from over. The women of the Ramsey family were anxious for him to come home.

In early May, German forces in Italy, Holland, Denmark, and Germany officially surrendered to the Allied armies, and news swept around the globe that the war in Europe was over. On May 8, 1945, Americans filled their city streets in throngs, cheering and weeping, celebrating Victory in Europe, or V-E, Day.

The next day, May 9, was Ed's twenty-eighth birthday—the fourth of the war. He was now stationed at new headquarters on Luzon in Meycauayan, and after almost exactly four years in the Philippines, he weighed less than one hundred pounds. Although he was no longer starving or sleeping in the jungle, he had continued to lose weight, and he was suffering from extreme fatigue.

On the morning of his birthday, Ed awoke to the sounds of a native band outside his window; a huge party had been planned in his honor. He learned that he was being promoted to lieutenant colonel—becoming one of the youngest men in the army to achieve that rank—and had been recom-

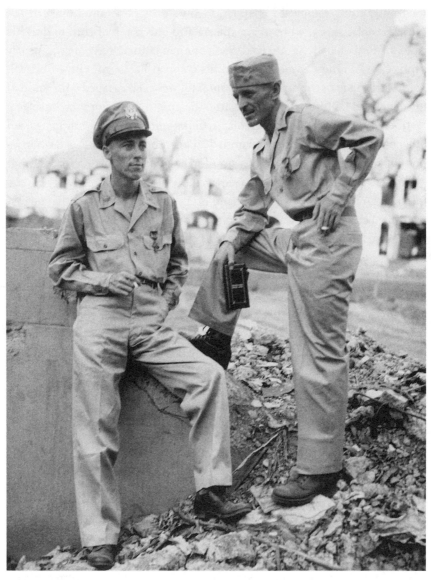

Ed (left) and fellow officer John Boone wearing their Distinguished Service Crosses amid the rubble of Manila, Philippines, June 1945

mended for the Distinguished Service Cross, the second-highest military award possible, awarded for extreme valor during combat. Though weary, he danced and celebrated with his soldiers all that day and late into the night.

The next morning, he had a nervous breakdown and was hospitalized. After ten days of rest, he was released and tried to resume his duties. On May 23, Mother's Day, Nelle received a telegram from the army: "The secretary of war desires me to inform you that your son 1/Lt. Ramsey Edwin Price returned to military control." A brief note from Ed concluded: "Feeling fine. Love on Mother's Day. See you soon."[26] It was the first time Nelle had heard directly from her son in three years; with it came relief and the hope that his health was improving.

Ed, however, knew that something was deeply wrong, describing this time in his memoir:

Everyone was safe, I told myself; no one would be killed now, no one was in danger, there would be no more raids, no hiding out in barrios, no alarms. I had brought them all through, and I deserved this despair. I had held it off with all my strength for three years through thousands of deaths, under a pressure of fear and loss so great I could not have afforded to face it. Gradually I had absorbed it all, and now here it was laying waste to me. . . . What kind of war was this? I wondered. What were the rules, who was the enemy, how could I win? There had been so many fronts in my war; which one was I on now?[27]

Ed had another nervous breakdown three weeks later and was hospitalized once again. General MacArthur personally intervened and ordered him to return to the States. Earlier, at the headquarters of the southwest Pacific forces, the general had made sure that Ed understood how valuable he and his guerrillas had been. "I am here by the grace of God and your good work," he said. "Please, tell your people that for me."[28] On June 13, in his office at Manila City Hall, MacArthur pinned the Distinguished Service Cross on the front of Ed's uniform and thanked him again. Three days later, Ed was on a plane home.

When Nadine heard that Ed was being sent to Letterman Hospital in San Francisco, she immediately requested permission to see him. Upon receiv-

WESTERN UNION (59)

A. N. WILLIAMS
PRESIDENT

The filing time shown in the date line on telegrams and day letters is STANDARD TIME at point of origin. Time of receipt is STANDARD TIME at point of destination

KA127 31 GOVT=WUX WASHINGTON DC 23 952A

MRS NELLE RAMSEY=

319 HOTEL LASSEN WCHTA=

THE SECRETARY OF WAR DESIRES ME TO INFORM YOU THAT YOUR

SON 1/LT RAMSEY EDWIN PRICE RETURNED TO MILITARY CONTROL

QUOTE FEELING FINE LOVE ON MOTHERS DAY SEE YOU SOON UNQUOTE=

J A ULIO THE ADJUTANT GENERAL.

1/LT.

THE COMPANY WILL APPRECIATE SUGGESTIONS FROM ITS PATRONS CONCERNING ITS SERVICE

Telegram to Nelle announcing Ed is officially back in military service, with Mother's Day wishes from Ed, May 1945

ing permission, she borrowed an airplane and flew north. She was ready and waiting at the airfield when a big C-54 touched down, and Ed climbed out.

"Hello, Buddy," she said, hugging him fiercely. Both she and Ed stubbornly struggled not to cry. Nadine was shocked by Ed's appearance; he was emaciated, disease ravaged, and could barely stand. He couldn't even carry his few belongings, so Nadine did. Although they both wanted to fly straight home to Wichita and Nelle, Ed's condition prevented the journey for several days at least.

Nadine stayed with Ed in the hospital as long as possible, then returned to teaching in Long Beach. At last, when he was finally allowed to travel, she borrowed a slick red racer, flew back to San Francisco, and loaded Ed into it. He was under orders to report to Winter General Army Hospital in Topeka, Kansas, but Nadine was determined to stop in Wichita first to visit Nelle. She and Ed flew east.

Overwhelmed by the prospect of seeing her war-scarred son, Nelle asked

Nelle and aviation tycoon Walter Beech (left) greet Nadine and Ed upon Ed's return to Wichita after the war, June 1945

her friend Walter Beech to accompany her to the Wichita Municipal Airport to welcome him home. As Nadine came in for a landing on the familiar runway, she joked that Beech would be sore she wasn't flying a Beechcraft.

Instead, after the plane stopped, Beech walked solemnly up to the small aircraft, opened the door, and helped Ed out. Nelle was already crying, and Ed fell into her arms. "Oh my god, Buddy," she managed to whisper through tears.

The war dragged on in the Pacific through the summer of 1945. After leaving Ed at the hospital in Topeka, Nadine flew a navy nurse and a marine back from Kansas to Long Beach with her. Shortly after passing over Riverside, California, the plane developed serious engine trouble and began losing altitude.

With the end of the war in sight and Ed finally back home and safe,

The Ramseys, reunited at Nelle's home, Wichita, June 1945

Nadine couldn't crash now—not after all that her family had been through. She turned the plane around and headed for March Air Force Base in Riverside. She wasn't even sure she could find the field, as the ceiling and visibility were both below minimums. Somehow, she managed to make it. After landing, she learned that all planes in the area had been grounded. Once again, she felt blessed. She thought about Ed; good luck was becoming a theme in her life.

In early August the United States dropped atomic bombs on the Japanese cities of Hiroshima and Nagasaki, decimating them and killing more than two hundred thousand people, mostly civilians. On September 2 General MacArthur accepted Japan's unconditional surrender, and World War II was officially over.

At Winter General Army Hospital, Ed was diagnosed with malaria, amoebic dysentery, anemia, acute malnutrition, and general nervous collapse. He had weighed almost 170 pounds before his deployment to the Philippines;

he now weighed only ninety-three. Nadine knew that Ed would recover: he was a Ramsey and therefore indefatigable. But she also knew that recovery, real recovery—for Ed and the rest of the world—would take years.

Nadine stayed on with the Sixth Ferrying Group. She was truly happy with her work, now earned $2,600 a year (more than $37,000 in 2020 dollars), and loved living in Long Beach. She had made new friends but also enjoyed spending time with her wartime friends who were still in the area. Some had even returned to Long Beach, including her former commanding officer, B. J. Erickson. From her home in the Pacific Northwest following deactivation, Erickson had heard about a potential job from WAFS Original Betty Gillies, whose husband was an executive at Ryan Aircraft in San Diego, so Erickson drove back down to Southern California.

On April 9, 1945, in a small ceremony at Long Beach's famous Breakers Hotel, Erickson married Major Jack London, whom she had been dating casually while ferrying for the ATC; he was still stationed with the Sixth Ferrying Group and was one of Nadine's superiors. Originally from Long Beach, London had grown up sailing and surfing. A childhood accident left him with permanently damaged eyesight, so he was unable to fly in combat. Even so, he had become a smart, instinctive pilot. Early in the war, he had ferried B-24s into Africa, then became the head of Flight Transition in the Sixth Ferrying Group. Soon after the wedding, London was named commanding officer at Hickam Air Force Base (formerly Pearl Harbor) in Hawaii, where the couple lived for the remainder of the war.

In the fall of 1945, B. J. and Jack moved back to Long Beach, pooled their resources, and bought a house near the airport. Biographer Sarah Byrn Rickman quotes B. J.'s recollections about this time: "In 1945, we each had $500 in savings and we each had a car. We were in good shape. We found a house in Long Beach, 900 square feet, for $9,000. The sellers were divorcing and left everything—dishes, furniture, washing machine. We bought it all."[29] Like most of the other former WASPs, B. J. Erickson had settled down.

While working in Long Beach, Nadine also met a dark-haired, mustachioed, and dashing young flight officer, John Percy "Jack" Gardner. Born April 12, 1923, in Redlands, California, Gardner was twelve years younger than Nadine. His parents, Percy Clayton Gardner and Ethel May Gardner (née

Stebbins), neglected Jack in early childhood. His grandfather, George Gardner, took him in and raised him.

A busy contractor in Redlands, George didn't have much time for discipline. Jack grew up wild and loved breaking the rules. He learned to fly at age fourteen by "borrowing" his cousin Harold's flying license and got one of his own at age sixteen in 1939.

Like Nadine, Jack was always eager to fly bigger and more powerful planes. He tried to join the army but was turned down for being too young. Undeterred, he enrolled in a flight instructor's course and taught older students to fly until he could finally enlist in the ATC in 1942. Originally stationed at Deming Army Air Field in New Mexico, he transferred to Long Beach in July 1944. At the time Nadine met him, he was only twenty-three—particularly young for an instructor. Writing about his transfer, the *San Bernardino County Sun* called him "the youngest instructor of an accredited Army Air School in the United States."[30]

Nadine already knew her fair share of hotshots and daredevils, but she was still charmed by Jack. Funny and utterly fearless, his personality was full-speed-ahead—exactly the approach to life that had compelled Nadine to fly pursuits. He also did more than just teach others to fly during the war. In 1944 he was assigned to fly a supply route in and out of the Pacific; he dropped off supplies and flew home wounded veterans and prisoners of war. On August 28, 1945, before Japan's surrender, he participated in the first flight of C-54 aircraft carrying men and supplies into Tokyo's Atsugi Airfield. That mission was considered extremely dangerous: under threat of enemy action, the pilots flew without navigational aids or information regarding weather, runway, or field conditions. Later, Jack received the Air Medal and Purple Heart for the mission. Danger meant nothing to him.

Not surprisingly, Jack went through relationships at the same breakneck pace that he flew airplanes. In 1945 he already had a reputation as a ladies' man and was married to his second wife. He had married his first wife, Belinda Bartlett, when they were both seventeen, but the marriage was quickly annulled (even though they had a baby girl, Jackie). On August 1, 1943, he married Louise Joy Hollingshead and became the father of another little girl, Paula Ann, in early 1945. A son Michael was born soon after.

In some ways, Jack's story must have reminded Nadine of her own; she, too, had married young and foolishly, the marriage was annulled, and she

was drawn to flying and living dangerously. Then again, she liked working for the army because she knew that the organization provided some much-needed discipline in her life.

Nadine liked Jack and thought he was handsome and brave, but as far as she was concerned, he was unavailable. She had no desire to get involved with a married man and the father of three young children. She determined to stay focused on her flight instruction job for the Sixth Ferrying Group as long as she could. Soon, however, a new opportunity arose that called Nadine back into the sky.

CHAPTER 11

HER OWN P-38

Beginning in the spring of 1945, surplus war planes were ferried to sales centers across the country, some of them by former WASPs.[1] The aircraft ran the gamut from war-weary and damaged to those with fewer than a hundred flying hours. In early February 1946, Nadine learned that nearly five hundred P-38 Lightnings were for sale at Storage Depot No. 41 of the War Assets Administration, formerly the Kingman Army Air Field in Kingman, Arizona. There, thousands of war-surplus and decommissioned aircraft were lined up in rows across four thousand acres of desert, waiting to be turned into scrap metal.

The Lightnings, which had each cost $115,000 to make (more than $1.6 million in 2020 dollars), were going for $1,250 per plane (less than $18,000 in 2020 dollars). A P-38 at that price was a steal, but on her instructor's salary, Nadine didn't even have that much money readily available. She knew her brother would understand her reason for buying a P-38, so she called Ed and asked for a loan. When he heard what she wanted, he laughed and said yes.

On Valentine's Day, Nadine went to Kingman and found the plane of her dreams. She bought it on the spot, making her P-38 one of only ten planes that were ultimately purchased in Kingman. She flew it back to Long Beach the same day.

Sure enough, Nadine's purchase made the news. On February 15 the *Los Angeles Times* printed a two-column article headlined "Woman goes shopping; flies home with P-38," noting that "while most women are still waiting for their postwar dreams of nylons, clothing, and household articles to materialize, Nadine Ramsey, of 5300 Hanbury St., Long Beach, had hers all wrapped up yesterday. Only it wasn't a feminine item." Nadine, the reporter wrote, had "stepped figuratively and actually into the stratosphere when she picked off a bargain at such a saving that womankind everywhere can envy her without reserve." She "not only scored a neat victory over all bargain-hunting competitors, but so far as is known, she became the first female civilian in the world to own outright one of the world's fastest airplanes."[2]

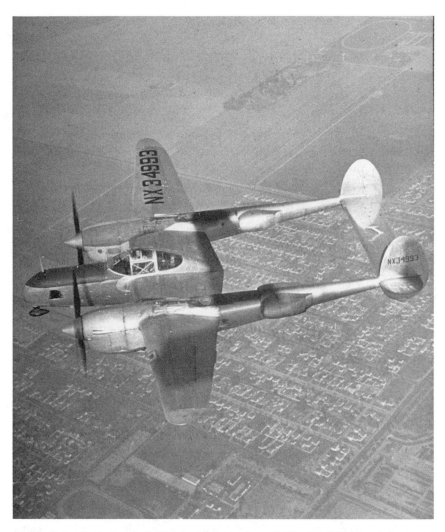

Nadine flying Lucky in the California skies, March 1946 (The LIFE Picture Collection/ Getty Images: photograph by Peter Stackpole)

The following day, the *Dayton Herald* verified the claim. "Girl Purchases P-38 and She Can Handle It!," the headline enthused, adding that Nadine "was the only girl in the world today to own a P-38—one of the twin-engined, twin-tailed, single-seater fighter planes that were the curse of the German Luftwaffe."[3]

Still another newspaper printed a photo of Nadine receiving her insurance certificate for the P-38. It opened, "Well known to both civilian and military flying circles, Nadine Ramsey, ex-WASP from Long Beach, Calif., recently acquired the distinction of being the only member of the fair sex to own one of the world's fastest pursuit planes—the Army P-38." Nadine had explained, "It's the plane I've been dreaming about."[4]

Less than a week later, Nadine flew her new plane in an airshow in Phoenix, performing harrowing acrobatics with a dead engine. Several local Arizona publications covered the event, noting Nadine's war record and her job with the Sixth Ferrying Group.[5]

Before the end of the month, Nadine was contacted by a reporter from *Life* magazine, who wanted to come, along with staff photographer and celebrated photojournalist Peter Stackpole, to photograph Nadine with her new plane in Long Beach. She happily agreed. The reporter and Stackpole showed up on a bright, calm day in late February, just as the sun was lengthening the shadows of buildings and airships surrounding Long Beach Army Air Field.

Peter Stackpole had worked for *Life* since its founding in 1936 and had made a name for himself photographing celebrities. In fact, he was the same photographer who had visited Avenger Field in 1943. Stocky, brown haired, and two years younger than Nadine, he was still a young man at thirty-three. He photographed Nadine in and around her Lightning, both in flight, suspended dramatically thousands of feet above the Southern California landscape, and as the P-38 sat on the runway in the softening late afternoon sun.

Overall, the photographs juxtaposed Nadine's femininity—red lipstick, slender figure, and loose curls—against the impressive, industrial bulk of the fighter plane. For one series of photos, she was dressed with modern flair in a long-sleeved blouse, wide-legged trousers, and woven leather sandals. It was easy for her to look enamored with her plane.

One of these photographs featured Nadine holding the propeller of the P-38's left engine. On March 25 it ran on the back cover of *Life* magazine's international edition. Under the headline "Personal P-38," the brief cover article distinguished Nadine as the only woman in the world to own one of her own.[6]

Though she enjoyed the brief fame that the P-38's purchase had brought

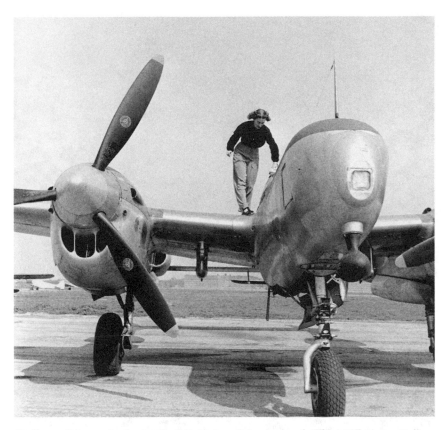

Nadine walking on Lucky, her P-38 Lightning, February 1946 (The LIFE Picture Collection/Getty Images: photograph by Peter Stackpole)

her, Nadine was mostly excited just to be able to fly her own Lightning, which she nicknamed Lucky, whenever she wanted.

A few months later, in June, Ed was approaching the end of his first grueling year of recovery. Although he had faced incredible adversity during the war, he was surprised at just how much he struggled to get well. He was damaged in both mind and body and was frequently plagued by nightmares. Later, he would say that "winning the war" of recovery took all the faith and love he had learned in Luzon.[7]

Meanwhile, the story of Ed's heroism in the Philippines had spread, and he became the subject of much praise and notoriety. Of course, Wichita

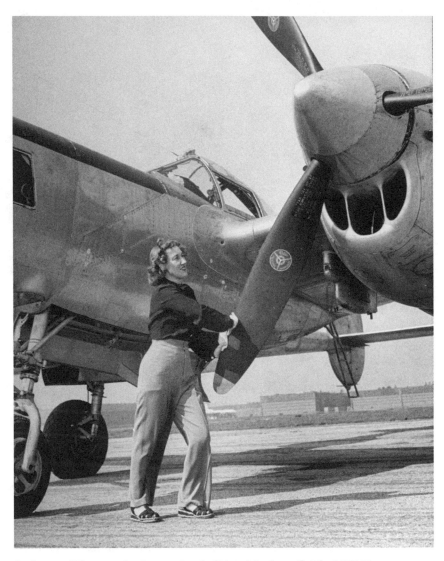

Back cover, Life *magazine international edition, March 1946 (The LIFE Picture Collection/Getty Images: photograph by Peter Stackpole)*

newspapers particularly lauded Ed's courage and celebrated their local hero. Other accolades came pouring in. In addition to the Silver Star and the Distinguished Service Cross he had already received, Ed was awarded the Bronze Star Medal and the Purple Heart, along with Philippine equivalents of his many awards. He was also named a commander in the Philippine Legion of Honor.

For his twenty-ninth birthday, Ed made a special request: he wanted to see the rest of his family. On May 9, 1946, he and Nelle headed back home to the Ramsey farm in Odin, Illinois. Ed's aunt and uncle, Dennis and Winnie Branch, hugged them both soundly and insisted on taking photographs of everybody to commemorate the visit. Their daughter, Barbara, then twenty-three, was simply happy to see Ed alive and posed for a photo beside him in his decorated uniform. Aunt Winnie prepared a grand feast in Ed's honor; other Ramsey family members shared the meal, too, including his Uncle Verbie and oldest aunt, Daisy Williams.

The *Centralia Sentinel* printed a small item about the dinner headlined "Hero of Guerilla Fighting Visits Aunt in County." It noted Ed's high rank as a lieutenant colonel at the age of only twenty-eight, concluding, "He has been awarded the highest honors given to members of the armed forces with the exception of one [the Medal of Honor]. He was sent to the Philippines in 1941 and in the fight on Bataan served in a cavalry unit."[8]

All of the honors Ed received were important to him, but the gesture that meant the most came in the form of a resolution. Almost one year before the United States officially recognized the Philippines' independence on July 4, 1946, the newly liberated Philippine government convened a special session of the First Philippine Congress. On this day, July 13, 1945, the House of Representatives voted on a Resolution Expressing the Profound Gratitude of the Filipino People to Major Edwin P. Ramsey.

Unanimously adopted, the resolution concluded:

The Filipino people owe him deep gratitude for his services which accelerated the liberation of the best organized and controlled area occupied by the ruthless enemy, thereby saving thousands of lives and property that otherwise would have been sacrificed: Now therefore be it resolved that the House of Representatives express, as it hereby expresses, the

profound gratitude of the Filipino people to Major Edwin P. Ramsey for his invaluable services to Philippine liberation.[9]

When Ed read those words, he began to think about all that he felt he owed the Filipino people. They had accepted him and fought at his side throughout his three years behind enemy lines, and many had died for him. He wanted to set something down on paper, something that could help others understand the courage of the Philippine guerrillas.

He began writing. Beginning with a copy of the resolution, he introduced the idea that gratitude should be reciprocal. He wrote that it was the courage and faith of the Philippine guerrillas that had enabled him to keep fighting: "Think about it for a minute. Here are Americans. We were supposed to be protecting the Filipino people. But at that moment, those black April days after Bataan, if anyone had a right to spit on men who'd let them down—the Filipinos had that right. But they didn't spit. They fed us, instead."[10]

As he wrote, Ed relived it all: three years of jungles, lowlands, and rice paddies, three years of machine-gun fire and the sound of Japanese Zeroes zooming overhead. He was revisited by fear prickling the back of his neck and the gnawing of constant hunger in his stomach. Though still recovering from his ordeals, he wrote it all down. He didn't want to forget anything that had happened.

In the summer of 1946, the Sixth Ferrying Group scaled back its operations dramatically. On July 11 Nadine received official notice of a "reduction in force"; her job as a preflight instructor for the military was coming to an end. Signed by the Air Corps commanding officer, Colonel K. C. McGregor, the notification formally thanked her for her service: "This agency appreciates your efforts and devotion to duty during and since the period of the emergency and regrets the necessity for this action. You should carry with you a feeling of personal satisfaction in having materially aided this organization in successfully carrying out its mission in the war effort."[11]

Nadine's last day was set for July 25, but she hoped it still might be possible to stay at Long Beach Army Air Field. After learning about an opening for a clerk-stenographer in the engineering department, she quickly applied for the position. The job would mean yet another demotion and pay cut, but Nadine loved working on the base; it was near her house and made an

especially convenient landing spot as she flew her P-38 around the area, flying in airshows and making appearances. Most importantly, it was a second home to her. Nadine was hired for the position and started her new job on July 22, 1946.

In August she decided to enter the famous Bendix trophy race, a cross-country speed dash from Los Angeles to Cleveland, Ohio. Automobile and aviation mogul Victor Bendix, who wanted to entice engineers to build faster and more durable aircraft, had established the annual race in 1931 as part of the National Air Races. The races were suspended during the war; Nadine and many other pilots were eager to sign up for the prestigious Bendix when it resumed in 1946 for the first time since 1939.

Due to the incredible wartime progress in airplane design and engineering, the fastest planes then available were former army pursuit aircraft and military jets—including the first operational US fighter jet, the Lockheed P-80. However, the Bendix 1931 charter stipulated that military aircraft were not allowed to compete, so organizers created two divisions for the 1946 competition: an R Division for civilian-piloted reciprocating engine airplanes, like Nadine's P-38, and a J Division for service-piloted military jets. Because active-military pilots weren't allowed to win prize money, Bendix officials decided to recognize their participation with a plaque. The jets also required longer runways for takeoff, which necessitated moving the starting point of the race from Burbank Airport to the Metropolitan Airport in Van Nuys.

Nadine considered her P-38, Lucky, one of the fastest and most powerful planes in the race; she figured she had a good chance at the trophy and a share of the $25,000 prize (more than $330,000 in 2020 dollars), which was to be distributed among the top R Division finishers. She was even more confident she'd win the special subcategory for women pilots, which came with its own $1,000 prize (more than $13,000 in 2020 dollars).

On August 19 Nadine checked in with Lucky at the Aviation Maintenance Corporation in Van Nuys, some forty-five miles from Long Beach over the Santa Monica Mountains. She was the first pilot to sign up for the race, and reporters and photographers were waiting. One from Fortune Illustrators in Cleveland, Ohio, took several photographs of Nadine in her bright printed blouse, posing in and around her plane; one featured her fixing her hair in a compact while seated primly on one of Lucky's tail fins. The *Bradford*

Evening Star ran another shot of Nadine in the Lightning's cockpit, powdering her nose.[12]

Still another photographer for the *Valley Times* snapped a photo of Nadine smiling beside the president of Aviation Maintenance Corporation, Colonel John H. Fite. "Red-headed Nadine Ramsey, who taught Army pilots how to fly fighter planes during the war," the accompanying article opened, "yesterday became the first pilot officially to check in at the starting line for the $25,000 Los Angeles to Cleveland Bendix Trophy Race." The caption offered another distinction: "Thus far, Miss Ramsey is the only woman pilot entered in the cross-country race."[13]

Nadine told the reporter, "So far, it looks as if I'm a cinch to be in the money at Cleveland. There's $1,000 up for the winning woman pilot and unless Jackie Cochran manages to get in, I'm the gal." The *Los Angeles Times* reported on the story as well, and the *New York Times* ran a short item about Nadine's entrance into the race, quoting her: "I'll win, if Jackie Cochran doesn't get in it."[14]

While Nadine knew that Lucky was fast, she was up against some stiff competition. Of the twenty-six planes registered in the R Division, seventeen were P-38s. There were five P-51s and a rumor that another would be flown by Jackie Cochran.[15]

Two of the registered P-51s belonged to famed Hollywood stunt pilot Paul Mantz. A notorious daredevil, Mantz had flown with the First Motion Picture Unit during the war, making public relations and training films. After the war, like Nadine, he took advantage of all the cheap war-surplus aircraft and purchased an entire fleet of 474 bombers and pursuit planes. He then sold the onboard fuel supplies of the decommissioned airships and resold most of the planes as scrap metal, making a tidy profit on his investment. He kept a dozen planes for himself to use in movie stunts and racing. Nadine knew that he would be one of her toughest competitors.

As the race approached, the registered pilots began readying their planes, removing all unnecessary weight and adding fuel supplies. Nadine had an extra gas tank installed in Lucky's nose. Mantz, who was planning to fly one of his own stripped-down P-51C Mustangs, also sponsored a friend, Thomas J. Mayson, providing him with a similarly modified P-51.

At the last minute, Jackie Cochran entered the race. She was the only other woman to register and, true to the rumors, signed up with a P-51 Mus-

Nadine registering for the Transcontinental Bendix Trophy Race (above) and checking her makeup while sitting on a tail fin (below), Van Nuys, California, August 1946 (Ben Franklin Collection; courtesy Al and Bob Chute; photographs by Fortune Illustrators)

Nadine and Colonel John H. Fite, president of Aviation Maintenance Corporation, Van Nuys, August 1946 (Valley Times Photo Collection, Los Angeles Public Library)

tang. Cochran had already won the Bendix trophy once, in 1938. Nadine was set to race against one of the most famous female pilots in the country—and the woman who had given and lost the WASPs their wings.

By the last few days of August, Ed had recovered enough to travel, and he went to California to support Nadine and watch the start of the race. Excitement was running high. On August 29, the day both before the race and after her thirty-fifth birthday, Nadine spent the evening making final checks on her Lightning and ensuring that everything was in order. Like most of the other pilots, she went to bed early.

The next morning, she was up before dawn, and as she trotted toward Lucky, she could already sense that something was wrong. A close inspection revealed that the Lightning's tires had been slashed; the thick, military-grade rubber was torn by jagged cuts. Nadine knew instantly she had been sabotaged: someone wanted her out of the race. Not only did the tires need repair, but the whole aircraft had to be thoroughly inspected, in case whoever had cut the tires had also damaged the plane some other way. There was simply no time to make Lucky air ready. Nadine was out of the race, and she was furious, though she hadn't been singled out; several other pilots reported that their planes had been sabotaged as well.

The race started promptly at 7 a.m. on August 30, with twenty-two entrants taking off throughout the morning. Jackie Cochran had telephoned ahead all the takeoff times to her husband, Floyd Odlum, who was waiting in Cleveland. By the end of the day, the winners were announced: Paul Mantz first, William F. Eddy second, Jackie Cochran third, and Mantz's friend Thomas J. Mayson fourth. They flew P-51s.

Cochran, however, disagreed with the results; she believed she had beaten William Eddy by about forty minutes. On September 9 she wrote a letter of protest to Rear Admiral Luis de Florez, chairman of the National Aeronautical Association's Contest Board, asserting that mistakes had been made in the race's timing. She also pointed out several other errors she had uncovered in the official race records:

The typewritten "Timing Start Flash Bulletin D" handed out at Cleveland to the newspaper men, and I suppose to the judges also, had Eddy leaving at 11:42, although he actually left at 11:01. It also had my number 13, P-51 plane, as being flown by Nadine Ramsey (although she had

not taken off at all and her entry was a P-38 and not a P-51). This same bulletin had Eddy and [Harvey M.] Hughes taking off 17 seconds apart which should have shown, on its face, that there was an error somewhere because that isn't done. . . . I think steps ought to be taken that will avoid such things in the future.[16]

In the end, as she often did, Cochran got her way. The race times were investigated and adjusted. According to the new official times, Mantz completed the race in four hours, forty-three minutes, and fourteen seconds, only nine minutes ahead of Cochran. Cochran was officially named the second-place finisher and Thomas J. Mayson named third. Ultimately, Mantz received $10,000 of prize money, Cochran's $5,500 (including the $1,000 prize for the winning woman pilot), and Mayson $3,000. Mantz would go on to win the next two Bendix races, beating Cochran again in 1948 by less than two minutes.

After her withdrawal from the Bendix race, there was nothing for Nadine to do but to repair Lucky. She was in low spirits. Though some WASPs had suffered accidents due to sabotage during the war, the idea that someone would want to harm a pilot such as Nadine during peacetime was puzzling and frightening.[17] Neither Nadine nor Ed, who had stayed on with her in Southern California, could understand the situation, and they were upset by its injustice.

After Lucky had been made whole again, Nadine took it up for a test flight. Ed and one of her fellow preflight instructors, along with hundreds of other interested spectators, were standing by the runway that day, and they watched as Nadine taxied and took off, retracting the landing gear as the plane lifted.

Suddenly, the Lightning's left engine sputtered and cut out, and the cockpit canopy pulled loose, striking her in the head and knocking off her headphones. The impact severely disoriented Nadine; she groped for the headphones but couldn't find them, which meant she couldn't hear any communication from the tower. Because the engine hiccupped just as the landing gear retracted, the plane dipped back toward the earth and scraped the runway, bending back five of the propeller blades into fishhook shapes. Fortunately, the tower could see that Nadine was in serious trouble and quickly cleared all traffic out of the area. Ed's heart was in his throat.

Nadine's head was spinning, but she instinctively realized that she didn't have room to stop before hitting a fence and plowing into a group of houses beyond. If she crashed there, innocent people would be killed. Though the plane was shaking violently due to buffeting from the damaged propellers and canopy, she knew she had to try to climb and circle back to the runway to make a safe landing. Fortunately, she had regained power in the left engine.

Somehow, she was able to pull the aircraft up and bring it around for a landing, but when she extended the landing gear, the P-38 started to roll onto its back. Making another split-second decision, she retracted the gear and climbed desperately to go around again. Miraculously, she was able to set the Lightning down on the second try by leaving the landing gear retracted until the very last second and cutting the power in both engines at the extreme end of the runway. Then she set down the P-38 on its wheels, relatively smoothly, and rolled to a stop.

Ed rushed to help Nadine out of the Lightning; she climbed down dizzily. She insisted on checking out the damage to her plane, and she and Ed were both shocked to discover that the propeller blades were bent backward almost eighteen inches. Engineers who later worked on the plane were amazed that she had been able to fly it at all.

Over Nadine's protests, Ed stubbornly took her to the hospital, where doctors found that she had a serious concussion. Still, she had survived, and no one else had been hurt. The *Los Angeles Times* ran a story about her incredible landing under the headline "Girl Pilot Saves Life by Executing Own Teachings." The piece emphasized that spectators on the ground had witnessed Nadine's remarkable recovery and speculated that the safety-focused mindset that characterized Nadine as an instructor was what had saved her during the accident. Accompanying the article was a photograph of Nadine crouching beside the Lightning, one arm wrapped around a propeller blade, with the broken canopy at her feet. It was captioned, "THANKFUL—Nadine Ramsey, girl civilian pursuit ship expert who narrowly escaped cracking up in her P-38, is shown kneeling beside the wrecked canopy after mishap."[18]

Once again, Nadine was lucky. Both she and her P-38 would continue to take to the skies.

In late 1946 the Sixth Ferrying Group was deactivated entirely, and Nadine was at last forced to look for work outside of the Army Air Forces. It was an

emotional blow. She had spent the last four years serving her country, and following military discipline had helped to provide stability in her life. Without it, she was restless and adrift.

In January 1947 she took a job as a secretary for the Servair Corporation at Clover Field (soon to be Santa Monica Airport) in Santa Monica, California. Reluctantly, she moved to nearby Los Angeles for the work. Within six months, she had assumed complete charge of the office and become the assistant sales manager for the sale of light planes. The job suited her, but perhaps not feeling at home in Santa Monica, she quit before the end of the year.

In early 1948 Nadine moved back to Long Beach and became the sales and office manager of Aircraft Aviation Specialists, which operated out of the familiar and beloved sprawl of the Long Beach Army Air Field, now the Long Beach Airport. Aircraft Aviation Specialists had a large stock of aircraft instruments and small component parts and the dealership for a light commercial plane. She returned to selling airplanes and continued performing in airshows and racing in her P-38, happy to be back in a familiar neighborhood.

Around this time, B. J. Erickson London and her husband, Jack, along with a few of their other pilot friends, established an aviation company, United States Aviation, which they also ran out of Long Beach Airport. There, Nadine's path occasionally crossed with B. J., who worked as an instructor at the company and flew in a war-surplus PT-19. Nadine was always glad to see her former WASP commander.

Nadine rented an apartment on Ocean Avenue, right across the street from the beach and the vast blue-green waters of the Pacific. A stately brick mansion that had served as the Army Navy Club during the war rested on a bluff near her new home. The Joint Army and Navy battery, a simple two-gun concrete battery, still stood a block from the club. It had been erected immediately after Pearl Harbor to defend the city in case of enemy motor torpedo boats or submarine attack. Technically a subpost of nearby Fort MacArthur in San Pedro, the dual artillery guns were never fired in combat and had been deactivated. The concrete pedestals remained as they had during wartime, just steps from Nadine's door.

Her apartment building was also just a short walk from the rapidly changing outdoor entertainment area around the Municipal Auditorium, Rainbow Pier, and the Pike—a paved boardwalk and amusement zone stretching a mile along the coastline. Nicknamed the Walk of a Thousand Lights, the

Pike was a hub of daytime and nighttime entertainment, boasting a massive bathhouse, a ballroom, and a beautiful whirling carousel, along with dozens of games, popcorn and saltwater taffy stands, pony and goat rides, fortune tellers, tattoo parlors, theaters, restaurants, and bars. The wooden Cyclone Racer roller coaster stretched on pilings over the ocean and hurled hundreds of delighted riders around its curves daily.

The city's natural beaches were also a tourist draw. Throughout the summer of 1948, the golden stretches of sand between the Pike and the ocean were crowded to capacity with Technicolor beach umbrellas, and the water was filled with shrieking, plunging swimmers. Nadine was able to watch the sun sink into the dusky blue horizon every night; to her it was likely the most beautiful place on earth.

In August 1948, two of Aircraft Aviation Specialists' three business partners were killed in a plane crash, and the company filed for bankruptcy. Nadine was shocked and dismayed, but she saw a silver lining: the chance to own her own company. However, buying the company out of bankruptcy would require a lot more money than Nadine had.

Looking at her finances, she saw that one of the biggest drains on her income was Lucky. Maintaining the plane was expensive: while a P-38 was fast and handled beautifully, its twin engines together burned 100 to 120 gallons of costly high-octane fuel per hour. It was Nadine's dream ship, but it was financially impractical.

Nadine made the hard decision and sold Lucky for $4,000, almost four times what she paid for it. She used the money to buy a large stock of components from Aircraft Aviation Specialists and launched her own business under the name Aircraft Enterprises, Inc., taking over a warehouse and office space at 3165 Atlantic Avenue, three miles west of Long Beach Airport. Along with the aircraft equipment business, she also acquired the dealership and continued to sell airplanes.

At thirty-seven, Nadine was finally her own boss.

Meanwhile, Ed's life had turned completely upside down. After Nadine's thwarted attempt at the Bendix trophy, he decided to move back to the Philippines. Although he loved his mother dearly and cherished her support, Kansas didn't feel like home anymore. All throughout his recovery, he had dreamed of Luzon and the company of the people he'd fought beside. He

began to wonder if he might find peace by returning to the islands he'd grown to love, and so, without much of a plan, he bought a ticket to Manila.

Upon arrival in Luzon, Ed was welcomed as a hero. He was embraced warmly by Philippine army officials and government dignitaries and was invited to lavish banquets and events. By this time, he had regained his marvelous dancing abilities and immediately caught the eye of Madeleine Willoquet, the brilliant and beautiful daughter of the French minister, the top French diplomat in Manila. Though only twenty-four, she was sophisticated and metropolitan; she spoke four languages and could charm a roomful of people with ease.

Passionate and unpredictable, her moods ran hot and cold in a way that Ed found simultaneously thrilling and frustrating. The two of them fell into an intense romance, despite the disapproval of her parents, who felt that Ed was beneath her. When they were married on May 1, 1948, Mr. Willoquet was so upset that he refused to attend the wedding. The young couple then moved into a house on Penafrancia Street, two miles inland from Manila Bay.

Nadine and Nelle were startled to receive news that Ed had tied the knot in the Philippines, and neither was entirely pleased. Nadine was sad that she hadn't been able to attend her brother's wedding but was eager to meet her new sister-in-law. Nelle, on the other hand, felt uneasy. *Who was this European woman?* she wondered. How could she possibly understand a heartland-bred American cavalryman? Despite their mixed emotions, both mother and sister wished Ed all the happiness in the world.

In early 1949 romance returned to Nadine's life; she reconnected with Jack Gardner in Long Beach. By this time, he was twenty-six, divorced and single, and was working for a commercial airline.

Nadine remembered how much she and Jack had in common, despite the eleven-year difference in their ages. They bonded over their love of fighter planes; in fact, Jack's cousin Harold Gardner also had bought a war-surplus P-38. They both loved dogs and owned poodles. Unlike Nadine, Jack wasn't musical himself, but he adored jazz from the twenties and thirties and always looked for an opportunity to put on records and tap his toes. He was a snappy dresser and quick with a joke and loved to drink and dance the night away.

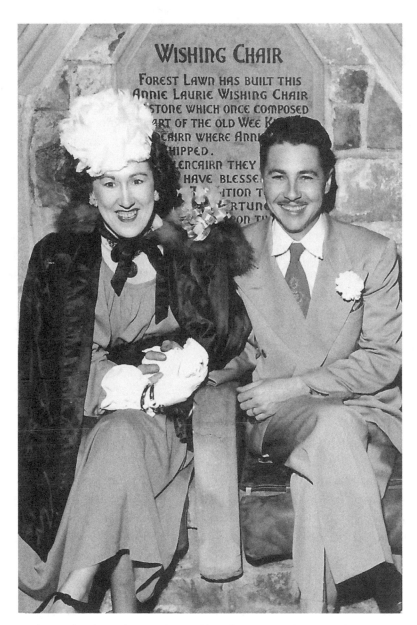

Nadine and Jack Gardner on their wedding day, Los Angeles, November 25, 1949

Of course, Nadine recognized that Jack wasn't entirely stable, but at the time, she was feeling more restless than ever. Approaching thirty-eight, she began to accept that she might never have children. Her twenties and thirties had been consumed by the Depression and the war. She likely felt she had missed her chance to have a "normal" domestic life. Then again, if she had really wanted to, she could easily have quit flying after the war, but over and over in her life, she was tugged skyward, pulled by her heart to some new and different place. This time she was feeling drawn to a life with Jack.

Nadine and Jack Gardner were married on November 25, 1949, at the Wee Kirk o' the Heather Chapel in Forest Lawn Memorial Cemetery in Glendale, a reproduction of the Scottish chapel where Annie Laurie, muse of the poet William Douglas, had supposedly worshiped. The chapel was an extremely popular wedding spot in Los Angeles between the world wars. After making their vows, couples would seat themselves in the twin Annie Laurie stone chair beside the chapel and recite a poem for good luck.

Nadine and Jack followed the tradition, plunking down happily side by side in the Annie Laurie chair. Together, they recited the words carved deep in granite at their feet:

Dressed in our best and all alone,
We sit within the wishing chair
Which bodes success for everyone
Exchanging bridal kisses there.[19]

Nadine was dressed in a blush-colored gown, a fur-trimmed cape, and white gloves. Jack wore a white carnation in his buttonhole. They posed for a photograph with their hands clasped, grinning broadly. A new chapter in Nadine's life was beginning, but her luck was about to change.

PART VI

RESTLESS

Nadine's car streaked north through a bleached Nevada desert toward high-rises shimmering in a blur of heat. A brand-new diamond-shaped sign emblazoned "Welcome to Fabulous Las Vegas" caught her attention as she zoomed past the city's southernmost point. Although it had been put up just a month before, in May 1959, tourists were already crowded around it, snapping photos. The sign twinkled and buzzed, promising nights of glamor, pleasure, and spectacle.

Nadine glanced to her right, listening to the snores of the hunched-over man asleep in the passenger seat. He had been out too late and was hungover; what she could see of his jaw was dark with stubble. Still, he was the man she loved. It will be different this time, *she thought.* He's different.

Like everywhere else in the country, Las Vegas was changing. Some even said city leadership was trying to cut its ties with organized crime and clean up the town. Nadine almost hoped Vegas would never become completely respectable, but as she pulled up beneath the Tropicana's huge, swooping porte cochère, she marveled at all the new resorts and buildings. During the war, she and her fellow WASPs had ferried trainers in and out of McCarran Field, a gunnery school. Now, fifteen years later, a commercial airport was called McCarran, and the original army field had been renamed Nellis Air Force Base. All the change was exhausting and hard to keep up with. Everything seemed to be moving too fast, but Nadine didn't know how to slow it down and wasn't sure she wanted to.

The man beside her jolted awake as Nadine put the car into park.

"Are we here?" he asked groggily.

"We're here," she replied.

Many hours later, Nadine—tipsy, clad in a new dress, and laughing breathlessly—accepted his outstretched hand as she climbed from a taxi beneath the towering red neon sign of the Sands Hotel. It had been a hot, full day of errands and ceremony, but she felt incandescent with happiness. Blinking lights dazzled her as she took the arm of her new husband, who gently folded a rough hand over hers. His familiar, masculine voice said, "Mrs. Donnelly." Nadine's heart gave a jump at the new name, and she smiled in response.

They weaved their way through the Sands's two-story glass entryway and up several sets of wide stairs into the casino. Her husband sat down at a roulette table, and Nadine ordered another drink at the bar, then thought suddenly about her family, about her mother and Ed. Was she really here, a bride again at forty-eight? Was this happening? At some point, she wandered into the Silver Queen Lounge, where young people jumped and jived to rock 'n' roll music. The world was bewildering.

Later that night, Nadine and her new husband, Tom, got a table in the Copa Room, where Frank Sinatra stood at the microphone, singing "Come Fly With Me." He wore a fedora tilted rakishly over one eye, but Frank himself was pushing fifty, Nadine reckoned, and the thought made her feel better. She ordered champagne. "We're newlyweds," she told the waiter, beaming.

The next morning, as they strolled arm in arm along Fremont Street, Nadine paused at a lurid sign for Binion's Horseshoe Club, advertising a view of "atom bomb blasts." The poster featured a series of time-lapse photographs of a blooming mushroom cloud on the horizon, and the images captured her attention. "It's just the bomb testing site," Tom said, when he noticed she had fallen behind. "I don't even think it's operating anymore."

But as Tom walked on, Nadine continued to stand, turning the new wedding band on her finger. Transfixed by the photographs of a nuclear bomb exploding in the remote Nevada desert, she stood frozen as the reality of a powdery atomic mushroom cloud—powerful, destructive, beautiful, Nadine thought—blossomed into the azure sky.

CHAPTER 12

SEARCHING FOR HOME

For several years, Nadine and Jack Gardner were very happy together. As the seasons turned, ushering in the 1950s, the couple made a home in Long Beach, where Nadine's successful business, Aircraft Enterprises, Inc., kept her busy. Her favorite part of the work was demonstrating and selling airplanes, but she enjoyed all the challenges of running a company. With Nelle as a role model and the skills Nadine had acquired at business school and as a secretary, office manager, and flight instructor, Nadine was well-prepared to step into the role of boss.

Jack, who was still in his twenties and flying for a commercial airline, lived a boisterous, wide-roaming life. He thought little of his previous marriages and had no contact with his ex-wives or children; instead, he threw himself headlong into his ongoing love of flying and his current romance with Nadine. Because of their busy schedules, sometimes several days would pass when they didn't see each other. The occasional distance just made their next reunions all the more happy and festive. The popular couple loved dressing up and going out on the town, and they had friends all over the city. Jack was hard charging and hard drinking, but Nadine had no trouble keeping up with him.

Their hobbies also kept them occupied. Whenever they could, they attended air races and air shows together, sometimes driving out to Palm Springs and the desert beyond. Jack loved to tinker and was adept at fixing airplane engines and cars. He also built model planes, littering the apartment on Ocean Avenue with glue and tiny bits of wood, plastic, and metal. Nadine bought an organ and filled the rooms with pop and classical music, effortlessly switching from Al Jolson to Strauss to Rachmaninoff, her high soprano voice accompanied by a chorus of barks from their fluffy white poodles.

Jack earned a good salary, but he had no concept of saving money, so Nadine handled their finances, trying to reasonably balance the budget for both of them. Nonetheless, Jack would sometimes fly into town and present

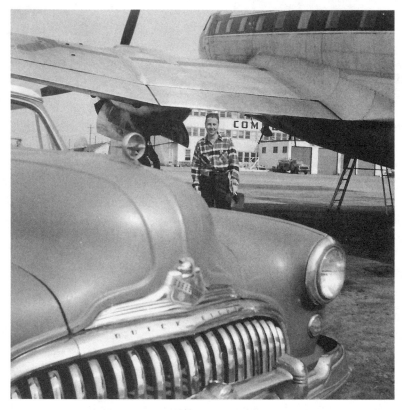

Jack before a takeoff from a Los Angeles-area airport, 1950

her with some lavish, impractical gift. He was inconsistent and irresponsible, but it was hard to stay mad at a man like Jack.

Now approaching forty, Nadine gradually began to accept that she would never be a mother. Ed, however, made her an aunt on March 3, 1949, when Madeleine gave birth to their first child, a boy, Edwin Ramsey Jr. Because Ed and Madeleine were still living in Manila, Nadine and Nelle heard the joyous news from a distance. Both mother and sister were thrilled.

In 1950 Ed decided to finish the law degree that he had abandoned at the University of Oklahoma to help take care of Nadine after her crash in 1940. Ed, Madeleine, and baby Ed Jr. moved from the Philippines back to the heartland and settled in the campus town of Norman, Oklahoma, a little more than 150 miles south of Wichita. Madeleine soon had her second child

Nadine playing the organ, with Jack's model planes P-38 and P-25, Long Beach, California, 1950

in June 1951, a son named Douglas, after Ed's wartime hero, General Douglas MacArthur.

Nelle couldn't have been happier. At sixty, she was at last a grandmother with her family close enough to visit by car. She doted on Ed Jr. and Doug, and when they grew old enough to talk, they called her Mimi. Ed Jr. had inherited the Cozad family's red hair and fair skin, while Doug's hair was light brown. Neither looked especially like beautiful, dark-haired Madeleine, whose mother was born in Brazil of French emigrants to that country. Indeed, everything about Madeleine seemed out of place in Oklahoma, and her personality clashed violently with Nelle's.

Nelle distrusted Madeleine's international upbringing. Although Nelle was progressive as a businesswoman, socially she was fiercely traditional.

She simply couldn't understand why Ed had married a foreigner. Madeleine wanted to raise the boys bilingually—speaking French as well as English—but Nelle objected. She believed a common misconception of the time: that children raised to speak more than one language would never truly master English. She wouldn't have her grandsons speaking French, she told Ed firmly.

Nelle also demanded that Ed Jr. and Doug receive a Christian education; specifically, she wanted them raised Baptist. Madeleine, who had been brought up Catholic but held no particular beliefs of her own, argued passionately against what she saw as Nelle's backward ideas. However, Ed agreed with Nelle, who took it upon herself to tell the boys Bible stories and sing them hymns.

In 1952 Ed graduated from law school, and at Madeleine's urging they moved the family from Oklahoma to Los Angeles—first to Westchester, then to Santa Monica, and later to Inglewood, right by the Inglewood Airport. That same year, their first daughter, Michele, was born, followed in December 1954 by their second daughter, Janine. By then, Ed was working at Hughes Aircraft Company.

That same year, Jack was offered a job as a flight instructor for Trans-Ocean Airlines. The company needed to train a large group of Indonesian pilots and could potentially provide steady work for both Jack and Nadine. The job also gave Jack a chance to stay home more, so Nadine agreed he should take it. She sold her company, and the two of them moved to Bakersfield, California, midway between Fresno and Los Angeles.

Sure enough, TransOcean hired Nadine as well, as a Link instructor; the blue box she had trained in during the war was back in her life. She was responsible for teaching the Indonesian students the basics of instrument flying. Once again, Nadine enjoyed the work, and she liked having Jack at home more frequently, but Bakersfield was hot, landlocked, and much less lively than Long Beach. When the Indonesian flight program concluded, she and Jack quit.

At this point, Nadine hoped to move back to Southern California. While living in Bakersfield, she sometimes flew down to visit Ed, Madeleine, and the kids, passing through their lives like a bright, glamorous comet, showing

Nelle and her grandchildren, Inglewood, California, 1956. Left to right: *Edwin Ramsey Jr., age 7; Janine, 2; Douglas, 5; Michele, 4*

them photos of herself and her airplanes. She longed for the opportunity to get to know her growing nieces and nephews.

Nelle, too, wanted to be closer to Ed's family. She had gotten used to spending time with them in Oklahoma. Now in her early sixties, she was eager to make her grandchildren the center of her life. It was a hard decision to leave Wichita, where she had built most of her life and career, but Nelle had always prioritized her family above all else. She closed down her cosmetology clinic and moved to Southern California, renting a house in Long Beach, about an hour south of Ed's home.

Jack, however, now accepted a new job as a pilot in Edmonton, Canada. Instead of moving south at the end of 1954, he and Nadine picked up and headed in the opposite direction, to a rapidly growing city of more than fifty

thousand about two hundred miles north of Calgary in Alberta. Edmonton also was the home of Canada's first licensed airfield, City Centre Airport, which had opened in 1929. Jack was hired to fly for the new Distant Early Warning Line, a communications network designed to warn Canada and the United States in the event of a Soviet attack from Russia over the North Pole. His job was to fly supplies and personnel in and out of remote radar installations that were being constructed across otherwise deserted regions of the far north. Jack was among the twenty-five thousand workers contracted by Western Electric to build the sixty radar stations, which would be manned around the clock by US or Canadian military personnel.

Nadine must have disliked Edmonton intensely. Poised over a stunning natural river valley, the city could be breathtakingly beautiful, but compared to Southern California, it was mercilessly cold. The temperature dipped below freezing as early as October, hovered around zero throughout the winter, and refused to warm up until well into April. Moreover, Jack was once again frequently away from home, and Nadine was lonely. Always one to try to make friends, she joined the American Women's Group, a charitable organization, and immersed herself in volunteer work. Still, her time in Canada was dismal. In 1956, when Jack was offered a job with General Airways in Portland, Oregon, Nadine insisted he take it.

For Nadine and Jack, Edmonton marked the beginning of the end of their marriage. Even after they moved to Portland and Nadine resumed working as a Link instructor, they couldn't seem to regain the happiness they'd felt in Long Beach. Nadine likely simmered in resentment at being isolated from her family and friends, and she began to suspect that Jack no longer loved her. She knew he was prone to chasing other women, and she was not about to tiptoe meekly around any suspected unfaithfulness. On the other hand, if she raged at him, Jack only became more distant.

In early 1957, Jack was hired by yet another commercial airline, and he and Nadine moved to Kingsport, Tennessee, just south of the Kentucky border. A small but bustling city of about twenty thousand, Kingsport was the home of one of the largest African American high schools in the state, Douglass High School. It was one of hundreds of Rosenwald schools throughout the South founded by the president of Sears, Roebuck, and Company, Julius Rosenwald. In 1957, despite the 1954 US Supreme Court ruling that

racial segregation in public education was unconstitutional, the city's public facilities had not yet been integrated. In that setting, Nadine was exposed to another ugly side of Jack's personality: he was extremely prejudiced against African Americans and did not hide his distaste for the growing national conversation about civil rights.

One day, Jack was staying in Knoxville with a pilot friend who invited him out on a double date. That evening, he met Jacqueline "Jackie" Rose, a pretty redheaded nursing student from Angelica, Tennessee, a town nestled in the foothills of the Great Smoky Mountains. At this time, Nadine was forty-six and Jack was thirty-five. Jackie was twenty-five but had already weathered some difficult life experiences. Her mother had died when she was nine, and her father had married a woman that Jackie fought with incessantly. At sixteen, she had run away from home and married a much older man, a professor named Fred Fisher. They had a daughter, whom Fred raised after their divorce.

While his marriage with Nadine deteriorated, Jack wooed Jackie. She had no idea he was married but was reluctant about his intentions. One day, when Jack told Jackie he was planning to marry her, Jackie laughed and said, "Yeah, right." Still, Jack poured all his energy into charming her, and Nadine noticed.

That spring, Nadine confronted Jack about his affair in Knoxville. Jack admitted he had fallen in love with someone else. Nadine was heartbroken, but she was certainly not going to stay with a man who couldn't be faithful. She filed for a divorce, which was finalized on June 6, 1957, then resolutely packed her things and flew back to California. She dropped Jack's last name immediately and became a Ramsey again.

Jack made good on his offer of marriage to Jackie, who was shocked when she learned he'd been married the whole time. The two were married in 1958 and had two daughters, in 1961 and 1964. However, Jack couldn't settle down with Jackie, either, and they split up before the end of the decade. Much later, Nadine learned that she was the third of Jack's six wives in total.

For Nadine, time felt like it was speeding up. Nationally, the 1950s brought myriad changes. After World War II, the United States became entangled

in the Cold War, a decades-long state of hostility with the communist Soviet Union. Meanwhile, families moved to the suburbs, the entertainment industry boomed, and teenagers rebelled and listened to rock 'n' roll music.

Though women no longer flew military aircraft, their work in aviation didn't abruptly end. The decade produced the founding of the Whirly-Girls, an international women's helicopter association. The Civil Air Patrol had also grown; of its roughly ninety thousand members in 1956, fourteen thousand were women or the teenage girls of the CAP Cadets program. On May 20, 1953, Jackie Cochran broke the sound barrier in a single-engine jet fighter, the F-86, and in 1959 she became the first woman president of the International Aeronautical Federation.[1]

After the war, some WASPs—like Nadine's 43-5 classmate Yvonne "Pat" Pateman—joined the newly created US Air Force, formerly the AAF, renamed when it became a separate military service on September 18, 1947, following passage of the National Security Act of 1947. When the Korean War broke out in June 1950, these women served in support capacities.[2]

Others were commissioned by the Air Force Reserve, including Nancy Love (who became a lieutenant colonel) and WAFS Originals Teresa James and B. J. Erickson London (who were majors). With her WASP accolades and her position as a commanding officer, London assumed she would eventually achieve flight status, but the air force never let her fly. The fifties also saw an increase in women's aviation organizations, but by and large, women struggled for a greater role in the industry.

Men were struggling as well. The repercussions of World War II reverberated throughout the country, shaking the lives of its millions of veterans and their families. In 1946 Congress passed the National Mental Health Act, which provided for expanded mental health facilities, particularly for veterans like Ed, who suffered from war trauma. Also called combat neurosis, combat exhaustion, or battle fatigue, the condition these veterans suffered is known today as post-traumatic stress disorder. In the 1950s an entire generation of men silently shouldered the weight of their war memories and tried to move on.

In May 1959 Ed had just turned forty-two. Like many of his fellow veterans, he felt he had left the war behind. He was a husband, father of four, and hardworking businessman. Fourteen years had passed since the trauma he

had endured in the jungles of Luzon, and he thought he had fully recovered. But like many other veterans, Ed could not bear to talk about what had happened to him. Although he had long since finished his manuscript about his war experiences, a 188-page memoir he called "Guerilla Command," he had never shown it to anyone.

In 1958 Ed began traveling to Japan for Hughes Aircraft. The company was hoping to win a major contract to supply Japan with an advanced early-warning radar system. The Japanese government solicited contract bids from large US aerospace companies, including Hughes Aircraft, Lockheed, and Grumman. Ed's superiors asked if he would be willing to move to Tokyo to represent Hughes Aircraft in the contest. The promotion also came with a new title: Far East vice president. Ed also led Hughes's joint venture with Nippon Electric, the Nippon Aviotronics Company, Ltd. Separately, on May 26, 1959, Tokyo was chosen as the host city for the 1964 Summer Olympic Games, and Hughes Aircraft recognized a potential market for its new, geosynchronous satellite technology to broadcast the Olympics internationally.

Ed considered the job offer carefully. He had traveled to Japan several times for business, but the prospect of moving there carried serious implications. He thought about the Japanese soldiers he had fought and killed—a lifetime ago, it seemed. Then again, he was still haunted by the ghosts of friends who had fallen under Japanese bullets and bayonets, and he recalled the incredible sacrifices of the Filipino people. The Kempeitai at one point had offered a substantial reward for Ed's capture or death, and they had nearly succeeded at killing him more than once. Could he really move to Japan?

Ed closely examined his own heart and surprisingly found no lingering hatred there for the Japanese. Yes, he had forgiven, and he could go. He accepted the position. The young Ramsey family boarded a Pan Am plane and flew first to Hawaii, then to Guam, and from there to Tokyo.

At first, Ed, Madeleine, and the children lived in Tokyo's landmark Frank Lloyd Wright–designed Imperial Hotel; a few months later, they moved into a spacious Western-style home provided by Hughes Aircraft in the wealthy Minato area of Tokyo. Minato was home to dozens of foreign embassies, including the US Embassy, as well as flourishing international companies and excellent schools. The Ramsey home, not far from the Imperial Palace, the birthplace and home of then-emperor Hirohito, came with a cook and

servants, and Ed was provided with a company car and driver. The children were even allowed to bring along their pet boxer, Tippy.

Living in Tokyo allowed Ed to renew his love of horseback riding, and he taught his children to ride. His role representing Hughes Aircraft gave him entrée to the country's leading riding club on the grounds of the Imperial Palace. One of Japan's top equestrians, Colonel Shunzo Kido, who rode for Japan in the 1928 and 1932 Summer Olympics, oversaw the children's equestrian training, notably in jumping and dressage. All four young Ramseys inherited their father's natural horsemanship and relished the opportunity to ride every Sunday within the lush confines of the stately palace grounds.

Madeleine did not ride, but she attended *gymkhana* equestrian competitions on the Imperial Palace grounds. She was active in the kids' schools and utilized the talents she'd developed as an ambassador's daughter. A skilled hostess, she threw stylish parties for other Hughes Aircraft and international families in Tokyo and the growing number of Ed's leading Japanese business partners (notably from the C. Itoh trading firm and Nippon Electric, the manufacturer today known as NEC).

Unfortunately, Ed's position required him to work ten- to twelve-hour days and travel frequently, which put a strain on his and Madeleine's relationship. Even though they were living a world away from the United States, Ed and his wife fell into the traditional gender roles of most US households of the time: he worked ceaselessly to provide for the family, and she was a mother and homemaker. Whether or not they wanted or were well suited to those roles didn't matter; that was simply the way things were done.

CHAPTER 13

A DECADE OF CHANGE

In 1957, after returning to California, Nadine decided she had had enough of pilots. She became a licensed real estate agent and joined the popular Kelly Girl Service, a nationally respected agency that loaned secretaries out to companies on temporary assignments. She used her Kelly Girl jobs to supplement her income from real estate sales and bought herself a simple little home on a cul-de-sac in Sun Valley, near Lockheed Air Terminal (now Hollywood Burbank Airport) in Burbank.

Hard as she tried not to meet or date pilots, Nadine once again found herself in a romance with a flier—this time a tall, black-haired, blue-eyed Irish American named Thomas Joseph Donnelly. Born in Saint Louis, Missouri, Tom had quit his mechanic's job at a carburetor company in 1940 to sign up with the army and become a pilot. He left the army in 1948, but he had the spirit of an aviator and continued flying.

When Nadine met him, likely in or around the airport, Tom was forty-three, four years younger than her, and married. Like Jack Gardner, Tom was almost certainly a drinker and a hotshot with a devil-may-care attitude. His eight-year marriage was on the rocks. In spite of herself, Nadine fell for him.

Tom's divorce from his wife officially came through on April 18, 1959. Within weeks, he had convinced Nadine to run away with him. They drove to Las Vegas, where they were married on June 20. On their Clark County, Nevada, marriage application, both listed the reason for their previous divorces: mental cruelty.

Time sped up further still, racing on to the dawn of the 1960s. On September 26, 1960, seventy million viewers crowded around their TV screens to watch the first-ever televised presidential debate between John F. Kennedy and Richard Nixon. Two months later, Kennedy won the closest presidential election since 1884.

The Cold War had brought the development of jet fighters, guided missiles, and the expansion of the aerospace industry into research, science,

and engineering. The concept of a female aerospace engineer had not yet taken hold; women were just beginning to break through social and gender stereotypes. Still, many women in the field saw the connection between the emerging women's rights movement and women fliers.

Such was the case with journalist Patricia Demarest, editor of *Flying* magazine, who wrote, "While a male student pilot is reviewing his last lesson and imagining his next, his student pilot wife is more likely to be cooking dinner and deciding if the ironing can wait until Wednesday." About the role of women in aviation, she observed, "To some the feminization of flying will be akin to holding a woman's bridge party in a monastery," concluding what Nadine herself surely could have written: "And for those to whom flying is an escape from the cares of the ground—something to be savored best when solo—the beauty of the sky is that it is big enough for both of us."[1]

In May 1961 President Kennedy announced his goal to land men on the moon by the end of the decade. He also made Americans aware of a new communist threat developing in Vietnam, contributing to anxiety already surrounding the United States' heated nuclear and space contests with the Soviet Union. In October 1961 he again used the national platform of television to warn American families to ready themselves for potential nuclear attacks by building bomb shelters in their backyards.

The sixties were off to a tumultuous start.

Nadine's third marriage wasn't going well, either. Like Jack, Tom was too often away from home, and Nadine bounced around the Los Angeles area working in real estate and as a Kelly Girl secretary. After their wedding, she worked as a bookkeeper at Porter Pipe and Supply in North Hollywood until September 1959.

The next year, she was hired as a secretary and assistant fundraiser at the prestigious Harvard School for Boys in the San Fernando Valley. Founded as a military academy in 1900 on the corner of Western Avenue and Venice Boulevard in Los Angeles, it quickly outgrew its campus. In 1937 the academy received a substantial grant from one of Nadine's former employers, aviation mogul Donald Douglas, and the campus moved into a spacious Spanish Revival building, formerly the Hollywood Country Club, on Coldwater Canyon Boulevard. Now, with the school scaling back its emphasis on

military training while increasing enrollment, Nadine assisted in developing procedures, manuals, and brochures about its changing programs.

When the school discontinued its fundraising in 1961, Nadine once again found herself looking for work. Possibly reasoning that with Tom's absences they were barely living together anyway, she decided to move back to Long Beach and rented a little apartment beside the Los Angeles River at 1926 San Francisco Avenue in the city's South Wrigley neighborhood. She was quickly hired at Guardtone, Inc., a burglar and fire alarm company. She ran the office there until the end of the year.

Although she wasn't living particularly close to the Long Beach Airport or near the beautiful Pacific Ocean, Nadine once again made a cozy nest for herself in Long Beach. For the first time in more than twenty years, she and her mother were living in the same city. Nelle joined a local Baptist church and, as usual, spent her time volunteering and organizing. Nadine frequently visited her by car, to catch up and commiserate. She still had friends in the area, too, and could easily borrow planes to fly on the weekends, though she was flying less often now due to increasing discomfort in her back and neck. Suspecting that her aches and pains were related to her 1940 crash, she soldiered on through them. She was getting older, and her marriage was falling apart, but Nadine was home at last.

In 1962 Hughes Aircraft granted Ed two months of home leave. Like military personnel, corporate employees stationed overseas were encouraged to return periodically to the United States to visit their extended families and recharge. Madeleine also saw it as a chance to expose her children—now thirteen, eleven, nine, and eight—to the world and international travel. She and Ed agreed to split the home leave into two parts, spending half on a trip around the world and devoting the other half to resting up at home in California.

The Ramseys boarded a cruise ship in Hong Kong, and after stopping in nearly a dozen countries along the way, they disembarked in Genoa, Italy. Then followed a trip around Western Europe by car. They were exposed to a whirlwind of cultures. Leaving Europe, the family flew to Los Angeles for the remainder of their home leave. Ed, Madeleine, and the kids also visited Nadine and Nelle in Long Beach, bombarding their Aunt Nadine and their

beloved Mimi with tales from their trip. At summer's end, the Ramseys returned by plane to Tokyo. Upon landing, they had circled the globe.

In 1963 Nadine and Tom realized that their four-year marriage simply wasn't working, and they divorced. Once again, Nadine placed the blame on Tom's absence and unreliable personality. At the time, she was working six-week clerical stints at various companies around Southern California, including Shell Chemical in Downey, Forest Lawn Memorial Park in Cypress, and Aeronutronic in Anaheim. As she had with Jack, when her divorce was finalized she dropped the Donnelly last name and resumed being a Ramsey.

On November 22 that year, President Kennedy was assassinated in Dallas, Texas, stunning the nation and the world. In the aftermath of the shooting, Vice President Lyndon Johnson was sworn in as president. In 1964, after a heated debate in Congress, he signed the Civil Rights Act into law, officially ending segregation and making discrimination based on race, color, religion, sex, or national origin illegal. That fall, Johnson ran for president against Republican Senator Barry Goldwater, who had strongly opposed the Civil Rights Act. He defeated Goldwater in a landslide.

To many former WASPs, the struggle for civil rights throughout the decade highlighted the injustice of their deactivation in 1944. As the Women's Movement gained traction throughout the 1960s, they grew more aware of their rights and the ways in which they were being discriminated against daily. Wrestling with these social changes, they turned to each other for support. As time passed and life changed rapidly for the army's former female fliers, the Order of Fifinella officially became part of the newly reorganized Women Airforce Service Pilots of WWII, or WASP, Inc., still helping to remind them of that essential time in their lives, the brief, happy time they'd been allowed to fly for their country. Later, this ongoing WASP solidarity inspired a more active fight for official military recognition.

For now, members of the order began publishing the *WASP Newsletter*, sharing information and the whereabouts of their fellow WASPs. Along with a "Class Notes" feature and postings of new WASP addresses, the first issue, in October 1964—now published officially under WASP, Inc.—recognized WASPs who had died in service during the war, as well as the seven WASPs who were members of the newly formed Federal Aviation Administration Women's Advisory Committee on Aviation. As might be expected

of a WASP publication during a time of transition for women, both aviation leaders and stay-at-home mothers were honored: in side-by-side photographs with captions, the newsletter featured Jackie Cochran, who flew to the 1964 reunion in Cincinnati, Ohio, in mid-August that year "at the controls of her own Lockheed Lodestar," and Jean Terrele (class 44-10), "now Mrs. Earl Moreo and Mother of 10!"[2]

Though she had not joined the Order of Fifinella, Nadine was invited to attend this first WASP, Inc. reunion. At the time, she worked at Turco Products in Wilmington—just over the Los Angeles River from her home in Long Beach—as the private secretary to a district sales manager of the company's aviation cleaning chemicals. However, the lingering headaches and back pain she had endured for years were growing worse. Citing her health, she sadly turned down the invitation.

In late 1964 a new injury brought Nadine to the hospital, where she was told she would need major surgery on her neck. It was a difficult diagnosis. Nadine, like many pilots, tended to ignore her physical limitations as much as possible. The surgery would require her to quit working and flying temporarily until she could recover. One bright spot was Nelle's offer to move in with her daughter during the post-surgery period. Determined to get well and resume flying, Nadine was prepared for the pain and hard work before her. But on July 1, 1965, eight painful months after her neck surgery, she suffered another injury, this time a hip fracture. When she awakened from surgery on her lower back, she was told that she would never fly again. Nadine had heard this grim statement before but hadn't heeded it. This time it was real, and it was heartbreaking.

At only fifty-four, she was grounded.

Thanks to Ed and his team's hard work, Nippon Aviotronics, the joint venture between Hughes Aircraft and Nippon Electric, was awarded the contract to supply Japan with its Base Air Defense Ground Environment early-warning air control radar system. The system would allow Japan to electronically and automatically detect, track, and identify airborne targets while providing to-the-target control of Japanese fighter-interceptor aircraft and surface-to-air defense missiles.

Ed was also instrumental in negotiating for broadcasting companies in Japan and the United States to use the newly launched Hughes-built

Syncom 3 satellite (the first satellite in geostationary orbit). Syncom 3 was launched successfully on August 19, 1964, allowing for the 1964 Summer Olympics to be broadcast live from Tokyo to the United States. It was the first overseas Olympics to be televised live to the United States via satellite. (The 1960 Rome Olympics had been televised live, via satellite, but only within Europe.)

With the Base Air Defense Ground Environment and satellite deals finalized, Hughes Aircraft transferred Ed back to its Los Angeles headquarters. Before heading to the United States, he and his family were invited to Manila for a month-long visit. Up until this point, Ed's children had little awareness of their father's war exploits or his status as a revered hero in the Philippines. Arriving in Manila, however, the family was treated like royalty.

Ed once again became the Filipinos' beloved Colonel Ramsey of wartime. He was embraced by many of the men and women he had served alongside at a reunion of his troops, the East Central Luzon Guerrilla Area Force. He was also welcomed by the country's then-president, Diosdado Macapagal, who had worked with Ed's guerrilla network during the war.

President Macapagal invited the Ramseys to stay in the Philippine presidential palace, Malacañang, the only major government building to have survived the bombing of Manila, and at a ceremony held on the palace grounds, he proudly awarded Ed the Philippine Medal of Honor. Ed now had more than a dozen US and Philippine medals and honors to his name. During their visit, the Ramseys were also provided with a Philippine Navy ship to shuttle them to visits on some of the country's more than seven thousand islands. Amazed, Ed's children began to suspect that there was much more to their father than they had realized.

Once back in Los Angeles, Ed's family moved an hour away from Nelle and Nadine in Long Beach. Although both women looked forward to spending more time with Ed and his children, Nadine didn't get along with Madeleine. They had little in common, and Nadine always took Ed's side in an argument. If Ed and Madeleine were at odds, then Nadine and her sister-in-law were too.

The boys struggled to adjust as well. Because they had been educated in Tokyo's more accelerated school system, they were placed several grades ahead when they entered Chaminade High School in the West San Fer-

Ed and family landing in the Philippines to attend the East Central Luzon Guerrilla Area reunion, Manila, 1964

nando Valley. Ed Jr., at fifteen, entered eleventh grade and Doug, at thirteen, tenth. To teenagers who had grown up overseas, sixties culture in the United States was disorienting.

In 1966 Hughes Aircraft offered Ed another overseas assignment, this time in London. Madeleine was thrilled. Although she wanted Ed to take the position, he declined it. Instead, he left Hughes and joined an engineering firm, Ralph M. Parsons Company, investors in an electronics factory in Taiwan. However, Parsons soon pulled out of the venture, putting Ed's job in jeopardy. The company made him a settlement offer: control of the factory in Taiwan.

Ed decided to create a company of his own at the Kaohsiung factory and accepted Parsons's severance package. Inspired by his mother's successful skincare business, he converted the former Parsons factory to manufacture handheld dermatological devices that used electrodes to tighten skin on the face, with the goal of selling them on the American market.

That year, while looking for a new, more spacious home for the family,

Ed and Madeleine found a stunning Spanish Revival house in West Los Angeles at 201 Tilden Avenue in Westwood. The house had been built in 1936 by legendary celebrity architect Wallace Neff, who designed in a variety of European Revival styles. Renowned as the man who had built Pickfair, the English Regency manor of Douglas Fairbanks and Mary Pickford, he had also designed homes for Charlie Chaplin, Greta Garbo, Claudette Colbert, Cary Grant, Katharine Hepburn, and many other celebrities. Known as the Galli-Curci House after its first owner, the Italian opera singer Amelita Galli-Curci, the home featured peaked ceilings with exposed dark wood beams, ornately carved fireplace surrounds, arched doorways, and a manicured garden protected by an intricate wrought iron gate.

The time spent at the home on Tilden Avenue was the last happy period for the Ramseys as a united family. The children had adjusted fully to life in the United States and began making friends. They loved swimming in the backyard pool, and Nelle and Nadine lived close enough to visit. After Ed Jr. graduated from high school in 1966, he and Doug spent the summer learning French intensively at the University of Grenoble in the foothills of the Alps. Returning to Los Angeles, Ed Jr. attended the University of California–Los Angeles, majoring in political science. Doug followed suit in 1967, after finishing high school at the *Lycée Français de Los Angeles*, a school founded three years earlier in Beverly Hills. Based on the French academic system, it offered classes in both English and French and was where Janine and Michele also attended—to their mother's great satisfaction.

Ed and Madeleine's relationship, however, continued to deteriorate as Ed struggled to run his new business. He could not get approval from the Food and Drug Administration to import and sell his dermatology devices in the United States. He also frequently traveled to the factory in Taiwan. Just as Ed's business seemed doomed to fail, so his marriage eventually passed the point of no return.

Nadine, meanwhile, tried to go back to work. In February 1967, when she had recovered enough to walk, Aztec Aircraft Sales at Long Beach Airport hired her as a dispatcher in the flight school. It wasn't flying, but it was the closest she could achieve, and even being back at the airport offered some relief from the dark clouds that seemed to be gathering.

The following year, she took a job at Golden Hours Villa, a convalescent

hospital owned and operated by investor Herbert A. Cook and his wife Joan, a registered nurse. Cook had built the facility at 2901 E. Pacific Coast Highway and opened it in 1966. In publicity materials, the hospital claimed it was "the newest, largest, most extravagant and plush convalescent hospital" in Long Beach and boasted of its large fountains, beautiful chandeliers, and a full-time chaplain and bakery on site.[3] Cook, who was thirty-six, hired Nadine as his executive secretary.

Immediately, Nadine sensed that something was wrong with the way Cook was conducting business. She quit after only a month, explaining to Nelle that the job "was not as represented" and that the pressure of working there was making her health worse. In fact, Cook and his wife were embezzling funds from their elderly patients and ran their bakery on more than $70,000 (about $560,000 in 2020 dollars) of stolen eggs and coffee. In 1971 Cook was convicted on six charges of receiving stolen property and was charged with fraud three years later.

Nadine's last day of work at Golden Hours was April 4, 1968—the same day Martin Luther King Jr. was shot and killed on a hotel balcony in Memphis, Tennessee. King's death incited riots across the country. That night, presidential hopeful Senator Robert F. Kennedy called on Americans to honor King's legacy and shared a message of unity. A civil rights champion, Kennedy himself was murdered only two months later, on June 6, at the Ambassador Hotel in Los Angeles.

On July 20, 1969, Neil Armstrong became the first man to walk on the moon, fulfilling President Kennedy's promise that the United States would be "the world's leading space-faring nation." At the same time, the Vietnam War was dividing Americans, and on December 1 the government held a draft lottery, the country's first since 1942. Thousands of young men were called up, willingly or unwillingly, to serve in Vietnam.

As the country struggled to absorb these events, Nadine fell into despair. To cope with the reality that she would neither fly nor ever really work again and wrestling with pain and emotional darkness, she began drinking more heavily.

At some point that year, in a rage, Madeleine threw Ed—who was now sleeping in the family den—out of the house on Tilden Avenue. The ensuing rift in the family would last for years.

The 1960s drew to a close, but peace was a long way off.

PART VII
RECOGNITION

Nadine shut the heavy front door, listening to its final click, and realized her hands were shaking. Pain, like an electrical current, shot from the base of her spine to her neck and seemed to radiate throughout her body. Pins and needles stabbed at her hip, where steel rods and joints held her leg together. Sometimes she thought of her bones as a skeleton of white-hot metal, a spacecraft reentering earth's atmosphere. Other times, she felt her flesh was a mass of earthbound, worm-like scars.

She gasped, leaning back against the door through which her friend and former commanding officer, B. J. Erickson London, had just left. Her vision swam, and she cursed softly. The living room, anchored by a goldenrod couch on one wall, seemed an empty ocean that stretched between her and the kitchen table, but Nadine gathered her courage and set out to cross it.

Pouring herself a drink, she gulped it down, refilled her glass, and dropped wearily back into the wooden chair she'd been working from for the last several hours. She reflected on London's kindness at coming over to help her; she would never have been able to pull down these boxes of papers without her friend's help. When London was there, filling out the honorable discharge application had seemed manageable, but now that Nadine was alone again, the process felt overwhelming.

She tried to calm herself and once more flipped through the thick stack of documents she and London had assembled. Most were boring, internal memos and flight assignments, but they meant something to Nadine. More importantly, she knew, they should mean something to the Air Force's Service Review Board. That she or any former WASP should have to prove her service to the country now, in May 1979, seemed like bureaucratic nonsense, but many of her peers had fought long and hard for this privilege. Nadine thought about how it would feel to be honorably discharged after all these years. She didn't know.

Then she paused. In the waning, late afternoon light, beneath a lattice of typed black-and-white pages, she saw the pale green corner of a book she recognized instantly: her class book from Avenger Field. Her eyes instantly filled with tears. The pain, which had been receding into the background, surged forward again in

another sickening wave. She took another sip from her drink and pulled out the book, almost not wanting to see what was inside.

Blinking rapidly, Nadine put her thumb between the covers and opened the book at random; the faces of half a dozen bright young women stared eagerly up at her. Flipping several pages hastily, she was met with her own much younger beaming face, the Fifinella patch on her jacket. Just below her photograph, she saw her friend Dawn Rochow's happy smile; she hadn't been in touch with Dawn in years. She froze. If she turned one more page, she would see the face of her lost friend, Helen Jo Severson, and that she just couldn't bear.

She slammed the book closed. Then, as she shoved it away, a newspaper clipping fell out and fluttered to the ground. Nadine bent forward gingerly to pick it up. The article was from only a couple of years earlier and the headline read: "WASPs Seek Status." The headline of our lives, *she thought.*

Suddenly, another photograph caught her eye: a glossy eight-by-ten print of Nadine and Lucky, her P-38 fighter plane, the one photojournalist Peter Stackpole had shot for a cover of Life *magazine. The magazine title jumped out at her. Now all of that life was gone; the sky was leaden and closed to her. In one wild, aching movement, Nadine got up and seized a pair of scissors from a drawer. Frantically, she drove the scissor blades through the glossy picture—a cut through the cloudless heavens, a cut across her Lightning's silver wings, a cut through her own smiling face, bisecting it down the middle. Dropping the photo scraps into the wastebasket, she collapsed on the couch, crying, tossing and turning fitfully until sleep claimed her at last.*

CHAPTER 14

NEW DIRECTIONS

Nadine wasn't the only former WASP to suffer from depression. Many had struggled with feelings of aimlessness for years. Like their male counterparts, few spoke in public or even in private about their wartime experiences, and those who did were frequently not believed.

And like many of today's women veterans who suffer long-term mental health implications from serving in a culture of bias and harassment, the WASPs were also not strangers to sexual harassment during their service—especially as they were the only women's unit employed in a men-only division of the army. Nor were they shielded, then or later, from the limitations imposed on them due to their gender. Both situations resulted in a sense of isolation.[1]

It was easy, then, for WASPs to feel they had no place in the world, despite their many accomplishments. Nevertheless, they continued to find ways to support each other, especially through the National Organization of Women Pilots, known as the Ninety-Nines. Established on November 2, 1929, by its charter members—ninety-nine female pilots, including Amelia Earhart—over the years the organization had attracted many WASPs to its various chapters. WAFS Original Betty Gillies had served as its fifth president before the war in 1939 and was one of ten founders of the San Diego chapter in 1946. In 1952 B. J. Erickson London helped to found the organization's first Long Beach chapter.

One of the most prominent women's flying events was an all-woman transcontinental air race, nicknamed the Powder Puff Derby; the first race had helped inspire the Ninety-Nines' founding in 1929. In 1947 some former WASPs and Ninety-Nines members decided to revive the derby, and Betty Gillies convinced London to fly in the third annual race in 1949. By 1950 race organizers officially incorporated as the All-Woman Transcontinental Air Race, and they named Gillies chairwoman. In turn, Gillies recruited London and former Long Beach WASP Iris Cummings Critchell to serve on the board. Together, Gillies and London administered the race for twelve years. London continued the work until 1967.

Aviatrixes of the first all-women transcontinental air race, including Amelia Earhart and Louise Thaden (fourth and fifth from right). Powder Puff Derby, Santa Monica, California, August 1929. (Courtesy Saint Louis University Libraries Archives and Digital Services)

Perhaps because Nadine moved so frequently during the 1950s and 1960s, she participated very little in these opportunities. She never joined the Ninety-Nines or flew in the Powder Puff Derby. Instead, following the devastating diagnosis in 1965 that she would never fly again, she withdrew into depression and despair, turning to alcohol in an attempt to dull the pain.

After moving out of the Tilden Avenue house in the late 1960s, Ed took up residence in the Oakwood Apartments—a huge, hip, gated apartment complex in Toluca Lake adjacent to Universal Studios. The apartments came fully furnished and the grounds featured several swimming pools, tennis courts, and clubhouses. At fifty-two, he was a newly minted bachelor, and he wasn't sure what he wanted to do. He bought a Jaguar sports car and returned to his former company, Hughes Aircraft.

For the next two years, Ed's divorce dragged on. Then, on March 31, 1971,

the couple's marriage legally ended. Ed Jr. and Doug finished their senior years at the University of California–Los Angeles in June 1970. Doug began graduate school at the College of Europe in Bruges, Belgium, while Ed Jr. joined the army after completing the university's US Army Reserve Officer Training Corps program. That June he was commissioned a second lieutenant and went on active duty in September.

Ed, however, felt directionless and alone. In the spring of 1974, he decided to take a trip to Jamaica. Having found solace in travel before, he hoped that seeing new sights would reinvigorate him. He found a room in one of the many new resorts in the town of Negril, on the westernmost point of the island, which was becoming a popular tourist destination. He also rented a motorcycle so he could more easily get around the area and view its famous beaches, which stretched in wide swaths of soft, white sand from the concrete lighthouse at the southern end to a rocky promontory at the northern end.

One day, Ed's motorcycle unexpectedly hit a rock and he was violently thrown from the bike onto the road. Seriously injured, he was rushed to the hospital. There he was treated for two broken ribs, contusions, and a ruptured spleen, which the doctors removed to stabilize him. Because three of his four children weren't in regular communication with him (by now Doug was writing for the *Washington Post* from Brussels, Michele was in Europe, and Janine attended at the University of Maryland–College Park), he spent a week in the Jamaican hospital alone, suffering greatly, psychologically and physically. Later, he would recall that during that week, he felt he was meant to die there.[2]

Eventually, one of Ed's friends and coworkers from Hughes Aircraft, Merritt Barker, convinced the company to send a jet to Jamaica to fly Ed home to Los Angeles. Once back, he was treated for a week at Saint John's Hospital in Santa Monica and spent an additional two weeks recovering at home before he could return to work. Although his body began to heal, loneliness and compounding trauma to his mind left Ed in great psychological despair.

In 1929, half a lifetime earlier, his father, Claude Ramsey, had killed himself in an El Dorado jail cell, leaving ten-year-old Ed and sixteen-year-old Nadine fatherless. At the time, they had been profoundly affected, but they had no way of knowing exactly how Claude's decision would shape them into the people they became.

Several times during the war, while starving in the jungles of Luzon, Ed had stared death in the face and even considered taking his life into his own hands. Nadine, in the latter part of her life, felt so lost because she was unable to fly and in so much chronic pain; she had to be hospitalized more than once for alcohol abuse. Yet, no matter how overwhelming the circumstances, the Ramsey spirit was stubborn and strong. Though it must have been tempting for both brother and sister to give up at certain times in their lives, the pact they had made when they were children to support each other and to never surrender carried them through.

In the late 1960s, WASP reunions inspired the women pilots to begin fighting for the military recognition they'd been denied so many years before. This meant they needed to be forthright and assertive about their service records. After the war, any official records pertaining to the WASPs had been sealed by the army and remained so throughout the fifties and sixties. In the early seventies, they finally were unsealed, and WASPs at last began telling their families and local newspapers about what they had done during the war.

In 1972 the WASPs' thirtieth anniversary reunion was held in Sweetwater, Texas. It was a triumphant moment for the pilots; nearly four hundred of them marched down the main street of the town, accompanied by their children and grandchildren. Even General Arnold's son, Colonel Bruce Arnold, and Jackie Cochran were in attendance. As the women reconnected with each other over the weekend, many WASPs who were still passionate about militarization formed the WASP Military Committee.

The reunion received national attention. In an article about the gathering, headlined "Lipstick Pilots of World War II Won Wings; Still Seek Status," the *Los Angeles Times* noted: "Despite the parade and the six-foot granite monument and a historical marker memorializing them on Interstate 20, some of the women said they felt as they always did—like the 'stepchildren of the Air Force.' It rankled them then, and it does today, that their pay came from Civil Service, and that they're not officially veterans." The article was written by Dorothy Townsend, herself a groundbreaking woman as one of the paper's first woman reporters.[3]

That year, Original Teresa James decided to campaign singlehandedly for former WASPs to receive veteran benefits. After all, Congress had mili-

tarized every other woman's group that served during the war—the Women's Army Corps, Women Accepted for Voluntary Emergency Services, the Women's Marines, the Women's Coast Guard, the Army Nurses Corp, and the Navy Nurses Corp.[4] Now, nearly thirty years later, she convinced Hawaii Congresswoman Patsy Mink to introduce a bill to the House Veterans Affairs Committee. However, the committee's chairman never allowed the bill to reach the House floor for a vote.

Undeterred, the newly organized WASP Military Committee reconnected with Colonel Bruce Arnold, who committed to helping the former WASPs gain military recognition. Arizona Senator Barry Goldwater, who had been a Ferrying Command pilot during the war, was acquainted with many former WASPs. He knew firsthand that they were excellent pilots who had served their country faithfully.

In 1975 Senator Goldwater and Representative Mink reintroduced WASP militarization bills. "These women are U.S. citizens who served with our Army Air Corps during World War II," Goldwater said. "This group of women was shunted aside by the country they served; and it is better that we should correct a past wrong now, rather than leave the record blemished."[5] The WASPs had fought for their country when it needed them most; now it was time for their country to fight for them.

The WASP militarization bill of 1976 passed in the Senate but was rejected by the House of Representatives four days later. The WASPs faced fierce opposition from the American Legion and Veterans Administration, which feared that if they were granted veteran status, every civilian organization that had supported the war—the Civil Air Patrol, Merchant Marines, and others—would also demand militarization. It was too expensive a proposition. Essentially, veterans' organizations argued, the WASPs were just trying to raid their benefits. This image of women pilots—scheming, aggressive, and out to steal jobs from men—was painfully similar to the one painted of them during the war.

By now, however, these women were thirty years older and wiser, and the world was changing. Following Public Law 94-106, which President Gerald Ford signed on October 7, 1975, US military academies were required to accept female applicants. In September 1976 ten women began flight training for the US Air Force at Lackland Air Base in Texas. They were lauded in a Pentagon press release as the "first women military pilots."[6]

When former WASPs around the country read those words, they were understandably outraged. Determined to sway public support to their side, they spoke out and were featured in newspapers around the country, frequently portrayed as unsung heroes who had been patiently waiting for rightful recognition. On October 10, 1976, the *Long Beach Examiner* published a piece on a Long Beach WASP reunion titled "A Gathering of WASPs," which lauded their diverse talents in flying multiple kinds of aircraft.[7]

In *Clipped Wings*, Molly Merryman explains: "These stories were very different from previous coverage, both because the complete history of WASP achievements was being told (as records and reports became declassified), and also because there was a distinctly sympathetic and supportive tone to the pieces. In the 1940s, the media was incredulous that the WASPs would demand or expect veterans' benefits; by 1977, it was incredulous that they had not received these benefits."[8]

With growing public opinion on their side, the WASP Military Committee, Colonel Arnold, and Senator Goldwater decided to try again. In the spring of 1977, Goldwater introduced S.247 in the Senate, and Louisiana Congresswoman Lindy Boggs submitted an identical bill in the House "to provide recognition to the Women's Airforce Service Pilots for their service to their country during World War II by deeming such service to have been active duty in the Armed Forces of the United States for purpose of laws administered by the Veterans Administration."[9]

Fortunately, Massachusetts Congresswoman Margaret Heckler, the second-ranking minority member of the House Veterans Affairs Committee, was cochair of the newly formed Congressional Women's Caucus. All four women in Congress at that time—Representatives Boggs, Heckler, and Elizabeth Holtzman of New York as well as Senator Margaret Chase Smith of Maine—decisively supported the WASP bill, making it the first piece of legislation in history cosponsored by every woman member of Congress.

Still the battle continued. Former WASPs began circulating petitions, helping to spread the word that women had flown for the army during the war, which was a surprise to many people. That summer of 1977, Dorothy "Dottie" Davis (class 44-10) gathered thousands of signatures in the San Francisco area from the lines of people waiting to see the movie *Star Wars*. Another, Dora Dougherty Strother-McKeown (class 43-4), had since become a PhD in aviation education, a lieutenant colonel in the Air Force Reserve,

Petition of names requesting WASP veteran status, US Capitol, 1977 (Courtesy WASP Archive, Texas Woman's University, Denton, TX)

and chief of human factors engineering and cockpit arrangement at Bell Helicopter. In a powerful presentation, she testified before Congress about the WASPs' service, safety record, and professionalism.

In September General Bill Tunner and gentle, eloquent Margaret Ann Hamilton (class 43-2) also testified before Congress. Decades earlier, in an interview published in the April 2, 1949, issue of *Colliers* magazine, Hamilton had expressed her view of the WASPs' role at home and in postwar international affairs:

> As a WASP during the war, I flew just about everything they'd let a woman handle. I know what it is to sit in the sky feeling the thrill of power in your hands. By the time you read this, I'll be in Japan with the military government helping to get the idea of democracy across to people who were once our enemies. . . . If there are going to be storms ahead, it will be our duty to stay on the beam, to keep our sights on basic

human rights. If we do that, we'll continue to be what I call the best bunch of people under God's blue sky.[10]

Tunner and Margaret Ann had married in 1951 and their daughter, Hamilton Suzanne Tunner, was born a year later. In their testimony, they spoke firmly about the necessity of honoring the WASPs' service. "I feel that those few of us still alive should be here in Washington to received national recognition, instead of this humble plea for positive identification as a veteran," Margaret Ann said.[11]

Another element was at work in the WASPs' favor: All the branches of the US military were hoping to recruit more women to join the armed forces. As a result, Assistant Secretary of the Air Force Antonia Handler Chayes stepped in to support the bill. In *On Silver Wings*, Marianne Verges points out, "The Defense Department was spending hundreds of thousands of dollars in advertising trying to convince women of the opportunities available and that they could expect to get a fair shake from the military. 'Be all you can be,' promised the Army. What would a public defeat for the WASP do for recruiting?"[12]

A final, crucial piece of evidence was a simple slip of paper: an honorable discharge. When the WASP was disbanded in 1944, Nadine's 43-5 classmate Helen Porter Sheffer was the only woman pilot stationed at Strother Field in Kansas. Because General Arnold had issued an order that all WASPs should receive "a certificate similar to an honorable discharge" but didn't specify further, the base commander at Strother Field simply gave Sheffer a regulation Army Honorable Discharge. Sheffer not only didn't correct this misunderstanding of her status, but she also kept the paper safe for decades. Then the WASP committee presented it in Congress. Her certificate turned out to be a piece of compelling evidence, as former chair of the Veterans Committee Congressman Olin E. "Tiger" Teague of Texas immediately recognized that Sheffer's discharge certificate was identical to his own, written proof, according to a long-established definition, that the women had been on "active military service."[13]

On October 19 the Senate added an amendment to the GI Improvements Act calling for former WASPs to be recognized as veterans. On November 3 the House passed the act, including the WASP amendment, and the next day the Senate passed it as well. One day before Thanksgiving, on November

23, 1977, President Jimmy Carter signed Public Law 95-202, officially grant-
ing veteran status to the WASPs of World War II. They would not receive
retroactive pay, nor would their families be allowed to display a gold service
star. However, they now had four specific privileges: they would be allowed
to receive treatment at Veterans Administration hospitals, they could go to
college under the GI Bill, they could have an American flag draped on their
caskets, and they could be buried or inurned at a military cemetery—though
not at Arlington National Cemetery, in Arlington, Virginia. For that last
right, they would have to wait another thirty-nine years.

Public Law 95-202 was a tremendous victory. However, to many others,
veteran status was a hollow gesture that simply came too late. B. J. Erickson
London explained:

> It gave the families of the girls that were killed a feeling that they died
> for their country. Six of my girls were killed. I had to go six times and
> tell their mothers that their daughters weren't coming home. . . . I think
> that's what really hurt during the war, is that we were put in a position of
> telling them that they did not get a flag or any other military recognition.
> And that was a shame.[14]

For Nadine, WASP militarization did not change the fact that the part of
her life that had made her the happiest was over. A year earlier, in the fall of
1976, she had been interviewed for an article in the *Long Beach Independent
Press-Telegram*. Even the reporter, whom Nadine hardly knew, could tell that
she was still grieving the loss of her life as a pilot. In "WASPs Seek Status,"
he described her career, singling out her experience with the P-38:

> One of the planes she flew was the fast, maneuverable P-38. The twin-
> engine fighter responded to fingertip control and Miss Ramsey fell in
> love with it. . . . There is excitement in her voice when she talks about
> owning and flying the glamorous World War II relic. It's as if she had
> tried to hold on to that part of her life she spent as a WASP for just a
> couple years more.[15]

One result of militarization for Nadine was that it seemed to revive her
interest in reconnecting with other former WASP. In June 1978, she wrote

Class 43-5 at the WASP Reunion, Colorado Springs, 1978. Nadine is seated in the front row, fourth from right. (Courtesy WASP Archive, Texas Woman's University, Denton, TX)

a summary of her life since the war, which the *WASP Newsletter* published. She included her purchase of a P-38, going into business for herself, and concluded with her address in Long Beach. Most importantly, she opened the door to future communication:

> Was married in 1949 to a former ferry command pilot, during which time we spent a year in Edmonton, Canada where he flew the D.E.W. line. Some years later we were divorced (male pilots are not the most dependable people in the world) and I resumed my maiden name. Have had several spinal operations since '65, but in pretty good shape, now. Hope to attend the WASP conference in Colo. Springs in Sept. if possible. Hooray for our gaining veteran status after so many years and a gallant fight by everyone on our side. I'd love to hear from you 43-5 WASPs.[16]

A few months later, in late September 1978, Nadine's hope of attending the Colorado Springs conference materialized. She posed with her class, 43-5, and was included in the conference publication's "Now and Then" fea-

ture.[17] After the reunion, she wrote to the *WASP Newsletter* with an update in April 1979: "Feel I must comment on the most successful WASP conference I attended in Sept. It was great—and what a thrill to see old friends and meet new ones. It was my first get-together, but I sincerely hope that it isn't my last."[18]

CHAPTER 15

SETTLING IN

On March 8, 1979, the secretary of defense determined that the WASPs' service during World War II was to be considered active military service, so honorable discharges—the linchpin for passage of the 1977 law granting WASP veteran status—could now become part of a WASP's military record. On May 21, 1979, the US Air Force issued its first WASP honorable discharge.

Nadine realized that in order to officially be recognized as a veteran under the new law, she needed to apply for an official honorable discharge from the US Air Force. Still beset with serious health problems, she contacted B. J. Erickson London, who agreed to help her gather materials to submit for her application, and together they put together a packet of paperwork that they felt would prove her service. The dossier included official records, newspaper clippings, photographs of Nadine and various planes she had flown and photocopies of pages from her Avenger Field class book.

They also wrote personal letters detailing Nadine's participation in the WASP program. London wrote, "I do hereby certify that Nadine B. Ramsey was a member of my squadron. . . . She was qualified as a pursuit pilot ferrying all types of pursuit aircraft. She was also qualified in twin engine aircraft and was classified as a 4-P pilot." In a cover letter dated May 29, 1979, and printed on Barney Frazier Aircraft stationery (the company London had helped to found), London concluded: "If there are any questions regarding this information, would you please contact me rather than Nadine as she is not well enough to be of much help and I will try and handle it for her."[1]

On July 18, the Individual Service Review Board met to review Nadine's documents and concluded decisively that she qualified for an honorable discharge. In a thick envelope postmarked July 30, 1979, Nadine received her DD Form 214, a Report of Separation from Active Duty, and DD Form 256 AF, her honorable discharge certificate. She was officially a veteran of the United States military.

Honorable Discharge

from the Armed Forces of the United States of America

This is to certify that

NADINE BERNIECE RAMSEY 559-18-4196 Women's Air Force Service Pilots

was Honorably Discharged from the

United States Air Force

on the 20th day of December 1944 — This certificate is awarded as a testimonial of Honest and Faithful Service

MILTON R. MCFARLAND, Major, USAF
AFMPC, Randolph AFB, Texas

DD FORM 256 AF
1 NOV 51

THIS IS AN IMPORTANT RECORD — SAFEGUARD IT!

Nadine's Honorable Discharge, dated retroactively to December 20, 1944, in July 1979

By now Ed Jr. had returned to Los Angeles and was living with his father in an apartment complex on a winding, hilly street in Bel Air. He was an engineer at Hughes Space and Communications, a division of Hughes Aircraft that was revolutionizing satellite technology in the late 1970s, and was concurrently an officer in the California Army National Guard.

Throughout the mid-1970s, every two weeks, Ed and Ed Jr. drove to Long Beach to visit Nelle and Nadine. They were extremely worried about the women; both were limited and frustrated by their physical conditions. Now in her sixties, Nadine was in nearly constant pain from her ongoing back and neck problems. Nelle was now in her mid-eighties and losing her mental agility. She strongly disapproved of Nadine's drinking. However, mother and daughter were always happy to see Ed and Ed Jr., and for the first time, Nadine became a more constant presence in her nephew's life. In person-

ality, Ed Jr. had become a man in some ways very similar to his father: thoughtful and even tempered.

In April 1977, as the fight over the WASP bill raged in Congress, Ed Jr. married. He and his wife, Monica, immediately moved into an apartment in nearby Sherman Oaks. About six months later, they bought a home in Canyon Country in the Santa Clarita Valley, north of Los Angeles. Still, Ed Jr. committed to staying as close as possible to Nadine and Nelle, who both desperately needed his support.

In 1979 Ed Jr. and Monica had a son, Stephen—a particularly joyous event for Nelle. At age ninety, she became a great-grandmother. In 1980 Ed Jr. and his wife moved Nelle from Long Beach into a nursing home in Granada Hills so she could be near them and Monica's parents. They had another son, James, in 1981.

That year, Ed decided to move back to the Philippines. Since the war, he had always felt at home in the islands and often longed to return whenever he felt lost. He arrived in Manila that year, drawn by his love of the country and its people, leaving Ed Jr. and Monica to look after Nelle and Nadine in Long Beach.

Despite the brief, happy victory of receiving her veteran status, Nadine continued to spiral into alcoholism as her pain continued. After Ed returned to the Philippines, she often fell into fits of rage and grief, during which she would pull out old photographs of herself in her WASP uniform and with her P-38 and cut them to pieces. Sometimes she called her nephew Ed Jr. in desperation; fearfully he would speed to Long Beach to help her off the floor or to take her to the hospital. Even as she hurt herself, she hurt every member of her family.

In August 1980, when she turned sixty-nine, Nadine sent one more update to the *WASP Newsletter*, offering a frank account of her health:

Last July, I slipped and fractured my hip. The first one, which was repaired with four steel pins, was not successful and necessitated my return to the hospital. . . . It has taken time to recover from [the] surgeries. I am going back to the hospital May 6 for the reconstruction of my right foot for loss of my ankle bone sustained in a plane crash in 1940—two years before my stint in the WASP.[2]

Nadine measured everything in her life by the time she had spent flying. Without the hope of ever flying again, she seemed lost in a great chasm from which she could find no way out.

Back in Manila, Ed once again was welcomed warmly and honored for his war record. He moved into the new Manila Garden Hotel, a stacked modern concrete high-rise near the Manila Polo Club. At the hotel's New Year's Eve party in 1979, he was celebrated as the guest of honor. There, he caught the eye of a beautiful young Spanish Filipina, Raquel "Raqui" Ramirez, who was attending the party as the guest of her brother Paul, a mechanical engineer and hotel employee.

Born in 1946, Raqui was thirty-two, twenty-nine years younger than Ed. Still a snappy dancer at sixty-one, he asked her to dance, and she was immediately enchanted by his magnetic presence and charm. He, in turn, fell head over heels for this petite, feisty, and highly intelligent woman whose outgoing passion it was impossible to resist.

At the time, Raqui, who came from a prominent family in Manila and had lost her mother when she was five months old, had been matched with several diplomats and naval officers of the Spanish Armada.

That evening, she learned more about Ed's contributions to the liberation of the Philippines. She had known about him from her student days at the University of Santo Tomas, one of the largest Catholic universities in the world and the oldest in the Philippines. It was where she had received most of her education, attending the university's associated elementary and secondary schools; receiving bachelor's degrees in education, foreign service, and Spanish; and earning a master's in education. Because some university buildings had housed Filipino and American prisoners of war during the Japanese occupation, she was aware of the horrors the Philippine people had endured during World War II, as well as their undeterred resistance with the support and leadership of Colonel Ramsey and other Americans. She was amazed that the man she was smitten with was the same Colonel Ramsey.

After his earlier divorce, Ed had sworn he would never marry again, but Raqui quickly changed his mind. Within months, they were engaged and planning a trip to the United States to meet the Ramsey family during the next holiday season. As she sat beside her much older fiancé on the plane,

Raqui thought about the accomplished Ramsey women and prayed they would accept her. Winging their way across the Pacific Ocean toward Southern California, she crocheted a shawl for Nelle as a gift.

During their time in the Los Angeles area, Ed and Raqui visited his friends from Hughes Aircraft, including his closest friend Merritt Barker, in Camarillo, California. There, Ed surprised Raqui with a civil wedding ceremony in their friends' home three days before Christmas, on December 22, 1980. Raqui was a lovely, radiant bride.

Nadine and Nelle met Raqui for the first time days later at Ed Jr. and Monica's home in Canyon Country. Ed jokingly introduced Raqui as his trophy wife, and indeed, she was only three years older than Ed's oldest son. However, the entire Ramsey family received her graciously and saw that she was a good match for Ed. Nelle was thrilled when Raqui presented the shawl she had crocheted; the very gesture of arriving with a handmade gift demonstrated her natural warmth. Ed's mother and sister took to her immediately, glad that Ed had at last found someone with whom he could spend his later years. More importantly, Raqui was determined to help Ed heal the divisions between him and his other far-flung children: Doug in New York, Michele in Los Angeles, and Janine in Bethesda, Maryland.

After a visit that seemed all too brief, the newlyweds returned to the Philippines. Raqui, a born teacher, decided to once again attend the University of Santo Tomas for a doctorate in development education.

In 1981 Ed and Nadine's dear cousin from childhood Barbara Stuntz reconnected with the Ramseys. She and her mother, Winnie, had moved to Wichita in the 1950s but only lived there at the same time as Nelle for a brief period. After Nelle closed her clinic and moved to California, they had fallen out of touch. Barbara missed the Ramseys. She hunted around until she found an address and wrote to Nadine, asking for family news.

Nadine was happy to receive Barbara's letter but struggled to discuss the many problems she was facing. In a typewritten letter dated March 15, 1981, she replied:

So sorry I haven't written you long ago, but I am a very poor correspondent, and what with three major spinal operations between '65 & '70 (from which I suffer) then major surgery some years ago for a clogged

artery. Then three more Major operations in less than a year and a half. Two for a fractured hip and then a total reconstruction of my ankle due to a badly damaged foot in 1940 from my plane crash. It is much better, but will never be perfect.[3]

She also recounted the story of Ed and Raqui's wedding, writing that her brother and his new bride were "like two love birds," and expressed wonderment at Raqui's influence in helping Ed to reconcile with his children. Finally, she described her mother's gradually failing health:

She had to be placed in a convalescent hospital, as she had become very weak. . . . [Ed] realized when he was home, as she wasn't safe at home. She is having difficulty adjusting to the hospital, and is not too rational at times. She is over in the San Fernando Valley where [Ed Jr.] can see her frequently and take care of all the business affairs. I had done all this for so long, and cared for her as best I could, but I really was not able to do more, and I was in constant fear that something would happen to her. I talk to her every night or so, but sometimes she doesn't seem to be aware that it is me.

On September 10, 1982, Nelle Ramsey passed away peacefully at the convalescent hospital. She was ninety-three years old. Ed and Raqui returned to the United States immediately, even as Ed Jr. and Monica handled all of Nelle's funeral arrangements at Westminster Memorial Park in Westminster, California.

Nelle had been a successful businesswoman and mother in the face of great adversity. Nadine and Ed knew how profoundly they had been influenced by her determination to raise them singlehandedly after their father's suicide, and they both credited her for instilling in them grit and determination. As Ed had written to Nelle from the Philippines before he was declared missing in action in 1943:

I hope you will always remember that the courage I have had to keep going was gained from thinking of you and remembering that your bravery and courage in giving me all the benefits of life and love would be poorly repaid and I would be unworthy of you if I failed to carry on to the last

with equal courage. For this reason, I have refused to surrender and am fighting and will continue to fight to the best of my ability and intelligence until the end, either of my life or the war.[4]

At the small chapel service, Ed spoke glowingly about his mother, as did Ed Jr. about his beloved grandmother Mimi. Those present sang "Amazing Grace." Nadine shed tears for the loss of the steadfast supporter and inspiration that her mother had been. Then, following the service, and surrounded by her children, grandchildren, and great grandchildren, Nelle Brown Cozad Ramsey was laid to rest.

In the wake of losing her mother, Nadine anticipated feeling even greater loneliness than before. However, Raqui and Ed were determined to support her as much as possible. Nadine felt that Raqui understood her, and the two naturally talkative women got along well.

Over the years, Raqui had worked with Ed to heal his long-broken relationships with his children and had brought a newfound faith into her husband's life. While Nelle had tried to raise her children in the Baptist faith, neither of them had regularly attended church or personally practiced Christianity. However, Raqui was a Catholic with deeply held beliefs, and Ed saw that she benefited from religion in a way he admired. He began to wonder if the peace and joy Raqui found in her faith could be possible for him.

Shortly before Nelle's death, Ed had told his mother that he was planning to convert to Catholicism. Nelle's reaction surprised him; she told him she was happy he was finding God. On the day of Nelle's funeral service, September 14, 1982, Ed told Raqui he wanted to convert. She cried and thanked the Blessed Mother, in whom she had always placed her trust. She viewed Ed's conversion as an answer to prayer.

In 1948, when Ed had married Madeleine in the Philippines, a Supreme Court justice had officiated their wedding. Therefore, he had never been married in the eyes of the church. Following his conversion, Ed returned with Raqui to Manila, where on December 22, 1982—the two-year anniversary of their civil wedding—they remarried in a Catholic ceremony at Don Bosco Parish Church in Makati. Raqui glowed in a white, long-sleeved lace gown and cascading veil. Dressed in a smart navy suit with a white flower in his buttonhole, Ed, at age sixty-five, looked twenty years younger.

Raquel and Ed with Nadine at Marlora Manor Post-Acute Rehabilitation Hospital,
Long Beach, 1995

In 1986 Raqui graduated with her PhD in development education from
the University of Santo Tomas. She and Ed moved back to Southern Califor-
nia into a cozy apartment near Santa Monica. From that point on, she and
Ed visited Nadine regularly. Nadine was still able to walk, with some dif-
ficulty, and she had begun tinting her hair to boost its natural russet color.

In 1987 Raqui went to work for Yeshiva University High Schools of Los
Angeles as an English teacher and speech and debate coach. In 1992 she
began teaching at Beverly Hills Unified School District after completing her
secondary teaching and administrative credentials under the mentorship of
Bruce Powell.

Eventually, as it grew harder and harder for Nadine to live on her own,
Raqui and Ed helped move her into Marlora Manor Convalescent Hospital
in Long Beach, a neat, forty-room facility three miles south of the airport.
The hallways were cold, polished, and lined with carefully neutral wallpa-
per; Marlora Manor did its best to look and operate like a hospital wing.
Nadine didn't like the clinical atmosphere, but she at least had access to
medical assistance if she needed it. Moreover, with proper care, she was
finally able to get her drinking under control.

Nearly every weekend over the coming years, Raqui and Ed drove to Long Beach. As a respite from cafeteria food, they took Nadine out for a hot, comforting meal—her favorite hamburgers, usually, or sometimes fried chicken. During these day trips, Ed and Nadine laughed uproariously and reminisced about old times growing up in Depression-era Wichita or riding horses across the Illinois farmlands. They were in complete agreement about almost everything, from current events and politics to movies and books. Both liked to read; Nadine particularly favored mysteries. Ed, Raqui, and Nadine cherished these Sundays. A long-awaited peace finally had come to the lives of the Ramsey family.

As Nadine settled into Marlora Manor, the long-delayed formal recognition of the WASPs at last began to yield under their ongoing pressure. In 1984 President Ronald Reagan awarded the WASPs the US Armed Forces World War II Victory Medal, and those who had been on duty for more than a year, including Nadine, received the American Theater Campaign Medal. While many former WASPs were grateful for the government's gestures, they still were heartbroken at how late the recognition arrived. By then, the number of surviving former WASPs had dropped to eight hundred and was decreasing steadily. For them, it was impossible to receive an honor without thinking of classmates who deserved it, too, but didn't live to receive it.

Still, with every acknowledgment, the WASPs' achievements grew more visible and celebrated. After the Victory Medal was awarded, local newspapers ran new articles about their hometown WASPs, telling their stories and covering their reunions. In 1990 the *Indianapolis Star* published one about Mary Anna Martin "Marty" Wyall (class 44-10), a member of the "forgotten" last class of WASP pilots to complete training at Avenger Field. When the article was published, she was living in Fort Wayne, Indiana, and running the state's first woman-owned air taxi business.[5]

Wyall's story and accompanying photograph caught the eye of Jack Gardner, Nadine's second ex-husband, then in his mid-sixties and living in Greenwood, just south of the state capital. He reached out to her to see if she could put him back in touch with Nadine. Fortunately, Marty was involved in the WASP organization and gave him Nadine's number in Long Beach. Jack called Nadine up. Two decades had passed since they had gone their

separate ways; a lot had happened in both their lives. Still, Nadine was glad to hear from him and listened interestedly as he told his story. He'd raised two daughters, worked for many commercial airlines, had a total of six marriages, and even spent a short stint in federal prison, where he was sent for a misguided attempt at drug smuggling.

Nadine was able to laugh at and sympathize with Jack's story. Although he had made many mistakes over the years, his life was never boring. He didn't want to live conventionally, and he hadn't. They decided to stay friends, and Jack agreed to call Nadine every year on her birthday, August 28. That was one promise he kept.

Nadine also maintained a firm friendship with B. J. Erickson London. B. J.'s husband, Jack, had been diagnosed with cancer in the early 1970s and passed away in 1973. Nadine was fond of their daughters, Terry (born in 1948) and Kristy (born in 1950). As she knew, having children was the reason the US Air Force Reserve had tried to decommission London, as per its policy at the time. Determinedly, she had fought back: "When the Air Force offered me a commission, they didn't ask me if I had kids," she explained. "It wasn't my fault they gave me a commission, and I wasn't about to give it back to them."[6] London had prevailed, and she and Jack had served in the same reserve unit for twenty years, until 1968.

London's children had been exposed to aviation all their lives. Terry had flown in the 1966 All-Woman Transcontinental Air Race with B. J. as a mother-daughter team and became one of a tiny fraction of female commercial airline pilots in the United States and the first female pilot for Western Airlines. After Jack's death, B. J. continued running their company, Barney Frazier Aircraft, with her daughter Kristy's help.

London regularly visited Nadine at Marlora Manor, joining her for ice cream on Saturdays. Nadine cherished their weekly visits.

In 1989 aviation art store owners Larry and Betty Bledsoe commissioned artist Dan Kelly to create a commemorative painting, *Young and Invincible*, in honor of the WASPs. Kelly depicted a P-38 floating against a stunning backdrop of gray-and-white clouds alongside a WASP with London's smiling face, her hair tossed in the wind. In June five of the Ferrying Command WASPs—including Nadine's fellow P-38 pilots London, Iris Cummings

Critchell (class 43-2), and Mary Lou Colbert Neale (class 43-1)—were invited to the Ramada Renaissance Hotel in Long Beach to sign the 1,500 special commemorative prints for buyers.

The *Long Beach Independent Press-Telegram* covered the event in an article on June 16, 1989, headlined "Women Who Ferried Planes in WWII Finally Get Their Due." The reporter told the story of the WASPs and their heartbreaking disbandment in 1944, quoting London: "After the war, they told us to go back to the kitchen." London also noted that the five women, all of whom wore pastel dresses to the print signing, had logged more than sixty-five thousand flying hours combined. As Iris Cummings Critchell said, "Today, we're accepted as equals."[7]

The following month, on July 15–16, *Young and Invincible* was officially unveiled at Long Beach Airport during its Salute to Aviation Weekend. Ferry Command WASPs who had flown the Lightning were invited to participate; this time Nadine was honored to join London, Critchell, Neale, Laura Beatty Foy, and Katherine Loft Strehle at the event. Her fellow pilots signed prints of the artwork, but Nadine's back pain prevented her from participating.

Over the years, the bustling airport made further efforts to honor its history, particularly the women who had ferried aircraft there. It still operated out of its original Streamline Moderne terminal building, which was named a City of Long Beach Cultural Heritage Landmark in 1990. Today, travelers and visitors can view a display honoring the airport's history and featuring the WASPs of the Sixth Ferrying Group on the terminal's second floor.

That summer, the Santa Monica Museum of Flying at Santa Monica Airport hosted its annual Aviation Week. Ed and Raqui, along with several family friends, accompanied Nadine to the event, taking turns pushing her in her wheelchair as she gazed around familiarly at many spectacularly restored World War II–era planes on the tarmac. When one of the event's organizers overheard Nadine's remark that she had flown every model of plane on display, he proudly announced over the loudspeakers that a former WASP was present and invited visitors to speak with her. It was the type of attention Nadine had never sought but that all were happy to celebrate.

Later, the museum's director asked Nadine if she'd like to fly the museum's old Ford Trimotor. Nadine was flattered but of course declined due to her health. She then joked that she'd "never liked those things" and said,

Nadine with her fellow former WASPs at a display of Dan Kelly's Young and Invincible, *Seattle, 1990.* Left to right: *Mary Lou Colbert Neale, Nadine Ramsey, Iris Cummings Critchell, Barbara Erickson London, Lauretta Beatty Foy, Katy Loft Strehle*

"You turn the wheel to the right, and five minutes later, it decided that's the direction it wanted to go anyway!"[8]

The following year, in July 1990, Kelly's *Young and Invincible* painting was again displayed, this time at the WASP reunion in Seattle. Nadine joined several former WASPs from the Sixth Ferrying Group, including the five women who had originally signed it. This time she proudly added her signature to the commemorative prints.

On May 9, 1991, Nadine received a Presidential Memorial Certificate from the Department of Veterans Affairs. Signed by President Bill Clinton, the certificate was part of the Presidential Memorial Certificate program, which since 1962 has honored the memory of deceased veterans who are eligible for burial in a national cemetery.

In 1992 a Women Airforce Service Pilots collection was established at Texas Woman's University in Denton, Texas. Now the official WASP ar-

chive—it contains donated documents and artifacts: more than 700 oral histories, 600 collections, and more than 12,000 digitized images and documents.

Throughout the late 1980s and early 1990s, the WASPs continued to inspire rising generations of young female pilots. Many books were written and published, frequently by former WASPs themselves. These included WAFS Originals Delphine Bohn's *Catch a Shooting Star* (1985) and Adela "Del" Riek Scharr's two-volume work *Sister in the Sky* (1986, 1988).

In 1991 Byrd Howell Granger (class 43-1) published *On Final Approach*, followed two years later by Lois Kay Gott Chaffey's (class 43-2) self-published *Women in Pursuit*. Still other publications informed old and new generations of a previously unknown part of the nation's history, including *In Memoriam: Thirty-Eight American Women Pilots Gave Their Lives in Performance of Duty with the United States Army Air Forces 1942–1943–1944*. Published in 1996 by Texas Woman's University Press and researched and written by former WASPs, it honors the WASPs who had died for their country during the war.

The WASPs' stories were being told.

PART VIII

LEGACY

March 4, 1997, dawned piercingly bright over the San Jacinto Mountains to the east, an early spring sun asserting itself into an unmarked ultramarine expanse of sky. Some of the more distant peaks still wore caps of snow, imitating the breakers rushing from icy deep waters in the west toward the shallows and the slowly warming sand. Powerful gusts propelling the waves bent towering palm trees like giant feathers, and sea birds crisscrossed, calling, over a jumble of sailboat masts and the iconic triple black-and-red smokestacks of the Queen Mary. *The grand old beauty of the seas was now docked permanently in Long Beach Harbor.*

Five miles inland, eighty-year-old Ed Ramsey climbed from the car, his jacket blowing open in a sudden blast of wind. As he straightened, he squinted at a glare off the Moderne-style white concrete terminal building. One of the most distinctive small air terminals in the world, *he thought.* Ed had always liked Long Beach Airport; it was a relic from his youth, from those glamorous days of flying when his sister had cut her name across the heavens. He had a sudden memory of riding bareback, galloping a powerful brown mare across a stretch of Kansas prairie grass, when all of a sudden a buzzy yellow Beechcraft zoomed overhead, and Nadine leaned out, waving and laughing. Had that really happened? *he wondered.* Or was it a dream? *His wife, Raqui, shut one of the car doors behind him, and Ed turned to take her arm.*

Minutes later, he took a deep breath and climbed aboard a tiny Cessna, buckling himself in beside the pilot. Before shutting the plane's door, Raqui handed him a rectangular container, which he clutched tightly in his lap, fighting the lump in his throat. She kissed him briefly and squeezed his hand, then backed away from the aircraft. The plane taxied, and Ed put on his headphones and readied himself for the familiar drop in his stomach as the plane accelerated and then lifted, surprisingly lightly, into the air.

Throttle! Brake! *He could hear Nadine's voice shouting. She had taught him to fly when he was a teenager, though he had never taken to it as she had. She'd criticized him mercilessly for playing polo, then for joining the cavalry. She said he was stuck in the past. The memory catapulted him slightly forward to another time, the feeling of his horse beneath him, mortar shells whistling, exploding, deaf-*

ening, his own voice screaming orders in the humid jungle air. We're all stuck in the past now, Big Sister, *he thought.*

The Cessna banked and headed west, engines roaring, the Pacific Ocean rising toward the plane, as big as the world, it seemed. More memories came flooding to Ed now, unbidden: his father, with whiskey on his breath, showing him arrowheads from Texas; Nadine in a cast hobbling toward a lone plane on a misty runway; his mother tickling his own baby girl in a pink dress; the sound of an organ; the smell of damp rice; the harsh scraping of propeller blades against a runway. Ed cried.

"Go ahead," he heard the pilot say over his headphones. *Ed gulped and lifted the box from his lap toward the window, opening it carefully. He thought of his mother Nelle, her kind brown eyes, the most sophisticated woman he had ever known. She had been laid to rest only a few miles from here, far from his father who was buried in a family plot in Illinois. Some people were like that, he supposed; they lived and died in one place, had only one adventure.* But not us.

Ed thought with resolve about the pact he and his sister had made so many years before: never look back, never surrender. *Firmly putting more memories out of his mind, he released Nadine's ashes and watched as they were swept away instantly by the wind, just how she had wanted to go. His brave sister was floating forever, riding the air currents, as part of the restless sea and sky. She was home.*

CHAPTER 16
A LOOK TO THE FUTURE

The retroactive militarization of the WASP in 1977, some thirty years in the making, was only a beginning. Over the next three decades, other historical, cultural, and educational milestones would serve to inspire future generations of women pilots, creating the WASP's legacy.

In the spring of 1993, the air force lifted restrictions on women flying combat missions, selecting, on April 28, Jean Marie "Jeannie" Flynn as the first woman for combat training. On February 10, 1994, Flynn completed her six months of training on the McDonnell Douglas F-15E Strike Eagle fighter plane at Luke Air Force Base in Arizona. In April she was assigned as an instructor pilot and training officer, becoming the US Air Force's first female fighter pilot.

In 1995 ground was broken for the National Women in Military Service for America Memorial just outside Arlington National Cemetery in Arlington, Virginia. The memorial, which received quite a bit of press throughout its planning and construction, was designed by Marion Weiss and Michael Manfredi. The architects utilized an existing semicircular Neoclassical granite structure called the Hemicycle, which stood at the entrance to the cemetery. Their plans called for an eighty foot circular pool in the center of the memorial surrounded by sections of lush green lawns. Atop the Hemicycle, they designed 108 glass panels, inscribed with the quotations of American servicewomen, saving some space for more to be added in the future.

A thirty-two-cent stamp commemorating women in the military was released in the fall of 1997, coinciding with the memorial's opening on October 18, 1997. It featured diverse women of all five branches of the armed forces, including the profile of a woman in a smart blue and white air force cap.

During the memorial's construction, another WASP statue was created for the honor court of the Air Force Academy, just north of Colorado Springs, Colorado. There it would join a display already commemorating Jackie Cochran. Designed and sculpted by Dorothy "Dot" Swain Lewis (class 44-5) and paid for by donations from the WASPs themselves, *The Trainee*

National Women in Military Service for America Memorial, Arlington, Virginia, ca. 2000 (Courtesy US Department of Defense)

depicts a young woman in belted "zoot suit" coveralls with a flight cap on and a Fifinella patch on her jacket, her chin lifted toward the sky. Inscribed are the words, "I salute ALL WASPS. You have been pioneers in a new field of wartime service. You have shown that you can fly wingtip to wingtip with your brothers."

Raqui, Ed, and Nadine eagerly followed the memorial's progress and other WASP projects in the news. As the years ticked forward toward the turn of the millennium, Raqui and Nadine discussed WASP news and all the events of their day during daily 4 p.m. phone calls. Despite Nadine's ongoing pain and struggles, she never complained. In true Ramsey fashion, she put on a brave face, even over the phone.

In 1996 Mary Anna Martin "Marty" Wyall (class 44-10), the former WASP who had reconnected Nadine and Jack Gardner in the late 1980s, wrote Jack, asking for an update on Nadine. Decades earlier, in 1978, Wyall had been elected the official WASP historian by her fellow former WASPs and was now serving as the president of WASP, Inc. Jack was working as an assistant veterans service officer in Vermillion County, Indiana.

In a letter dated September 11, 1996, Jack replied:

Yes, Nadine is still active as far as I know. Her birthday is August 28th, and I telephone her on that day each year. This year she said that she was feeling good and that a couple of weeks before that her brother [Ed] and

Commemorative stamp, Women in Military Service, Arlington, Virginia, October 18, 1997 (Courtesy US Post Office)

his wife had taken her to a restaurant for dinner. So she is at least getting out once in a while. I am sure that she is in a wheelchair. We discussed the old days and she seemed mentally alert. Asked me about my poodle, Buttons, by name.

The letter concluded, "Keep 'em flying, Jack Gardner."[1]

In the late 1990s, as computer technology gave birth to the internet, email and websites enabled the WASPs to connect with each other and collect their stories more easily. In 1998 Nancy Parrish, the daughter of Odean "Deanie" Bishop Parrish (class 44-4), teamed up with her mother to found Wings Across America, a multimedia group dedicated to preserving WASP history, based at Baylor University in Texas. Beginning with a simple website, Nancy and Deanie collected dozens of interviews with surviving WASP and later created the first WASP app.

In 2003 the Parrishes organized a group of citizens from Sweetwater and presented the Sweetwater City Council with plans to create a WASP museum. Avenger Field had served as a radar station during the Cold War

but had officially shut down in the fall of 1969. The city agreed to make the site the home of the National WASP World War II Museum and granted the group a two-hundred-year lease on the hangar and fifty-five acres adjacent to the airport. The WASPs would be remembered in their old home on the dusty, windswept Texas plains.

Over the years, the museum has become one of the primary collection repositories for WASP artifacts, in addition to the official archive at Texas Woman's University. Today, surviving WASPs are invited annually to a homecoming at Avenger Field, and the museum collects their handprints and stories. The hangar also houses planes the WASPs flew and an exhibit on Jackie Cochran, who passed away in 1980, and sponsors other projects year-round to help raise awareness about the WASPs and their legacy. Other museums have also added displays about the WASPs, including the Smithsonian's Air and Space Museum in Washington, DC, the National Museum of the US Air Force, the Texas State History Museum, and many more.

But the Parrishes weren't done. In 2009 Wings Across America teamed up with WASP, Inc. and Military Officers' Association of America and lobbied Congress to award the WASPs the Congressional Gold Medal—the highest civilian honor bestowed by Congress.

Spokeswoman Colonel Nicole Malachowski cited the WASPs as her inspiration in becoming a pilot. In an article about the Congressional Gold Medal published in *USO* magazine, she told her story: Growing up in the late 1980s, she had always wanted to become a pilot. However, she was distressed to learn that women were not allowed to fly in combat. Then she saw a display on the WASPs at the Air and Space Museum. As she told *USO*, "It was one of these women from World War II sitting in front of a P-51 with a flight suit on. . . . I said, 'Wait a second! They did this a long time ago!'"[2] Malachowski graduated from the Air Force Academy in 1996, became the first woman to pilot a Thunderbird, and was among the first women to fly combat missions during Operation Iraqi Freedom. She pushed hard for Congress to pass the Gold Medal legislation.

On July 1, 2009, President Barack Obama signed S.614 into law, officially awarding the Congressional Gold Medal to the Women Airforce Service Pilots of World War II. "I am honored to sign this bill to finally give them

President Barack Obama signing legislation awarding the WASP the Congressional Gold Medal, Washington, DC, July 2009 (Courtesy US Air Force)

some of the hard-earned recognition they deserve," he said. The bill itself recognized the WASPs as having "faced overwhelming cultural and gender bias against women in nontraditional roles" and overcoming "multiple injustices and inequities in order to serve their country." Highlighting their place in history, it added that "through their actions, the WASP eventually were the catalyst for revolutionary reform in the integration of women pilots into the Armed Service."[3]

The WASP Congressional Gold Medal depicts the bust of a female pilot and to her side three female pilots in flight suits with parachute bags, an aircraft flying overhead. On the reverse, the WASP legacy is clearly stated: "The First Women in History to Fly American Military Aircraft, Act of Congress 2009."

Although only one Congressional Gold Medal was symbolically presented to the WASPs, Wings Across America raised funds for replica medals to be delivered to the families of every WASP who served. To receive the Congressional Gold Medal in person, many surviving WASPs attended a formal ceremony in Washington, DC, on March 10, 2010. They included B. J. Erickson London, who had stopped flying in 2000 but remained a vis-

Left to right: *Women Airforce Service Pilots Congressional Gold Medal, front, 2010 (Photograph by Amy Barnard) and reverse (Photograph by Eric Long, Smithsonian National Air and Space Museum [NASM2011-2505])*

ible symbol of the WASPs in the media, especially in Long Beach. In 2005 a street connecting the east and westbound sections of Donald Douglas Drive at the airport was named Barbara London Drive.

When London's family asked if she wanted to attend the Gold Medal ceremony in Washington, Barbara initially said no, but her family eventually persuaded her to go. In a jet loaned by filmmaker Robert Zemeckis, three generations of female pilots flew to Washington for the ceremony: B. J., her daughter Terry and her husband Bob, and Terry's daughters Kelly and Lauren—under corporate pilot Kelly's able handling. Two other WAFS Originals, Gertrude Meserve Tubbs LeValley and Barbara Donahue Ross, also attended, along with another Long Beach P-38 pilot, Dorothy "Dottie" Kocher Olsen (class 43-4). Following the ceremony, Kelly flew her grandmother back to Long Beach. It would be London's final flight.

On July 7, 2013, Barbara Jane Erickson London passed away peacefully, surrounded by her family. She was ninety-three. It had been forty years and one day since her husband's death and nearly seventy years since the WASPs were disbanded.

London was honored across the country but primarily by her beloved city of Long Beach. In an article titled "Aviation Icon Barbara London Passes Away at 93" published in the Long Beach *Grunion Gazette*, her daughter

Kristy said, "She just wanted people to know how much she loved being a part of the Long Beach community and especially the Long Beach Airport. . . . She was such an amazing mentor and supporter." In an interview with author Sarah Byrn Rickman, London herself had explained, "I was the luckiest girl alive. I was in the right place at the right time and at the right age. An opportunity presented itself and I took it. I learned to fly and I stayed with flying all my life. And I was stationed at the best base." To many others, London often said, "I came to Long Beach Airport in 1943, and I never left."[4]

After her death, according to their mother's wishes, Terry and Kristy quietly scattered B. J.'s ashes at sea.

Although the WASPs were not allowed burial at Arlington National Cemetery, a change in army regulations in 2002 permitted them to have their ashes inurned there. However, in March 2015 Secretary of the Army John McHugh rescinded their eligibility. "While certainly worthy of recognition, [the WASPs' service] does not, in itself, reach the level of active duty service required for inurnment there," Arlington National Cemetery officials explained on the cemetery's website.[5] Once again, the surviving WASPs—in ever-dwindling numbers—were forced to fight for fair treatment from the US government.

Elaine Danforth Harmon (class 44-9) became the face of the WASPs' right for burial in the nation's most prominent military cemetery. When she passed away in April 2015, she left explicit written wishes for her ashes to reside there. However, her family was surprised when the cemetery rejected her request. The story caught the attention of Arizona Representative Martha McSally, a retired Air Force colonel who had been the first woman squadron leader of an all-woman squadron. "I was in serious disbelief when I first heard it," McSally told the *Christian Science Monitor*. "There's no possible way in 2016—after all this time, after all their service, after all the discrimination—that they're still being discriminated against. Then I confirmed it was in fact possible."[6]

In January 2016 Maryland Senator Barbara Mikulski introduced a bill, the Women Airforce Service Pilot Arlington Inurnment Restoration Act, to restore the WASPs' eligibility for aboveground inurnment. The bill was referred to the Committee on Veterans Affairs, where it was approved in late March. Then in May, Representative McSally sponsored a resolution

(HR4336) to allow WASPs to have their ashes inurned at Arlington. "These women fought, and died, in service of their country," she said in a press release. "They trained in the military style: sleeping on metal cots, marching, and living under military discipline. They deserve the full honors we give our war heroes."[7]

A number of the WASPs still living were involved in the fight to pass the legislation. Nell Stevenson Bright (class 43-7) traveled to Washington, DC to lobby for it. She had fought for veteran status in 1977. Although she didn't wish to be buried at Arlington herself, she thought the ban was "a slap in the face." As she told the *Christian Science Monitor*, "to not allow it would be "ridiculous. . . . We're veterans—and we should have that privilege."[8] Harmon's family, historians, and WASP, Inc. circulated a petition on Change. org to support the bill. They collected approximately 170,000 signatures.

On May 20, 2016, HR4336 was signed into law by President Barack Obama as Public Law 114-158. Harmon's ashes were at last inurned at Arlington in September that year. Her memorial service received a flyover of the World War II Warbirds, followed by "Taps" and a twenty-one-gun salute. Several of the surviving WASPs traveled to the funeral, and some even told reporters they were considering being inurned at Arlington too.[9]

Ironically, even as the WASPs fought in Congress over inurnment at Arlington, one final remarkable event in women's equality occurred. On December 3, 2015, Defense Secretary Ash Carter announced that, beginning in January 2016, all military occupations and positions would be open to women, without exception. In a statement given at the Pentagon, he proclaimed, "They'll be allowed to drive tanks, fire mortars and lead infantry soldiers into combat. . . . They'll be able to serve as Army Rangers and Green Berets, Navy SEALs, Marine Corps infantry, Air Force parajumpers, and everything else that was previously open only to men." He also noted that the United States military draws its strength from its diversity and considers itself to be a true meritocracy. "That's why we have the finest fighting force the world has ever known, and it's one other way we will strive to ensure that the force of the future remains so, long into the future," he said.[10]

Unfortunately, Nadine didn't live to see much of this progress. On February 16, 1997, as Raqui and Ed were at home having dinner, the telephone rang. When Raqui answered, a representative from Marlora Manor told her

the devastating news: her sister-in-law had passed away. Raqui sank into a chair as Ed grabbed the phone and demanded an explanation. Nadine was in chronic poor health, but she hadn't been ill. She had died from asphyxiation, the Marlora Manor representative said, choking on some food in her room alone. Raqui and Ed were stunned, and Ed was heartbroken. Nadine was eighty-five.

Years before, Nadine had made arrangements for her own funeral. She asked to be cremated and to have her ashes scattered over the Pacific Ocean from a plane. Ed set out to ensure that her wishes would be fulfilled. The family planned to have a small gathering to commemorate her on March 5, 1997. However, first, they had to inform Nadine's many loved ones that she was gone.

Ed wrote "To All Friends of Nadine Ramsey," sharing the sad news of his beloved sister's passing. He noted that she had been bedridden in steadily deteriorating health and constant pain for years, adding:

> Nadine will be sorely missed by my wife Raquel and myself, as well as her friends, and it will take a long time to get used to her no longer being with us. But it is a relief to know that this courageous and unique human being, who contributed so much to the advancement of women in aviation by being one of the earliest pioneers in that field, will no longer have to suffer and is now at peace. Her death marks the passing of a great lady.[11]

In response to the letter, messages of grief and consolation came flooding back. On February 23, cousin Barbara Stuntz sent a card from Wichita expressing her sadness: "I was sorry to hear Nadine had passed away, but really when one has suffered as long as she had, it is really a blessing. That doesn't stop us from missing them terribly. She had such a thrilling life for so many years, flying planes that she loved to do, until her back injury. We were always so thrilled to hear what she was doing. . . . We enjoyed her so much."[12]

Even Nadine's old friends from her time in Los Angeles remembered her. Dick Simmons, the actor who had played *Sergeant Preston of the Yukon*, wrote:

What a glorious, courageous lady. My dear, dear friend Nadine. How privileged each of us has been that God allowed us to share her company and friendship and love. I recall the very day she so proudly introduced her brother to me, an introduction I've cherished for these many years. Nadine is a very special lady. She has not gone. I know she's just parked on one of those soft, puffy clouds she used to dart in and out of. "I'll take this one" or "maybe that one." What a great gal. It runs in the family that I've always considered mine. Your wonderful mom did it all.[13]

On February 15, Raqui and Ed received a letter from Nadine's former commanding officer of the Fifth Ferrying Group, WAFS Original Florene Miller Watson, who was also WASP Inc.'s chaplain. She wrote: "Nadine served her country as she trained and served as a pilot during the time of war. We want you to know that her organization honors her and will miss her. . . . Nadine meant a great deal to her country and her friends throughout her lifetime. She will surely be missed."[14]

Nadine's 43-5 classmate Dawn Rochow Seymour also wrote, expressing her condolences: "Nadine was a classmate. I am saddened by her death." She concluded by inviting Raqui and Ed to the dedication of the WASP statue at the Air Force Academy. Barbara Erickson London wrote, "Nadine is not only my special friend, but part of the family."[15]

On March 4 Ed climbed aboard a Cessna at Long Beach Airport. It was a bright, warm day, but Ed's heart was heavy. He leaned out the plane's window and scattered his sister's ashes over the Pacific Ocean and Long Beach Harbor. He, Raqui, and a handful of other family members spent the rest of the day reminiscing and remembering the remarkable woman Nadine had been.

The WASPs' legacy continues. While these dedicated women aren't widely known or remembered today, they are the heroes of nearly every woman military pilot.

At Elaine Harmon's inurnment at Arlington National Cemetery, her daughter Terry received a folded flag from Air Force Captain Jennifer Lee. The flag had been flown in various places around the country by female pilots, who were invited to comment in a logbook about what the WASPs' contributions meant to them. One, Air Force Reserve Lieutenant Colonel

Nadine Ramsey's flag case containing her AAF WASP wings, World War II Victory Medal (awarded to all WASPs), and American Campaign Medal (awarded to WASPs who served at least one year). A plaque "In Living Tribute" from Nadine's "Brother and Sister Ed & Raquel Ramsey" recognizes her as "A great and courageous lady, far ahead of her time." (Photograph by Amy Barnard)

Nadine B. Ramsey, Certificate of Burial at Sea, 1997

Caroline Jensen, had written, "I'm humbled every time I think of the legacy of the WASPs."[16]

Another, who took the flag up in an F-16 at supersonic speed, wrote that she "drew on the strength of those who went before me." Still another said, "Their contributions were pivotal. . . . When it comes to overall mission success, [WASPs] are a key asset. I've always looked up to the WASPs, and I used them as an inspiration and motivation for what I do today. They paved the way for myself and the rest of the women in this book to do what we love, and for that we are very thankful."[17]

Following Nadine's death in 1997, Ed and Raqui were contacted by Mary Lou Colbert Neale (class 43-1), a Class IV-P pilot like Nadine and a member of the P-38 National Association. She wanted to write a story about Nadine's time flying her Lightning, Lucky, after the war and was looking for photographs. Raqui collected the scraps of photographs of Nadine and her plane that Nadine had cut up while in her darkest hours and took them to a photographer to be restored.

Mary Lou's story for the P-38 National Association newsletter, titled "Overcoming Odds, One Woman's Dream . . . to Own a Lightning," was published alongside Peter Stackpole's *Life* magazine photograph of Nadine lovingly holding the P-38's propeller. In it, she recounted the highlights of Nadine's life, including her extraordinary journey back to health following her 1940 crash, concluding, "Nadine Ramsey's story is more than just an answer to the trivia question: 'Name the only woman to ever personally own a P-38.' Her story is a lesson in true grit—working hard to pay for flight instruction and flight time to get her flying license and overcoming terrible injury and enormous odds to reach her goal to fly the P-38."[18]

Her family agreed. Ed and Raqui committed to making sure that Nadine would be remembered. They decided to attend ceremonies and reunions in Nadine's place, including the Women in Military Service Memorial in Arlington. Ed fought to preserve his sister's memory until his death on March 7, 2013. In his later years, he made Raqui promise to tell Nadine's story. "What do you want people to know?" Raqui asked him.

Ed, a highly decorated war hero, later buried with full military honors at Arlington National Cemetery replied, "She had more guts than I ever did."[19]

Nadine Berniece Ramsey (1911–1997)

EPILOGUE

In 1987, after reading Doug Ramsey's book *The Corporate Warriors*, Nadine and Ed's cousin Barbara Stuntz in Wichita wrote to Ed, asking if Doug was his son.

In a letter dated March 13, 1987, Ed typed a warm reply, confirming that he was Doug's father and stating how proud he was of his second child. He also recounted a substantial amount of family news: "I was divorced in 1970 but remarried in 1980 to a very lovely Spanish Filipina and I couldn't be happier or more content with my life. She is an educator who has Bachelor's degrees in three disciplines, two Master's degrees and one Ph.D. in Development Education. She is teaching here in Los Angeles while I am starting to write the story of my war years." Ed also included two photos, one of them a snapshot from his Catholic wedding in 1982. He signed off, "With love from your old cousin, Bud Ramsey."[1]

Ed also told Barbara that he had pulled out his old manuscript, "Guerilla Command," which he had written during his postwar recovery and completed in 1946. Around the same time, screenwriter Stephen J. Rivele, who was researching the history of the US Cavalry, attended the Horse Cavalry Convention at Fort Riley, Kansas. While there, someone asked him if he would like to meet the leader of the last horse-mounted cavalry charge in US military history. Interested, Rivele said yes, and he was introduced to Ed. Later, the two men were surprised to learn that they both lived in Los Angeles and made arrangements to meet so Rivele could look over Ed's manuscript.

Over the next five months, Ed and Rivele met almost daily at Ed and Raqui's apartment on the west side of Los Angeles, and Ed shared every detail of his story. Eventually, they coauthored *Lieutenant Ramsey's War*, a comprehensive narrative of Ed's amazing wartime perils, which was published in 1990 by Knightsbridge. The book was well received. *Kirkus Reviews* wrote that *Lieutenant Ramsey's War* was an "inspiring, unsentimental tale attesting to the reality that the costs of war cannot be wholly reckoned in blood and treasure."[2] The book was soon excerpted in *Reader's Digest* and sparked interest in Ed's story from several movie studios (though a film version has yet to be made).

In retelling his story, Ed was reminded that, like the WASPs, the United States had not properly recognized the Philippine guerrillas he had served with during the war. In 1944 the GI Bill of Rights extended benefits to soldiers from sixty-six countries who had fought alongside the United States forces but excluded the Philippines. Later, the Rescission Act of 1946 extended some aid to Filipino veterans, but only those who had been seriously injured or disabled, leaving thousands of men and women without benefits or even a gesture of gratitude from the United States.

Following the release of his book in 1990, Ed organized and lobbied lawmakers to honor the Philippine guerrillas who had fought under US officers by extending the benefits the Filipino veterans deserved. Beginning in 1993, he and other activists convinced legislators to introduce bills to Congress granting full status to Filipino veterans, but none of them ever reached a vote. Ed and Raqui attended cavalry and military events around the country, accepting awards and honorary titles. Ed would carry on until it became too difficult for him to travel—well into his nineties.

In 1992 Ed was presented with the Filipino American Community Los Angeles Award and in 1994 was inducted into the Oklahoma Military Academy Hall of Fame. A couple of years later, in 1996, he rode in Pasadena's Annual Rose Bowl Parade along with other mounted soldiers. In 2000 he was awarded the US Cavalry Medal and installed as a Distinguished Knight, Order of Saint George, in the US Third Cavalry. On November 11, 2010, Veterans Day, Ed was inducted into the Oklahoma Military Hall of Fame.

Yet all of these honors and tributes only inspired him to fight even harder for recognition for the Filipino veterans he had served alongside. Unfortunately, he didn't live to see the realization of this dream. In 2014 the volunteer Filipino Veterans Recognition and Education Project lobbied to award Filipino and Filipino American veterans the Congressional Gold Medal. At last, the bill passed in Congress. On December 14, 2016, President Barack Obama signed Public Law 114-265 honoring the 260,000 who had fought alongside American troops and by extension 57,000 Filipino troops who had died. Finally, on October 25, 2017, Filipino veterans received the Congressional Gold Medal in Washington, DC. They had waited more than seventy years.

Edwin Price Ramsey passed away on March 7, 2013, at age ninety-five. After a viewing and mass at Saint Paul the Apostle Catholic Community in West-

Ed signing copies of Lieutenant Ramsey's War *at the Pentagon with Filipino veterans, Washington, DC, 1996 (Courtesy Philippine Scouts Heritage Society)*

wood—near the home he had shared with Raqui for twenty-eight years—he was buried with full military honors in Arlington National Cemetery on June 28. His funeral was accompanied by a platoon of soldiers from the Third Infantry Division, a marching band, caisson and riderless horse, a gun salute, and the playing of taps—all hallmarks of the burial of a true American hero. Raqui, her eyes filled with tears, accepted the folded flag that had covered his casket, and she vowed to carry on his legacy and that of the Ramsey family.

Immediately after Ed's death in 2013, she established two scholarship funds in his memory: the Colonel Edwin Ramsey Endowment Fund at the University of Oklahoma, awarded annually for Reserve Officer Training Corps outstanding cadets, and the Ed Ramsey Scholarship Endowment, which inaugurated the return of a cadets program to the Oklahoma Military Academy, now Rogers State University.

Over the years, she has donated Ed's memorabilia to permanent exhibitions and displays throughout the United States: National World War II Museum (New Orleans), US Army Museum of Hawaii (Honolulu), MacArthur

Memorial (Norfolk, Virginia), Marines' Memorial Club (San Francisco), US Cavalry Association Museum (El Reno, Oklahoma), Mount Soledad National Veterans Memorial (La Jolla, California), Philippine Scouts Heritage Society (San Antonio), and the new National Museum of the United States Army (Fort Belvoir, Virginia). She also co-curates temporary displays, such as those organized for both the Philippine Consulate and the Presidio in San Francisco and the Beverly Hills Public Library.

In 2015 filmmakers Steven C. Barber, Tamara Henry, and Matt Hausle approached Raqui about helping them create a documentary about Ed's life and military service. Thrilled, she stepped in as executive producer. The resulting documentary, written by the late John Travers and narrated by Oscar-nominated actor Josh Brolin, features interviews with military historians and Ed's friends and family, along with powerful reenactments of his wartime adventures in the Philippines.

Never Surrender: The Ed Ramsey Story premiered in Los Angeles on Veterans Day weekend, November 13, 2016. Subsequently, it was screened at several film festivals, but the screenings that meant the most to Raqui were personal. On May 8, 2017, the film was shown at the Reagan Library and Museum in honor of what would have been Ed's one-hundredth birthday. Later that year, it was screened by the National Federation of Filipino American Associations at the Veterans' Museum and Memorial Park in San Diego. Another Veterans Day weekend screening marked the Philippine premiere of the film, hosted by the Central Luzon Chapter of the American Chamber of Commerce and the VFW in Pampanga.

On July 20, 2018, Raqui received her husband's Congressional Gold Medal (which had been awarded to the Filipino veterans the previous fall) as part of the Twenty-Sixth Cavalry (Philippine Scouts). A ceremony was held at the Philippine Scouts Heritage Society in San Antonio, Texas, where Raqui accepted the replica medal with great emotion, knowing how proud Ed would have been to see his dream realized. She was surrounded by family, including Ed's sons, and decorated members of the Philippine Scouts Heritage Society, whose work today maintains the legacy of those faithful soldiers Ed fought alongside.

In October, Raqui and Ed's daughter, Janine, with Ed and Nadine's cousin Barbara Stuntz, then ninety-seven, attended a screening of *Never Surrender*

World premiere, Never Surrender: The Ed Ramsey Story, *Los Angeles, 2016. Raquel Ramsey (executive producer), Stephen C. Barber (producer, Vanilla Fire Productions), current members of the Twenty-Sixth Cavalry (Philippine Scouts), and General Douglas MacArthur reenactor Robert Tidwell*

at the Third Annual All-School Reunion of Wichita North High School, Ed's alma mater. Raqui thanked Barbara for her continued help and support in telling the story of the Ramsey family. That same month, she established the Edwin Price Ramsey Collection at the Library of Congress in Washington, DC.

The publication of this book marks the most recent addition to Raqui's legacy projects for the Ramsey family and sets the stage for those that follow. Currently, Nadine is represented in the WASP display at the Women's Memorial outside Arlington National Cemetery. Fittingly, the P-38 Association and Museum (Riverside, California) honors her in its WASP exhibition as well as in the association's book *P-38 Lightning.* The WASP Museum at Avenger Field (Sweetwater, Texas) and the Army Women's Museum (Fort

Raquel Ramsey and Barbara Stuntz at a screening of Never Surrender, *Wichita, 2018*

Display containing the contributions of twenty-one WASP P-38 fliers, WASP exhibition, P-38 National Association and Museum, Riverside, California (Courtesy P-38 National Association and Museum)

Lee, Virginia) also include Nadine in their exhibitions. As she did to honor Ed, Raqui will contribute a Nadine Ramsey Collection to the Library of Congress archives.

Just as the courage of Ed and Nadine's generation carried the United States through its crisis during World War II and beyond, so the Ramseys' legacy sustains Raqui daily. She reflects constantly on the remarkable family she is honored to have joined. She knows her inheritance is strength and love.

NOTES

Ramsey Collection	Nadine Ramsey Collection, Los Angeles
Woman's Collection	Woman's Collection, Texas Woman's University, Denton, TX
WASP Archive	MSS 250 Women Airforce Service Pilots Records, Woman's Collection, Texas Woman's University, Denton, TX
Weatherby Collection	MSS 288c Mary Weatherby Collection, Woman's Collection, Blagg-Huey Library, Texas Woman's University, Denton, TX
Severson Collection	MSS 329c Helen Severson Collection, Woman's Collection, Blagg-Huey Library, Texas Woman's University, Denton, TX
Oral History Collection	Oral History Collection, Woman's Collection, Texas Woman's University, Denton, TX
National Archives, Nadine Ramsey Veteran Personnel File	National Archives, National Personnel Records Center, Saint Louis, Army Air Forces Veteran Personnel File: Nadine Ramsey

CHAPTER I. FARMERS AND OILMEN

1. "Illinois Central Railroad: Mainline of Mid-America," American Rails, 2019, https://www.american-rails.com/illinois-central.html.
2. Illinois, 1940, United States Census Bureau, Census of Population and Housing, 304.
3. Vol. P. Mooney, *History of Butler County, Kansas* (Lawrence, KS: Standard Publishing Company, 1916), 150–151.
4. "Kansas Oil Boom," American Oil and Gas Historical Society, 2019, https://aoghs.org/petroleum-pioneers/kansas-oil-boom. For more about the early oil industry, see Christy Davis, "Oil Boomtowns," *Symphony in the Flint Hills Field Journal*, 2014, https://newprairiepress.org/cgi/viewcontent.cgi?article=1094&context=sfh; Aspen Junge, "Petroleum Refining: A 125 Year Kansas Legacy" (Topeka, KS: Kansas Department of Health and Environment, 2010), 1–26.
5. Barbara Stuntz, "Oil Boom in El Dorado" (unpublished manuscript, August 2018), typescript.
6. Edwin Price Ramsey and Stephen J. Rivele, *Lieutenant Ramsey's War* (New York: Knightsbridge Publishing Co., 1990), 5.
7. Ramsey and Rivele, 6.
8. Ramsey and Rivele, 8.
9. Barbara Stuntz, "Memories of Aunt Nelle, Nadine, and Edwin" (unpublished manuscript, October 2013), typescript.
10. Ramsey and Rivele, *Lieutenant Ramsey's War*, 8.

CHAPTER 2. A FAMILY OF THREE IN WICHITA

1. Rob Nixon, "Hell's Angels (1930)," Leonard Maltin Classic Movie Guide, 2005, 2010, http://www.tcm.turner.com/tcmdb/title/77738/Hell-s-Angels/articles.html.

2. Dennis Farney, *The Barnstormer and the Lady: Aviation Legends Walter and Olive Ann Beech* (Kansas City, MO: Rockhill Books, 2010), chap. 2.

3. Farney, chap. 2.

4. "Wichita—'The Air Capital of America,' Location, Terrain, and Weather Make City Aviation Center," *The Wichita*, August 1927, 11, 23–25.

5. Susan Thompson, *Prairie Runways: The History of Wichita's Original Municipal Airport* (Wichita, KS: Air Capital Press, 2000), 49.

6. Thompson, 68.

7. Farney, *The Barnstormer and the Lady*, chap. 2.

8. Joseph J. Corn, "Making Flying 'Thinkable': Women Pilots and the Selling of Aviation, 1927–1940," *American Quarterly* 31, no. 4 (1979): 556–571.

9. Louise Thaden, *High, Wide and Frightened* (New York: Air Facts Press, 1973), chap. 5.

10. Ramsey and Rivele, *Lieutenant Ramsey's War*, 10.

11. "Solos after 6½ Hours in Air," *Wichita Beacon*, n.d., Ramsey Collection.

12. "The Bendix Trophy," Air Racing History, 2019, http://www.airracinghistory.freeola.com/Between%20the%20wars(2).htm.

13. Thompson, *Prairie Runways*, 76.

14. Ramsey and Rivele, *Lieutenant Ramsey's War*, 9.

15. Richard J. Cawthon, "National Register of Historic Places Inventory/Nomination: Lassen Hotel / Market Centre," https://npgallery.nps.gov/NRHP/GetAsset/NRHP/84000108_text.

16. "NAA chapters," National Aeronautics (February 1938), 31, Ramsey Collection.

17. Mary Chance VanScyoc, *A Lifetime of Chances* (Wichita: Parkwood Press, 1996), 148.

CHAPTER 3. AT HOME IN THE SKY

1. Edward A. Keogh, "A Brief History of the Air Mail Service of the U.S. Post Office Department (May 15, 1918–August 31, 1927)," Air Mail Pioneers, http://www.airmailpioneers.org/content/Sagahistory.htm.

2. Thompson, *Prairie Runways*, 65.

3. "National Air Mail Week, 05/1918–1938m," US National Archives, https://www.youtube.com/watch?v=v5hRE08qgpc.

4. "Wichita Aviatrix May Become First Woman to Fly U.S. Mail," *Wichita Eagle*, May 17, 1938.

5. "Women Mail Pilots," *Evening Wichita Eagle*, May 9, 1938.

6. Kelli Gant, "Women Involved in Aviation," The Ninety-Nines, 2019, https://www.ninety-nines.org/women-in-aviation-article.htm.

7. Ramsey and Rivele, *Lieutenant Ramsey's War*, 13–14.

8. Ramsey and Rivele, 15–19.

9. Ramsey and Rivele, 23.

10. "Sued Aviatrix Denies Drinking," *San Francisco Union*, October 8, 1941.

CHAPTER 4. AT WAR

1. Ramsey and Rivele, *Lieutenant Ramsey's War*, 26.

2. Ramsey and Rivele, 51–68.

3. "Speed Queen Captures Bendix Trophy," *Salt Lake Tribune*, September 4, 1938; "Jacqueline Cochran Wins $30,000 Bendix Air Derby," *Wisconsin State Journal*, September 4, 1938; "Woman Wins Bendix Race," *Coshocton (OH) Tribune*, September 4, 1938.

4. "Harmon Trophy to Jacqueline Cochran of New York," *Manhattan (KS) Mercury*, April 4, 1938; Jacqueline Cochran, *The Stars at Noon* (Boston: Little, Brown, 1954), 106–107.

5. John Wheeler, "Rear Guard in Luzon," *Life*, March 2, 1942, 51–55.

6. "Magazine Gives Tip on Son's Location," *Wichita Beacon*, March 2, 1942, Ramsey Collection.

7. Franklin D. Roosevelt, "Fireside Chat," December 9, 1941, National Archives and Records Administration, https://www.archives.gov/education/lessons/fdr-fireside.

8. "Wichitan Certain Brother Is Alive, Safe on Bataan," unidentified newspaper clipping, n.d., Ramsey Collection.

CHAPTER 5. A BUNCH OF GALS

1. Sarah Byrn Rickman, *The Originals: The Women's Auxiliary Ferrying Squadron of World War II* (Sarasota, FL: Disc-Us Books, 2001), 42.

2. Army Air Forces, Air Transport Command, Ferrying Division, "WASPs—Women's Airforce Service Pilots," *Informational Bulletin*, March 8, 1944, WASP Archive.

3. Quoted in Debra G. Douglas, "United States Women in Aviation: 1940–1985," *Smithsonian Studies in Air and Space*, no. 7 (1990): 46.

4. Nadine Ramsey to Jackie Cochran, February 9, 1943, Ramsey Collection.

5. Claire V. Eberhard, character reference, 1943, Ramsey Collection.

6. William R. Hunt, "Sweetwater, Texas," Texas State Historical Association, https://tshaonline.org/handbook/online/articles/hes09.

7. Vera S. Williams, *WASPs: Women Airforce Service Pilots of World War II* (Osceola, WI: Motorbooks International, 1994), 51; Jean Landis, interview by Sarah Byrn Rickman, May 13 and September 16, 2012, Oral History Collection.

CHAPTER 6. AVENGER FIELD

1. Irma "Babe" Story to Mary Weatherby, July 13, 1943, Weatherby Collection.
2. Helen Severson to her parents, August 17, 1943, Severson Collection; Irma "Babe" Story to Mary Weatherby, July 13, 1943, Weatherby Collection.
3. Rickman, *The Originals*, 117.
4. Quoted in Williams, *WASPs*, 106.
5. Quoted in Williams, 109.
6. Williams, 98.
7. Quoted in Williams, 66.
8. Karen Lee Ashcraft and Dennis K. Mumby, *Reworking Gender: A Feminist Communicology of Organization* (Thousand Oaks, CA: Sage Publications, 2004), 137. For more on WASP portrayals in the media, see Molly Merryman, *Clipped Wings: The Rise and Fall of the Women Airforce Service Pilots (WASPs) of World War II* (New York: New York University Press, 1998), 65–69; and Williams, *WASPs*, 96.
9. Rickman, *The Originals*, 153–155.
10. Rob Simbeck, *Daughter of the Air: The Brief Soaring Life of Cornelia Fort* (New York: Atlantic Monthly Press, 1999), 225.
11. Yvonne Pateman to Mary Weatherby, June 11, 1943, Weatherby Collection.
12. "Girl Pilots: Air Force Trains Them at Avenger Field, Texas," *Life*, July 19, 1943, 73–81.
13. Irma "Babe" Story to Mary Weatherby, August 31, 1943, Weatherby Collection.

CHAPTER 7. BECOMING A WASP

1. Helen Jo Severson to her parents, August 17, 1943, Severson Collection.
2. Helen Jo Severson, August 25, 1943, Severson Collection.
3. Nadine Ramsey to Mrs. Amy Anderson [Helen Jo Severson's mother], September 19, 1943, Severson Collection.
4. 318th Army Air Forces Flying Training Detachment Classbook, Avenger Field, Classes 43-W-4 and 43-W-5, Ramsey Collection.
5. Marianne Verges, *On Silver Wings: The Women Airforce Service Pilots of World War II, 1942–1944* (New York: Ballantine Books, 1991), 103.
6. Quoted in Rickman, *The Originals*, 182; Irma "Babe" Story to Mary Weatherby, August 19, 1943, Weatherby Collection.

7. "Army Air Forces Regulation 40-9: Wearing of the WASP Uniform," February 14, 1944, Wings Across America, http://www.wingsacrossamerica.us/wasp/documents/uniform_regulation.pdf.

CHAPTER 8. FERRY PILOT

1. Ruth Dailey Helm, interview by Tracey MacGowan, October 3, 2002, Oral History Collection.
2. Quoted in Rickman, *The Originals*, 123.
3. Elizabeth "Betty" Whitlow Rummerfield Smith, interview by Dawn Letson, August 4, 1999, Oral History Collection.
4. Sarah Byrn Rickman, *WASP of the Ferry Command: Women Pilots, Uncommon Deeds* (Denton: University of North Texas Press, 2016), 155–156.
5. Lorraine Rodgers, interview by Jean Hascall Cole, June 19, 1989, Oral History Collection.
6. Cathcrine McBride D'Arezzo, interview by Dawn Letson, February 29, 1996, Oral History Collection.
7. Quoted in Rickman, *The Originals*, 217.
8. "WASP Celebrate First Birthday November 12," *The Avenger*, November 19, 1943.
9. Headquarters Ferrying Liaison, Public Relations Section, "Ferrying WASPs," ca. 1944, 2, MSS 865, H. O. Malone Research Collection, Woman's Collection.
10. Headquarters Ferrying Liaison, Public Relations Section, 1, H. O. Malone Research Collection, Woman's Collection.
11. Jean Landis, interview by Sarah Byrn Rickman, May 13 and September 16, 2012, Oral History Collection.
12. "Pilots Pursuit Plane," unidentified newspaper clipping, Ramsey Collection.
13. Rickman, *WASP of the Ferry Command*, 245.
14. Rickman, *The Originals*, 278.
15. Drew Pearson, "Merry Go Round," *Washington Times-Herald*, August 6, 1944.
16. Jacqueline Cochran to Commanding General, Army Air Forces, *WASP Report*, August 1, 1944, WASP Archive.
17. Captain Walter J. Marx, "Women Pilots in the Air Transport Command" (unpublished manuscript, January 1945), WASP Archive.

CHAPTER 9. IN PURSUIT

1. Julian DelGaudio and Craig Hendricks, *A Big Change for Long Beach: World War II Transforms the City* (Long Beach, CA: Historical Society of Long Beach, 2017), 40.

2. DelGaudio and Hendricks, 27.
3. Quoted in Sarah Byrn Rickman, *B. J. Erickson: WASP Pilot* (Palmer Lake, CO: Filter Press, 2018), 60.
4. Larry Bledsoe, *The Few: Women Who Flew the P-38* (Portland, OR: Bookbaby, 2017), chap. 7.
5. Douglas, "United States Women in Aviation," 51.
6. Iris Cummings Critchell, email correspondence with Raquel Ramsey, August 24 and September 15, 2013.
7. Quoted in Bledsoe, *The Few*, chap. 6.
8. Betty Huyler Gillies, interview by Dawn Letson, October 6, 1996, Oral History Collection.
9. "Policy and Status Report of the Order of Fifinella," *WASP Newsletter*, December 20, 1944, WASP Archive.
10. Kay Gott, *Women in Pursuit: Flying Fighters for the Air Transport Command Ferrying Division during World War II: A Collection and Recollection* (self-published, 1993), 71; Rickman, *WASP of the Ferry Command*, 319.
11. Dawn Seymour, interview by Rebecca Wright, July 19, 1999, NASA Oral History Collections, https://historycollection.jsc.nasa.gov/JSCHistoryPortal/History/oral_histories/NASA_HQ/Aviatrix/SeymourD/Seymourd_7-19-99.htm.
12. Quoted in Williams, *WASPs*, 124.
13. "They Are Willing," *Fresno (CA) Bee—The Republican*, December 26, 1944.
14. "WASP Ferry Offer Spurned," *Los Angeles Times*, December 21, 1944.
15. Barbara London, WAFS, interview by Sarah Rickman, March 17 and 19, 2004, Oral History Collection.
16. Quoted in Rickman, *The Originals*, 329.
17. General H. L. George, Commendation to Air Transport Command WASP, December 20, 1944, National Archives, Nadine Ramsey Veteran Personnel File.
18. General William H. Tunner, Commendation to Commanding General, Ferrying Division, ATC, October 16, 1944, National Archives, Nadine Ramsey Veteran Personnel File.
19. Quoted in Douglas, "United States Women in Aviation," 56.
20. Jacqueline Cochran, to Commanding General, Army Air Forces, *WASP Report*, August 1, 1944, WASP Archive.
21. Tunner, Commendation to Commanding General.

CHAPTER 10. ON THE WING

1. Stephanie Michelle Cavin, "Women, War, and Planes: Women Airforce Service Pilots' Experience Working alongside the Army Air Force during World War II," Master's thesis, University of Texas-Pan American, May 2015, 116;

"Women Ferrying Pilots' Service Ends Next Week," *Long Beach Independent Press-Telegram*, December 15, 1944.

2. *WASP Newsletter*, December 1, 1944, December 10, 1944, December 20, 1944, January 25, 1945, March 15, 1945, WASP Archive; Nancy Baker, class 43-W-4, interview by Dawn Letson, September 5, 1977, Oral History Collection.

3. M. Allaire Bennett, class 43-W-7, interview by Dawn Letson, September 30, 1995, Oral History Collection; Dorothy Allen, class 44-W-4, interview by Dawn Letson, December 3, 1997, Oral History Collection; *WASP Newsletter*, December 1, 1944, March 15, 1945, May 20, 1945, WASP Archive.

4. Nancy Baker, class 43-W-4, interview by Dawn Letson, September 5, 1977, Oral History Collection; Peggy Eccles, class 44-W-4, interview by Dawn Letson, December 4, 1977, Oral History Collection.

5. M. Allaire Bennett, class 43-W-7, interview by Dawn Letson, September 30, 1995, Oral History Collection.

6. *WASP Newsletter*, January 25, 1945, WASP Archive.

7. *WASP Newsletter*, January 25, 1945, December 1, 1944, WASP Archive.

8. Katherine Elizabeth [Sharp] Landdeck, "Pushing the Envelope: The Women Airforce Service Pilots and American Society," PhD diss., University of Tennessee, 2003, 130.

9. Peggy Eccles, class 44-W-4, interview by Dawn Letson, December 4, 1977, Oral History Collection.

10. Barbara London, WAFS, interview by Sarah Rickman, March 17 and 19, 2004, Oral History Collection.

11. Quoted in Landdeck, "Pushing the Envelope," 114.

12. Quoted in Katherine S. Gray, "Flying in Formation: Creating a Place for Women in Aviation through the Ninety-nines, the WASP, and the Whirly-Girls," Master's thesis, Miami University, Oxford, OH, 2007, 24.

13. *WASP Newsletter*, February 1946, WASP Archive.

14. Landdeck, "Pushing the Envelope," 130.

15. Cavin, "Women, War, and Planes," 18; Gray, "Flying in Formation," 54; Angele Farizo, "Women in a Warzone: Participation Precedes Policy," Master's thesis, Southeastern Louisiana University, May 2012, 129–130; Landdeck, "Pushing the Envelope," 108.

16. Dorothea Moorman, class 43-W-4, interview by Ziggy Hunter, October 24, 1976, Oral History Collection; Gray, "Flying in Formation," 55.

17. Edgar A. Guest, "How to Stay Young," *Wichita Beacon*, n.d., Ramsey Collection.

18. David A. Keeps, "Girl Pilot Saves Life by Executing Own Teachings," *Los Angeles Times*, 1946.

19. Sarah Rickman, email correspondence with the authors, September 18, 2018.

20. "The Battle for Luzon," *New York Times*, January 11, 1945.

21. Ed Ramsey to Nelle Ramsey, April 7, 1945, Ramsey Collection.

22. Ed Ramsey to Nelle Ramsey, May 15, 1945, Ramsey Collection.

23. Frank Good, "Wichitan Hero in Luzon as Leader of Guerillas," *Wichita Beacon*, June 5, 1945; Ed Ramsey to Nelle Ramsey, May 15, 1945.

24. Good, "Wichitan Hero in Luzon."

25. Good.

26. United States Army to Nelle Ramsey, telegram, May 23, 1945, Ramsey Collection.

27. Ramsey and Rivele, *Lieutenant Ramsey's War*, 328.

28. Ramsey and Rivele, 322.

29. Rickman, *B. J. Erickson*, 134.

30. "Jack Gardner to New Post," *San Bernardino County Sun*, July 14, 1944.

CHAPTER 11. HER OWN P-38

1. Douglas, "United States Women in Aviation," 60.

2. "Picks Up Plane Bargain: Woman Goes Shopping; Flies Home with P-38," *Los Angeles Times*, February 15, 1946.

3. "Girl Purchases P-38 and She Can Handle It!" *Dayton (OH) Herald*, February 16, 1946.

4. "Nadine Ramsey, L.B. Ex-WASP Now Owns Ex-Army Fighter," unidentified newspaper clipping, February 15, 1946, Ramsey Collection.

5. "Marines Due for Air Show," *Arizona Republic (Phoenix)*, February 16, 1946.

6. "Personal P-38," *Life* (International), March 25, 1946.

7. Ramsey and Rivele, *Lieutenant Ramsey's War*, 333.

8. "Hero of Guerilla Fighting Visits Aunt in County," *Centralia (IL) Sentinel*, April 17, 1946.

9. Ed Ramsey, "Guerilla Command" (unpublished manuscript, 1946), preface.

10. Ramsey, 3.

11. Colonel K. C. McGregor to Nadine Ramsey, Notice of Reduction in Force, July 11, 1946, Ramsey Collection.

12. "Around the World with the Bradford Evening Star Cameraman," *Bradford (PA) Evening Star*, August 29, 1946.

13. "Woman First Entrant in Bendix Trophy Race," *Valley Times* (San Fernando Valley, CA), November 11, 1946.

14. "Fast Planes 'Souped Up' for Attack on Records," *Los Angeles Times*, August 25, 1946; "Miss Ramsey in Race," *New York Times*, August 25, 1946.

15. Bendix Trophy Race List of Participants, August 30, 1946, National Archives, Nadine Ramsey Veteran Personnel File.

16. Jacqueline Cochran to Admiral Luis DeFlores, Chairman, National Aeronautical Association Contest Board, September 9, 1946, Ramsey Collection.

17. Lois K. Merry, *Women Military Pilots of World War II: A History with Biographies of American, British, Russian, and German Aviators* (Jefferson, NC: McFarland, 2011), 101.

18. Keeps, "Girl Pilot Saves Life."

19. Nadine Ramsey and Jack Gardner, Christmas card, December 1949, Ramsey Collection.

CHAPTER 12. SEARCHING FOR HOME

1. Douglas, "United States Women in Aviation," 69–70, 74.

2. Rickman, *The Originals*, 335–336. See also Martha Lockwood, "Women's Legacy Parallels Air Force History," *US Air Force News*, September 18, 2014, https://www.af.mil/News/Article-Display/Article/497548/womens-legacy-parallels-air-force-history/.

CHAPTER 13. A DECADE OF CHANGE

1. Quoted in Douglas, "United States Women in Aviation," 84.

2. *WASP Newsletter*, October 1964, WASP Archive.

3. "Announcing Golden Hours Villa," *Long Beach Independent Press-Telegram*, November 9, 1966.

CHAPTER 14. NEW DIRECTIONS

1. Dackri Davis, "Navigating Discrimination: A Historical Examination of Women's Experiences of Discrimination and Tirumph with the United States Military and Higher Educational Institution," PhD diss., Georgia State University, 2014, 8n10; Maureen Murdoch et al., "Women and War: What Physicians Should Know," *Journal of General Internal Medicine* 21 Suppl 3:S5–10 (April 2006), 57; Service Women's Action Network, "The Mental Needs of Military Women: Community Driven Solutions, 2018 Report," 2, https://www.servicewomen.org/wp-content/uploads/2018/02/2018-Annual-Summit-Report-Final.compressed.pdf.

2. Douglas Ramsey, correspondence with the authors, December 7, 2017.

3. Dorothy Townsend, "Lipstick Pilots of World War II Won Wings, Still Seek Status," *Los Angeles Times*, June 25, 1972.

4. Jessica Wilson, "Waiting in the Wings: A History of the Women Air Force Service Pilots of World War II," Master's thesis, Sarah Lawrence College, May 2015, 4.

5. Quoted in Rickman, *The Originals*, 336.

6. Verges, *On Silver Wings*, 232; Williams, *WASPs*, 135; Rickman, *The Originals*, 336.

7. "A Gathering of WASPs," *Long Beach Examiner*, October 10, 1976.

8. Merryman, *Clipped Wings*, 139.

9. Rickman, *The Originals*, 337.

10. Margaret Ann Hamilton, "Cover Story: What America Means to Me," *Collier's*, April 2, 1949, in Linda Burdette, "Anne Tunner: A Life Well Lived," Virginia Aeronautical Historical Society, virginiaaviationhistory.org.

11. Quoted in Rickman, *The Originals*, 338.

12. Verges, *On Silver Wings*, 235.

13. Merryman, *Clipped Wings*, 155.

14. Quoted in Williams, *WASPs*, 137.

15. "WASPs Seek Status," *Long Beach Independent Press-Telegram*, October 10, 1976.

16. *WASP Newsletter*, June 1978, WASP Archive.

17. "Now and Then," *1978 The Year of the WASP*, Colorado Springs Conference program (June 1978), 24, WASP Archive.

18. *WASP Newsletter*, April 1979, WASP Archive.

CHAPTER 15. SETTLING IN

1. Barbara Erickson to Air Force Military Personnel Center, cover letter, Application for Honorable Discharge for Nadine Ramsey, May 29, 1979, National Archives, Nadine Ramsey Veteran Personnel File.

2. *WASP Newsletter*, August 1980, WASP Archive.

3. Nadine Ramsey to Barbara Branch, March 15, 1981, Ramsey Collection.

4. Edwin Ramsey to Nelle Ramsey, April 7, 1943, Ramsey Collection.

5. Beth Rosenberg Zweig, "Fort Wayne Woman Keeps Female Fliers' Sagas Alive," *Indianapolis Star*, June 10, 1990.

6. Rickman, *B. J. Erickson*, 140.

7. Kathleen Cairns, "Women Who Ferried Planes in WWII Finally Get Their Due," *Long Beach Independent Press-Telegram*, June 16, 1989.

8. Stephen J. Rivele, email correspondence with Tricia Aurand, December 14, 2018.

CHAPTER 16. A LOOK TO THE FUTURE

1. John Percy Gardner to Mary Anna Wyall, September 11, 1996, MSS 802c, Nadine Ramsey Collection, Woman's Collection.

2. "On a Wing and a Prayer," *USO Magazine* (Summer 2010): 20.

3. House Congressional Record, June 16, 2009, H6840, https://www.congress.gov/111/crec/2009/06/16/CREC-2009-06-16-pt1-PgH6840.pdf.

4. Harry Saltzgaver, "Aviation Icon Barbara London Passes Away at 93," *Grunion Gazette* (Long Beach, CA), July 10, 2013; Rickman, *B. J. Erickson*, 142.

5. Quoted in Anna Mulrine, "The Female WWII Pilots Who Got All Congress on Their Side," *Christian Science Monitor*, May 11, 2016, https://www.csmonitor.com/USA/Military/2016/0511/The-female-World-War-II-pilots-who-got-all-Congress-on-their-side.

6. Mulrine.

7. Don Vaughn, "A Worthy Cause," *Military Officer* (May 2016): 81.

8. Max Lewontin, "Bill to Restore Burial Rights to Female WWII Pilots Flies through Congress," *Christian Science Monitor*, May 13, 2016.

9. Anna Mulrine, "Memorial, and a Milestone, for Pioneering Female World War II Pilot," *Christian Science Monitor*, September 8, 2016, https://www.csmonitor.com/USA/Military/2016/0908/Memorial-and-a-milestone-for-pioneering-female-World-War-II-pilot.

10. Cheryl Pellerin, "Carter Opens All Military Occupations, Positions to Women," *DoD News*, December 3, 2015, https://dod.defense.gov/News/Article/Article/632536/carter-opens-all-military-occupations-positions-to-women/.

11. Edwin Ramsey to All Friends of Nadine Ramsey, Spring 1997, Ramsey Collection.

12. Barbara Stuntz to Edwin and Raquel Ramsey, February 23, 1997, Ramsey Collection.

13. Dick Simmons to Edwin and Raquel Ramsey, March 21, 1997, Ramsey Collection.

14. Florene Miller Watson to Edwin and Raquel Ramsey on behalf of WASP Organization, February 15, 1997, Ramsey Collection.

15. Dawn Seymour to Edwin and Raquel Ramsey, April 9, 1997; Barbara Erickson London to Edwin and Raquel Ramsey, December 3, 1997, Ramsey Collection.

16. Meredith Tibbets, "At Long Last, WWII WASP Pilot Elaine Harmon Is Home at Arlington," *Stars and Stripes*, September 7, 2016, https://www.stripes.com/news/us/at-long-last-wwii-wasp-pilot-elaine-harmon-is-home-at-arlington-1.427789.

17. Tibbets.

18. Mary Lou Neale, "To Own a Lightning," in Steve Blake and Dayle L. DeBry, *P-38 Lightning: Unforgettable Missions of Skill and Luck* (March Air Reserve Base, CA: P-38 National Association, 2011), 234–235.

19. Stephen J. Rivele, interview with Raquel Ramsey, December 1989.

EPILOGUE

1. Edwin Ramsey to Barbara Stuntz, March 13, 1987, Ramsey Collection.

2. "Review: *Lieutenant Ramsey's War*." *Kirkus Review*, 1990, https://www.kirkusreviews.com/book-reviews/edwin-price-stephen-j-rivele-ramsey/lieutenant-ramseys-war/.

BIBLIOGRAPHY

BOOKS AND PERIODICALS

American Psychiatric Association. *Diagnostic and Statistical Manual of Mental Disorders (DSM-1)*. 1st ed. Washington, DC: American Psychiatric Association, 1952.

Ashcraft, Karen Lee, and Dennis K. Mumby. *Reworking Gender: A Feminist Communicology of Organization*. Thousand Oaks, CA: Sage, 2004.

Bartels, Diane, and Ruth Armour. *Sharpie: The Life Story of Evelyn Sharp*. Lincoln, NE: Dageforde, 1996.

Bledsoe, Larry. *The Few: Women Who Flew the P-38*. Pennsauken, NJ: Bookbaby, 2017.

Churchill, Jan. *On Wings to War: Teresa James, Aviator*. Manhattan, KS: Sunflower University Press, 1992.

Cochran, Jacqueline, and Maryann Bucknam Brinley. *Jackie Cochran: An Autobiography of the Greatest Woman Pilot in Aviation History*. New York: Bantam, 1987.

Cochran, Jacqueline, and Floyd Odlum. *The Stars at Noon*. Boston: Little, Brown, 1945.

Cole, Jean Hascall. *Women Pilots of World War II*. Salt Lake City: University of Utah Press, 1992.

Corn, Joseph J. "Making Flying 'Thinkable': Women Pilots and the Selling of Aviation 1927–1940." *American Quarterly* 31, no. 4 (1979): 556–571.

Courtwright, Julie. "'Want to Build a Miracle City?': War Housing in Wichita." *Kansas History: A Journal of the Central Plains* 23 (Winter 2000): 218–239.

DelGaudio, Julian, and Craig Hendricks. *A Big Change for Long Beach: World War II Transforms the City*. Long Beach, CA: Historical Society of Long Beach, 2017.

Douglas, Debra G. "United States Women in Aviation, 1940–1985." *Smithsonian Studies in Air and Space* 7 (1990): 1–142.

Farney, Dennis. *The Barnstormer and the Lady: Aviation Legends Walter and Olive Ann Beech*. Kansas City, MO: Rock Hill, 2011.

"Female WWII Pilots: The Original Fly Girls." *Homeland* 2, no. 3 (March 2015): 20–22.

"Girl Pilots: Air Force Trains Them at Avenger Field, Texas." *Life*, July 19, 1943, 73–81.

Gott, Kay. *Women in Pursuit: Flying Fighters for the Air Transport Command Ferrying Division during World War II: A Collection and Recollection*. Self-published, 1993.

Granger, Byrd Howell. *On Final Approach: The Women Airforce Service Pilots of W.W.II*. Scottsdale, AZ: Falconer, 1991.

Hatch, Gardner N. *P-51 Mustang*. Nashville, TN: Turner, 1987.

Hope, Clifford R., Sr. "Kansas in the 1930s." *Kansas History: A Journal of the Central Plains* 36, no. 1 (Spring 1970): 1–12.

Jessen, Gene Nora. *The Powder Puff Derby of 1929: The True Story of the First Women's Cross-Country Air Race*. Naperville, IL: Northam, 2002.

Junge, Aspen. *Petroleum Refining: A 125 Year Kansas Legacy*. Topeka: Kansas Department of Health and Environment, 2010.

Keil, Sally Van Wagenen. *Those Wonderful Women in Their Flying Machines: The Unknown Heroines of World War II*. New York: Four Directions Press, 1990.

"Kelly Honors WASP Pilots: Mayor Recognizes Long Beach Women's Air Force Service Pilots Bravery Cited for Service to U.S." *Long Beach Today*, 1, no. 3 (April 1994): 1.

"Long Beach Based World War II Women Pilots Ferried Aircraft Coast-to-Coast." *Long Beach Business Journal*, July 11–24, 1989.

Merry, Lois K. *Women Military Pilots of World War II: A History with Biographies of American, British, Russian, and German Aviators*. Jefferson, NC: McFarland, 2011.

Merryman, Molly. *Clipped Wings: The Rise and Fall of the Women Airforce Service Pilots*. New York: New York University Press, 1998.

Mooney, Vol. P. *History of Butler County, Kansas*. Lawrence, KS: Standard, 1916.

Morgan, Len. *Famous Aircraft: The P-47 Thunderbolt*. Dallas: Morgan Aviation Books, 1963.

———. *Famous Aircraft: The P-51 Mustang*. Dallas, TX: Morgan Aviation Books, 1963.

Murdoch, Maureen, Arlene Bradley, Susan H. Mather, Robert E. Klein, Carole L. Turner, and Elizabeth M. Yano. "Women and War: What Physicians Should Know." *Journal of General Internal Medicine* 21 Suppl. 3:S5–10 (April 2006): 55–59.

Neale, Mary Lou. "To Own a Lightning." In *P-38 Lightning: Unforgettable Missions of Skill and Luck*, by Steve Blake and Dayle L. DeBry, 234–235. March Air Reserve Base, CA: P-38 National Association, 2011.

"Personal P-38." *Life International*, March 25, 1946.

Poole, Barbara E. "Requiem for the WASP." *Flying Magazine*, December 1944, 55–56, 146, 148.

Ramsey, Edwin Price, and Stephen J. Rivele. *Lieutenant Ramsey's War*. New York: Knightsbridge, 1990.

Reese, Robert L., with Todd Depastino. "Women in World War II." *Military Order of the World Wars: Officer Review*, May 2015.

Rickman, Sarah Byrn. *B. J. Erickson: WASP Pilot*. Palmer Lake, CO: Filter Press, 2018.

———. *Nancy Love and the WASP Ferry Pilots of World War II*. Denton: University of North Texas Press, 2012.

———. *The Originals: The Women's Auxiliary Ferrying Squadron of World War II*. Sarasota, FL: Disc-Us Books, 2001.

———. *WASP of the Ferry Command: Women Pilots, Uncommon Deeds*. Denton: University of North Texas Press, 2016.

Scharr, Adela Riek. *Sisters in the Sky.* 2 vols. Saint Louis, MO: Patrice Press, 1986.

Seymour, Dawn, Clarice I. Bergemann, Jeannette J. Jenkins, and Mary Ellen Keil. *In Memoriam: Thirty-Eight American Women Pilots Gave Their Lives in Performance of Duty with the United States Army Air Forces 1942–1943–1944.* Denton: Texas Woman's University Press, 1996.

Simbeck, Rob. *Daughter of the Air: The Brief Soaring Life of Cornelia Fort.* New York: Atlantic Monthly Press, 1999.

Sloan, Charles William, Sr. "The Newelletters: E. Gail Carpenter Describes Life on the Home Front, Part I." *Kansas History: A Journal of the Central Plains* 11, no. 1 (Spring 1988): 54–72.

———. "The Newelletters: E. Gail Carpenter Describes Life on the Home Front, Part II." *Kansas History: A Journal of the Central Plains* 11, no. 2 (Summer 1988): 123–142.

———. "The Newelletters: E. Gail Carpenter Describes Life on the Home Front, Part III." *Kansas History: A Journal of the Central Plains* 11, no. 3 (Autumn 1988): 150–170.

———. "The Newelletters: E. Gail Carpenter Describes Life on the Home Front, Part IV." *Kansas History: A Journal of the Central Plains* 11, no. 4 (Winter 1988–1989): 243–259.

Thaden, Louise. *High, Wide and Frightened.* New York: Air Facts Press, 1973.

"This Week's Cover." *Collier's*, April 2, 1949.

Thompson, Susan. *Prairie Runways: The History of Wichita's Municipal Airport.* Wichita: Air Capital Press, 2000.

VanSycoc, Mary Chance. *A Lifetime of Chances.* Wichita: Parkwood Press, 1996.

Verges, Marianne. *On Silver Wings: The Women Airforce Service Pilots of World War II 1942–1944.* New York: Ballantine Books, 1991.

Wheeler, John. "Rear Guard in Luzon." *Life*, March 2, 1942.

Williams, Vera S. *WASPs: Women Airforce Service Pilots of World War II.* Osceola, WI: Motorbooks International, 1994.

NEWSPAPERS AND NEWSLETTERS

"A Bargain's A Bargain." *Deadwood (SD) Pioneer Times*, February 19, 1946.

"Aeronautical Women to Have Fireside Meeting." *Wichita Eagle*, 1939.

"Air Show Will Open New Port." *Arizona Daily Star*, February 26, 1946.

"Announcing Golden Hours Villa." *Long Beach Independent Press-Telegram*, November 9, 1966.

"Around the World with the Bradford Evening Star Cameraman." *Bradford (PA) Evening Star*, August 29, 1946.

"Aviatrix To Visit: Nadine Ramsey Is En Route to Ohio." *Wichita Eagle*, May 4, 1940.

"The Battle for Luzon." *New York Times*, January 11, 1945.

Belk, Sean. "Woman Aviator Barbara Erickson London Remembered for Playing Pivotal Role in Long Beach Aviation History." *Long Beach Signal Tribune*, July 12, 2013.

"Bendix Trophy Race On, Rich Purse Posted." *Miami (OK) Daily News-Record*, August 30, 1946.

Bowers, Carol L. "Women Pilots of WWII Inspired Generations." *American Forces Press Service*, March 10, 2010.

Branson-Potts, Hailey. "Rose Parade Float Honors Female Pilots." *Los Angeles Times*, January 1, 2014.

Cairns, Kathleen. "Women Who Ferried Planes in WWII Finally Get Their Due." *Long Beach Independent Press-Telegram*, June 16, 1989.

Christensen, Joyce. "A Gathering of WASPs." *Long Beach Independent Press-Telegram*, October 10, 1976.

"Cosmetologists' President Speaks to Local Chapter." *Hutchinson (KS) News*, January 8, 1935.

"Cosmetologists to Meet." *Lincoln Evening Journal*, January 12, 1934.

"Cosmetologists Want an Advisory Board." *Emporia (KS) Gazette*, January 16, 1939.

"Crash Is Blamed on Inexperience." *San Francisco Union*, September 4, 1940.

"Dignity and Pride of Skill." *Los Angeles Herald-Examiner*, September 14, 1975.

Djurklou, Alessandra K. "Sky Queen." *Los Angeles Times Magazine*, January 22, 1995.

"Ex-WASP Runs Sales Division." *Long Beach Independent Press-Telegram*, February 19, 1948.

"Fast Planes 'Souped Up' for Attack on Records." *Los Angeles Times*, August 25, 1946.

"Festive Luau Aids New Camp." *Long Beach Independent Press-Telegram*, October 8, 1969.

"A Gathering of WASPs." *Long Beach Examiner*, October 10, 1976.

"Girl Purchases P-38 and She Can Handle It!" *Dayton Herald*, February 16, 1946.

Good, Frank. "Wichitan Hero in Luzon as Leader of Guerillas." *Wichita Beacon*, June 5, 1945.

"Guerilla Leader Returns." *Daily Journal World* (Lawrence, KS), June 26, 1945.

"Gutsy Women Rose above Obstacles To Fly." *San Antonio Express-News*, November 24, 1991.

Hagmann, Tony. "COAST-ing the Clouds." *Skylady*, May–June 1946.

Harmetz, Aljean. "Laraine Day, B+ Movie Star, Dies at 87." *New York Times*, November 13, 2007.

"Harmon Trophy to Jacqueline Cochran of New York." *Manhattan (KS) Mercury*, April 4, 1938.

"Hero and Sister." *Decatur Press*, June 11, 1943.

"Hero of Guerilla Fighting Visits Aunt in County." *Centralia (IL) Sentinel*, April 17, 1946.

"Honoring Women Airforce Service Pilots." *Military Order of the World Wars: Officer Review*, April–June 2017.

"Jack Gardner Tells 20–30 about Army." *Chula Vista (CA) Star*, January 26, 1945.

"Jack Gardner to New Post." *San Bernardino County Sun*, July 14, 1944.

"Jacqueline Cochran Wins $30,000 Bendix Air Derby." *Wisconsin State Journal*, September 4, 1938.

"Keeping One Legacy Alive, Starting Another." *Army Times*, December 25, 1995.

Keeps, David A. "For Neff, An Era of Glamour Came First." *Los Angeles Times*, March 18, 2004.

Kelly, Kate. "Recognizing Progress: The 1938 Celebration of National Airmail Week." *Huffington Post*, May 18, 2010.

"Kingman Girl Buys P-38 as a 'Bargain.'" *San Bernardino County Sun*, February 15, 1946.

Kushner, Ella R. "From the Cockpit." *Skylady*, May–June 1946.

Lewontin, Max. "Bill to Restore Burial Rights to Female WWII Pilots Flies through Congress." *Christian Science Monitor*, May 13, 2016.

"Local Officer Is Called Back to Philippines." *Wichita Evening Eagle*, July 24, 1946.

"Lone Navy Plane Enters Air Race." *Los Angeles Times*, August 23, 1946.

Mader, Vint. "Convalescent Home Owner Convicted on 6 Charges." *Long Beach Independent Press-Telegram*, March 16, 1971.

"Mail Pilots on Schedule." *Wichita Eagle*, May 19, 1938.

"Maj. Edwin Ramsey Flown to Wichita by Sister, Nadine." *Wichita Eagle*, June 25, 1945.

"Marines Due for Air Show." *Arizona Republic* (Phoenix, AZ), February 16, 1946.

"Miss Bartlett Weds John Gardner Friday." *San Bernardino County Sun*, March 24, 1940.

"Miss Cochran Leading Her Girls on Good Will Hop." *Star-Telegram* (Fort Worth, TX), April 24, 1943.

"Miss Ramsey in Race." *New York Times*, August 25, 1946.

"Mrs. Sellhorn Again Heads Cosmologists." *Lincoln Star*, January 28, 1936.

Mulrine, Anna. "The Female WWII Pilots Who Got All Congress on Their Side." *Christian Science Monitor*, May 11, 2016.

———. "Memorial, and a Mile Stone, for Pioneering Female World War II Pilot." *Christian Science Monitor*, September 8, 2016.

"NAA Chapters." *National Aeronautics*, February 1938.

"New Oil Leases Made in Walnut River Valley." *Butler County Democrat*, December 19, 1913.

"Nico to End Meet." *Lincoln Journal Star*, February 13, 1935.

"On a Wing and a Prayer." *USO Magazine*, Summer 2010.

"Once No Planes over Wellington." *Wellington Daily News*, August 23, 1971.

"Overdue Honor." *Military Officer*, October 2009.

"P-38 Painting Honors WASP." *WASP News*, September 1989.

"P-80 First over Bendix Line." *Wilmington (CA) Daily Press Journal*, August 30, 1946.

"Paul Mantz Wins Race in Mustang Fighter." *Los Angeles Times*, August 31, 1946.

Pearson, Drew. "Merry Go Round." *Washington Times-Herald*, August 6, 1944.

"Picks Up Plane Bargain: Woman Goes Shopping; Flies Home with P-38," *Los Angeles Times*, February 15, 1946.

"Recognition Due." *Military Officer*, June 2010.

"Rest Home Owner Fined and Jailed." *Long Beach Independent Press-Telegram*, April 13, 1971.

Rickman, Sarah Byrn. "WAFS B. J. Erickson London Takes Her Last Flight." *WASP News*, Summer 2013.

Rickman, Sarah, with Nora Montoya. "Barbara Erickson London WAFS/WASP." New Horizons, Long Beach Chapter. *99 News*, September/October 2013, 31.

Rosenberg Zweig, Beth. "Fort Wayne Woman Keeps Female Fliers' Sagas Alive." *Indianapolis Star*, June 10, 1990.

Saltzgaver, Harry. "Aviation Icon Barbara London Passes Away at 93." *The Grunion* (Long Beach, CA), July 10, 2013.

"Second Class Graduates." *The Avenger*, June 28, 1943.

Sherman, Gene. "Warplanes Go to Arizona Desert to Die." *Los Angeles Times*, April 1, 1946.

"Speed Queen Captures Bendix Trophy." *Salt Lake Tribune*, September 4, 1938.

"State Airmail 'Pickup' Planes Leave at 10 a.m." *Wichita Eagle*, May 18, 1938.

Stuart, John. "Airlines Planning to Penalize 'No Shows' by Charging 25 Percent for Unused Tickets." *New York Times*, August 25, 1946.

"Sued Aviatrix Denies Drinking." *San Francisco Union*, October 8, 1941.

Summers, Juana. "Recognition at Last for Female WWII Pilots." *Austin American-Statesman*, June 22, 2009.

"WASP Celebrate First Birthday November 12." *The Avenger*, November 19, 1943.

"The Watchman." *Los Angeles Times*, March 25, 1941.

"They Are Willing." *The Fresno (CA) Bee–The Republican*, December 26, 1944.

Townsend, Dorothy. "Lipstick Pilots of World War II Won Wings, Still Seek Status." *Los Angeles Times*, June 25, 1972.

"Two Women in Bendix Classic." *Wilmington (CA) Daily Press Journal*, August 26, 1946.

Vaughn, Don. "A Worthy Cause." *Military Officer*, May 2016.

Warth, Gary. "Remembering Role of Women in WWII." *San Diego Union-Tribune*, March 29, 2016.

"WASP Ferry Offer Spurned." *Los Angeles Times*, December 21, 1944.

"WASP's Eye View." *World War II*, October 2010.

"WASPs Seek Status." *Long Beach Independent Press-Telegram*, October 10, 1976.

Weiner, Rachel. "Female WWII Pilots Were Barred from Arlington. Not Anymore."
 The Washington Post, May 20, 2016.

"Wichita Aviatrix May Become First Woman to Fly U.S. Mail." *Wichita Eagle*, May
 17, 1938.

"Wichita Aviatrix to Pause Here on Plane Trip East." *Wichita Beacon*, May 31, 1940.

"Wichita—'The Air Capital of America,' Location, Terrain, and Weather Make City
 Aviation Center." *The Wichita*, August 1927.

Willman, Tom. "Financial Woes Hit Rest Homes." *Long Beach Independent Press-
 Telegram*, December 14, 1974.

"Woman Air Crash Victim Moved Here." *Los Angeles Times*, September 4, 1940.

"Woman First Entrant in Bendix Trophy Race." *Valley Times* (San Fernando Valley,
 CA), November 11, 1946.

"Woman Pilot Crashes Plane." *Los Angeles Times*, September 3, 1940.

"Woman Wins $28,233 Damages." *San Francisco Union*, October 9, 1941.

"Woman Wins Bendix Race." *Coshocton (OH) Tribune*, September 4, 1938.

"Women Ferrying Pilots' Service Ends Next Week." *Long Beach Independent Press-
 Telegram*, December 15, 1944.

"Women Kin of Missing Men Win Air Forces Wings." *Salt Lake Tribune*, September
 12, 1943.

"Women Mail Pilots." *Evening Wichita Eagle*, May 9, 1938.

"Women: Unnecessary and Undesirable?" *Time*, May 29, 1944.

"Work Begun on Hospital." *Long Beach Independent Press-Telegram*, August 4, 1963.

"Young Matron Arrives for Stay in Former Home." *Santa Ana (CA) Register*, June
 25, 1942.

ARCHIVES AND COLLECTIONS

Nadine Ramsey Collection

Correspondence

Bellafaire, Judith. Letter to Raquel Ramsey on behalf of Women in Military Service
 for America Memorial Foundation. August 6, 1997.

Cochran, Jacqueline. Letter to Admiral Luis DeFlores, Chairman, National Aeronau-
 tical Association Contest Board. September 9, 1946.

Cohen, Gil. Letter to Raquel Ramsey. June 23, 2014.

Critchell, Iris Cummings. Email correspondence with Raquel Ramsey. August 24
 and September 15, 2013.

Faculty and Students, Wichita North High School. Letter to Nelle Ramsey. July 19, 1942.

Grantham, Kevin A. Letter to Nadine Ramsey. February 28, 1990.

Hamilton, Capt. John C. Letter to Nelle Ramsey on behalf of Oklahoma Military Academy. August 4, 1942.

Landis, Jean. Letter to Raquel Ramsey. October 23, 2014.

London, Barbara Erickson. Letter to Edwin and Raquel Ramsey. December 3, 1997.

Neale, Mary Lou. Letter to Edwin Ramsey. March 18, 1997.

Ramsey, Edwin. Letter to All Friends of Nadine Ramsey. February 1997.

———. Letter to Barbara Stuntz. March 13, 1987.

———. Letter to Nelle Ramsey. April 7, 1943.

———. Letter to Nelle Ramsey. April 7, 1945.

———. Letter to Nelle Ramsey. May 15, 1945.

Ramsey, Edwin, Jr. Email correspondence with the authors. November 15 and November 20, 2017.

Ramsey, Nadine. Letter to Jackie Cochran. February 9, 1943.

Seymour, Dawn. Letter to Edwin and Raquel Ramsey. April 9, 1997.

Seymour, Dawn Rochow Balden. Email correspondence with Raquel Ramsey. July 9, 2014.

Simmons, Dick. Letter to Edwin and Raquel Ramsey. March 21, 1997.

Stuntz, Barbara. Letter to Raquel Ramsey. December 8, 2013.

———. Letter to Edwin and Raquel Ramsey. February 23, 1997.

Watson, Florene Miller. Letter to Edwin and Raquel Ramsey on behalf of WASP Organization. February 15, 1997.

Interviews

Landis, Jean. Telephone interview with Raquel Ramsey. October 25, 2014.

Lutz, Shelby Jean Gardner. Telephone interviews with Tricia Aurand. March 3 and March 12, 2018.

Ramsey, Douglas. Personal interview with the authors. December 7, 2017.

Ramsey, Raquel. Personal interview with Tricia Aurand. October 5, 2017.

Rinehart, Terry London. Telephone interview with Raquel Ramsey. December 17, 2017.

Rivele, Stephen. Telephone interview with Raquel Ramsey. December 1989.

Rivele, Stephen. Email correspondence with Tricia Aurand. December 14, 2018.

Stuntz, Barbara. Personal interview with Tricia Aurand. October 22, 2017.

Personal and Family Records

Affidavit of Application for Marriage License, Thomas J. Donnelly and Nadine Ramsey. Issued by State of Nevada. June 20, 1959.

Annual Sports Registration. Landplane. FAI 8937. August 13, 1946.

Branch, Winnie Ramsey. Recollections on Claude Ramsey. March 13, 1997.

Branch, Winnie Ramsey, comp. My Family Genealogy. March 1, 1997.

Burial remembrance of Otero Beeson (1889–1944). 1944.

Certificate of Birth, Nadine Ramsey. August 28, 1911.

Certificate of Burial at Sea, Nadine Ramsey. March 4, 1997.

Certificate of Death, John Percy Gardner. Issued by State of Indiana, April 5, 2002.

Certificate of Death, Nadine Ramsey. Issued by State of California, February 24, 1997.

Certificate of Marriage, Nadine Ramsey and John Percy Gardner. Issued by Los Angeles County, CA, November 23, 1949.

Certificate of Participation, National Air Mail Week. US Post Office Department. May 19, 1938.

Fifth Ferrying Group Yearbook. Love Field, Dallas, TX. ca. 1943/1944.

Graduation Program, Class 43-W-5. September 11, 1943.

Marriage Record of Nelle Brown Cozad and Claude Ramsey. Clinton County, IL, 1911.

Murphy, Catherine A., comp. WASP 1994 Roster. 1994.

Press Release on Bendix Trophy Race. Frost & Crawford, August 19, 1946.

Ramsey, Ed. "Guerilla Command," unpublished manuscript, 1946.

Ramsey, Edwin Price. Audio recording. March 1997.

Ramsey, Nadine. Autobiography. n.d.

Ramsey, Nadine, and Jack Gardner. Christmas card. December 1949.

Stuntz, Barbara. "Memories of Aunt Nelle, Nadine, and Edwin." October 30, 2013.

———. "Oil Boom in El Dorado." Unpublished manuscript, August 2018.

Stuntz, Barbara, comp. Ramsey Family Genealogy. March 1, 1997.

318th Army Air Forces Flying Training Detachment Classbook, Class of 43-W-4 and 43-W-5. Avenger Field, Sweetwater, TX. 1943.

WASP Banquet Program. 1978.

WASP Newsletter. June 1978.

WASP Roster Fifth Ferrying Group. Dallas, TX, September 30, 1943.

Willard, Marie Cozad, comp. Cozad Family Genealogy. March 1, 1987.

Women in Military Service for America Memorial Registration. 1977.

Yearbook. El Dorado Central High School. 1929.

Military Records

Certificate of Honorable Discharge. Issued by United States Air Force, July 1979.

Commercial Pilot's License. Issued by National Aeronautical Association, September 13, 1946.

DD-214 and DD-256 Card. Issued by United States Air Force, March 20, 1985.

DD-2168. Application for Honorable Discharge. May 24, 1979.

Identification Card, Women Airforce Service Pilots. ca. 1943.

Notice of Reduction in Force. Col. K. C. McGregor to Nadine Ramsey. July 11, 1946.

Pursuit Training Certification. Issued by Ferrying Division, Air Transport Command, April 30, 1944.

Qualifications Statement for Promotion and/or Reassignment, December 23, 1944.

Ramsey, Nadine, with Barbara Erickson. Application for Honorable Discharge. May 29, 1979.

Record or Request for Approval of Promotion and/or Reassignment. Instructor, A/C Mechanics, Sixth Ferrying Group, Long Beach, CA, January 16, 1945.

United States Army. Telegram to Nelle Ramsey. May 23, 1945.

War Department Air Forces. Transfer to Sixth Ferrying Group, Ferrying Division, ATC. Notice of Personnel Action. September 1944.

Miscellaneous

Eberhard, Claire V. Character reference. 1943.

Guest, Edgar A. "How to Stay Young." *Wichita Beacon*, n.d.

Keeps, David A. "Girl Pilot Saves Life by Executing Own Teachings." *Los Angeles Times*, 1946.

"Magazine Gives Tip on Son's Location." *Wichita Beacon*, March 2, 1942.

"Nadine Ramsey, L.B. Ex-WASP Now Owns Ex-Army Fighter." Unidentified newspaper clipping, February 15, 1946.

"Officer from Wichita Bags Japs in Fight." *Wichita Beacon*, 1942.

"Pilots Pursuit Plane." *Wichita Beacon*, n.d.

"Solos after 6½ Hours in Air." *Wichita Beacon*, n.d

"Wichitan Certain Brother Is Alive, Safe on Bataan." Unidentified newspaper clipping, n.d.

Woman's Collection, Blagg-Huey Library, Texas Woman's University, Denton

MSS 250 Women Airforce Service Pilots Records

Army Air Forces. Cornelia Fort accident report.

Army Air Forces. Dorothy Nichols accident report.

Army Air Forces. Evelyn Sharp accident report.

Army Air Forces. Marie Sharon accident report.

Army Air Forces, Air Transport Command, Ferrying Division. "WASPs—Women Airforce Service Pilots," *Informational Bulletin*, March 8, 1944.

Cochran, Jacqueline. Final Report, Women Pilot Program. February 1945.

———. WASP Report, to Commanding General, Army Air Forces, August 1, 1944.

Colorado Springs Conference Program. June 1978.

Committee on Military Affairs. Hearings before the Committee on Military Affairs. January 20, 1942.

———. Hearings before the Committee on Military Affairs. May 1, 1942.

———. Hearings before the Committee on Military Affairs on HR 4219. 78th Congress, 2nd Session, March 22, 1944.

Costello, John. HR 3358: A Bill to Provide for the Appointment of Female Pilots in the Air Forces of the Army. 78th Congress, 1st Session, September 30, 1943.

Gillies, Betty. Notes for talk about the Ferry Command. Biographical File.

Porter, Helen. Certificate of Honorable Discharge from the Army. December 20, 1944.

Ramsey, Nadine. Biographical File.

Severson, Helen. Photocopy of letter from Leoti Deaton. Biographical File.

Silver Wings and Santiago Blue. Documentary, 1981.

"Waiting for Ships at the Main Field." *The Avenger* (Sweetwater, TX). June 28, 1943.

WASP Newsletter, December 1, 1944, December 10, 1944, December 20, 1944, January 25, 1945, March 15, 1945, May 20, 1945, February 1946, October 1964, June 1978, April 1979, August 1980, August 1989, September 1989.

Weingarten, Joe. "The History of the WASP Wings." MSS 250. Historical Files.

Yonally, Lillian. Biographical File.

Additional Collections

Cowden, Violet "Vi," class 43-W-4. Interview by Krista Cooke. November 16, 1998.

MSS 253 Marion Hodgson Collection. Letters to family, summer to fall 1943.

MSS 263 Jill McCormick Collection. Letters to family, July to August 1943.

MSS 288c Mary Weatherby Collection. Letters received from classmates, June 1943 to September 1943.

MSS 295c Solange D'Hooghe Collection. "The Trainee's Alphabet."

MSS 299 Madge Minton Collection. Letter to parents, June 1943.

MSS 318c Dorothy Ebersback Collection. Army Air Forces. Orders to report to Love Field.

MSS 329c Helen Severson Collection. Letters to family, letters from Ed and Nadine Ramsey to Helen's family.

MSS 369c Adeline Wolak Ellison Collection. Letters to parents, June 1943 to August 1943.

MSS 507c Jane Campbell Collection. Army Air Forces. 43-W-5 Graduation Announcement, September 1943.

MSS 529c Lola Ricci Collection. Photo of Avenger Field floods, June 1943.

MSS 633c Ellenor Schaffer Collection. Army Air Forces. Class 43-W-5 academic sections.

MSS 773 Krista Cooke Collection. Calhoun, Helen B. "Peg" Brownell, class 43-W-4. Interview by Krista Cooke. December 4, 1998.

MSS 802c Nadine Ramsey Collection. Autobiographical sketch, biographical materials.

MSS 827 Sally VanWagenen Keil Research Papers. Interview with Jean Landis.

MSS 837c Ruth Lindley Muller Collection. Army Air Forces. Avenger Field schedule for class 43-W-5, April 1943.

MSS 865 H. O. Malone Research Collection. Interviews for unpublished book.

MSS 928 Claire Archambault and Pat Jernigan. WASP Research Collection. Army Air Forces. Fifth Ferrying Group Roster, 30 September 1943.

AAF School of Applied Tactics roster, August 1944.

Orders to report to Ferrying Commands, September 1943.

WASP Roster with aircraft classification, May 1944.

Oral Histories

Allen, Dorothy, class 44-W-4. Interview by Dawn Letson. December 3, 1997.

Baker, Nancy, class 43-W-4. Interview by Dawn Letson. September 5, 1977.

Bennett, M. Allaire, class 43-W-7. Interview by Dawn Letson. September 30, 1995.

Blake, Betty C. Tackaberry, class 43-W-1. Interview by Maura Mackowski. August 6, 2003.

Bridge, Catherine "Cappy" Vail, class 43-W-2. Interview by Dawn Letson. October 27, 2003.

Chaffey, Kay Gott, class 43-W-2. Interview by Dawn Letson. November 11–12, 2008.

Clayton, Sylvia Dahmes, class 43-W-5. Interview by Dawn Letson. October 6, 2002.

D'Arezzo, Catherine McBride, class 44-W-4. Interview by Dawn Letson. February 29, 1996.

Eccles, Peggy, class 44-W-4. Interview by Dawn Letson. December 4, 1977.

Gillies, Betty Huyler, WAFS. Interview by Dawn Letson. October 6, 1996.

Harding, Lela Louder, class 43-W-7. Interview by Dawn Letson. June 11, 2003.

Helm, Ruth Dailey, class 43-W-2. Interview by Tracey MacGowan. October 3, 2002.

Krahn, Virginia Luttrell, class 43-W-4. Interview by Helen Schaefer. February 9, 1997.

Landis, Jean, class 43-W-4. Interview by Sarah Byrn Rickman. May 13 and September 16, 2012.

Lesnikowski, Anne Berry, class 44-W-2. Interview by Jean Hascall Cole. 1989.

London, Barbara, WAFS. Interview by Sarah Byrn Rickman. March 17 and 19, 2004.

Maloney, Florene Phillips, class 44-W-4. Interview by Julia Lauria-Blum. January 20, 2005.

McKay, Mary Catherine "Jary" Johnson, class 43-W-2. Interview by Dawn Letson. October 14, 1994.

Moorman, Dorothea, class 43-W-4. Interview by Ziggy Hunter. October 24, 1976,

Pfister, Betty, class 43-W-4 and 43-W-5. Interview by Nancy Durr. 1996.

Rodgers, Lorraine, class 44-W-2. Interview by Jean Hascall Cole. June 19, 1989.

Rownd, Helen Ricketts Hooks, class 43-W-2. Interview by Dawn Letson. May 28, 1998.

Smith, Elizabeth "Betty" Whitlow Rummerfield, class 43-W-2. Interview by Dawn Letson. August 4, 1999.

Other Sources

Army Air Force Historical Office. *Women Pilots with the AAF: 1941–1944.* Washington, DC: GPO, 1946.

Army Air Forces, Air Transport Command. History of the Women Pilots of the Ferrying Division, Air Transport Command: September 5, 1942, to December 20, 1944. February 1, 1945.

Marx, Captain. Women Pilots in the Air Transport Command. January 1945.

Report of Investigation Regarding Proper Use of Women Pilots in the Army Air Forces. August 5, 1943.

WASP Base Assignment Map, Digital Collection.

National Archives, National Personnel Records Center, Saint Louis.

Army Air Forces Veteran Personnel File: Nadine Ramsey

Arnold, General H. L. Commendation to Air Transport Command WASP. December 20, 1944.

Bendix Trophy Race List of Participants. August 30, 1946.

Cochran, Jacqueline. Letter to Nadine Ramsey with Certificate of Honorable Service. February 10, 1945.

Erickson, Barbara. Cover letter to Air Force Military Personnel Center. Application for Honorable Discharge for Nadine Ramsey. May 29, 1979.

George, H. L. Commendation to Air Transport Command WASP, December 20, 1944.

Tunner, General William H. Commendation to Commanding General, Ferrying Division, ATC. October 16, 1944.

FILMS AND VIDEO CLIPS

Ladies Courageous. Universal Studios, 1944.

"National Air Mail Week, 05/1918–1938." U.S. National Archives. YouTube. September 29, 2014. https://www.youtube.com/watch?v=v5hREo8qgpc.

She Wore Silver Wings. Spring Valley, CA: American Dream Cinema, 2010.

ONLINE SOURCES

"Airmail to Airlines: How Mail Made Commercial Aviation." Smithsonian National Postal Museum, 2019. https://postalmuseum.si.edu/Airmail-to-Airlines/.

"Army Air Forces Regulation 40-9: Wearing of the WASP Uniform." February 14, 1944. Wings Across America. http://www.wingsacrossamerica.us/records_all /DOCUMENTS/uniform_regulation.pdf.

"The Bendix Trophy." Air Racing History, 2019. http://www.airracinghistory.freeola .com/Between%20the%20wars(2).htm.

Burdette, Linda. "Anne Tunner: A Life Well Lived." Virginia Aeronautical Historical Society. Virginiaaviationhistory.org.

Cawthon, Richard J. "National Register of Historic Places Inventory/Nomination: Lassen Hotel/Market Centre." August 21, 1983. National Park Service. https://np gallery.nps.gov/NRHP/GetAsset/NRHP/84000108_text.

Civil Air Patrol: Our Congressional Gold Medal Journey. Civil Air Patrol National Headquarters, 2019. capgoldmedal.com/.

Davis, Christy. "Oil Boomtowns." In *Symphony in the Flint Hills Field Journal*, 2014. https://newprairiepress.org/sfh/2014/people/5.

Denfield, Duane Colt. "Women Airforce Service Pilots from Washington." History Link, March 11, 2013. http://www.historylink.org/File/10339.

Fad to Fundamental: Airmail in America. Smithsonian National Postal Museum, 2019. https://postalmuseum.si.edu/airmail/index.html.

Foreign Relations of the United States: Franklin D. Roosevelt Administration (1933– 1945). US State Department, Office of the Historian, 2019. https://history.state .gov/historicaldocuments/roosevelt-fd.

Gant, Kelli. "Women Involved in Aviation." The Ninety-Nines, 2019. https://www .ninety-nines.org/women-in-aviation-article.htm.

Hunt, William R. "Sweetwater, Texas." Texas State Historical Association, 2019. https://tshaonline.org/handbook/online/articles/hes09.

"Illinois Central Railroad: Mainline of Mid-America," American Rails, 2019. https:// www.american-rails.com/illinois-central.html.

"Illinois, 1940." United States Census Bureau, Census of Population and Housing. https://www.census.gov/prod/www/decennial.html.

Kansas Digital Newspapers. Kansas Historical Society, 2019. https://www.kshs.org /p/kansas-digital-newspaper-program/16126.

"Kansas Oil Boom." American Oil & Gas Historical Society, 2019. https://aoghs.org /petroleum-pioneers/kansas-oil-boom/.

Keogh, Edward A. "A Brief History of the Air Mail Service of the U.S. Post Office Department (1918–1927)." Air Mail Pioneers, 1999. http://www.airmailpioneers .org/content/Sagahistory.htm.

Lockwood, Martha. "Women's Legacy Parallels Air Force History," *U.S. Air Force News*, September 18, 2014. https://www.af.mil/News/Article-Display/Article/497548 /womens-legacy-parallels-air-force-history/.

"The Mental Needs of Military Women: Community Driven Solutions, 2018 Report." Service Women's Action Network. https://www.servicewomen.org/wp-content /uploads/2018/02/2018-Annual-Summit-Report-Final.compressed.pdf.

"Milestones in the History of U.S. Foreign Relations: Japan, China, the United States, and the Road to Pearl Harbor (1937–1941)." U.S. State Department, Office of the Historian, 2019. https://history.state.gov/milestones/1937-1945/pearl-harbor.

Naylor, Roger. "Arizona's Military History: Kingman Army Air Field." *Arizona Republic*, February 20, 2015. https://www.azcentral.com/story/travel/local/history /2015/02/20/arizona-military-history-kingman-army-air-field/23618689/.

Nixon, Rob. "Hell's Angels." Leonard Maltin Classic Movie Guide, 2005, 2010. http://www.tcm.turner.com/tcmdb/title/77738/Hell-s-Angels/articles.html.

Pellerin, Cheryl. "Carter Opens All Military Occupations, Positions to Women." *DoD News*, December 3, 2015. https://dod.defense.gov/News/Article/Article/632536 /carter-opens-all-military-occupations-positions-to-women/.

"Review: *Lieutenant Ramsey's War*." *Kirkus Reviews*, 1990. https://www.kirkusreviews .com/book-reviews/edwin-price-stephen-j-rivele-ramsey/lieutenant-ramseys -war/.

Roosevelt, Franklin D. "Fireside Chat." December 9, 1941. National Archives and Records Administration. https://www.archives.gov/files/education/lessons/fdr -fireside/images/chat-01.gif.

Seymour, Dawn, class 43-W-2. Oral history interview by Rebecca Wright. July 19, 1999. Oral History Collection, NASA. https://www.jsc.nasa.gov/history/oral_his tories/NASA_HQ/Aviatrix/SeymourD/DS_7-19-99.pdf.

Tibbets, Meredith. "At Long Last, WWII WASP Pilot Elaine Harmon is Home at Arlington." Stars and Stripes, September 7, 2016. stripes.com/news/us/at-long -last-wwii-wasp-pilot-elaine-harmon-is-home-at-arlington-1.427789.

Wings Across America. 2019. http://www.wingsacrossamerica.us/wings/.

The Women's Memorial. 2017. https://www.womensmemorial.org/.

THESES AND DISSERTATIONS

Cavin, Stephanie Michelle. "Women, War, and Planes: Women Airforce Service Pilots' Experience Working alongside the Army Air Force During World War II." Master's thesis. University of Texas–Pan American, May 2015.

Davis, Dackri. "Navigating Discrimination: A Historical Examination of Women's Experiences of Discrimination and Triumph with the United States Military and Higher Educational Institution." PhD dissertation. Georgia State University, 2014.

Farizo, Angele. "Women in a Warzone: Participation Precedes Policy." Master's thesis. Southeastern Louisiana University, May 2012.

Gray, Katherine S. "Flying in Formation: Creating a Place for Women in Aviation through the Ninety-Nines, the WASP, and the Whirley-Girls." Master's thesis. Miami University, Oxford, OH, 2007.

Landdeck, Katherine Elizabeth, "Pushing the Envelope: The Women Airforce Service Pilots and American Society." PhD dissertation. University of Tennessee, 2003.

Wilson, Jessica. "Waiting in the Wings: A History of the Women Air Force Service Pilots of World War II." Master's thesis. Sarah Lawrence College, May 2015.

ADDITIONAL READING

Dobler, Grace. "Oil Field Camp Wives and Mothers." *Kansas History: A Journal of the Central Plains* 10 (1987): 29–42.

Graves, Celeste. *A View from the Doghouse of the 319th AAFWFTD*. Bloomington, IN: Author House, 2004.

LaFarge, Oliver. *The Eagle in the Egg*. Boston: Houghton, Mifflin, Riverside Press, 1945.

Tunner, William H., with Boot on Herndon. *Over the Hump*. New York: Duell, Solan, and Pearce, 1964.

Turner, Betty Stagg. *Out of the Blue and Into History*. Arlington Heights, IL: Aviatrix, 2001.

ABOUT THE AUTHORS

Raquel Ramsey is executive producer of the documentaries *Taking Flight: The Nadine Ramsey Story* (Vanilla Fire Productions, forthcoming 2021) and *Never Surrender: The Ed Ramsey Story* (Vanilla Fire Productions, 2016). Screened in museums and universities across the country and internationally, *Never Surrender* is based on *Lieutenant Ramsey's War*, the memoir of Ramsey's late husband, Edwin P. Ramsey. Originally published in 1990 by Knightsbridge Publishing, *Lieutenant Ramsey's War* was later published by Brassey's (1996), Potomac (2005), and, in a Philippine edition, the University of Santo Tomas Press (2016). With Raquel's continued involvement in the book's promotion, it is still in print today.

A retired teacher with a doctorate in education, Raquel Ramsey continues to carry her husband's legacy. For decades, she has been actively engaged in several military organizations related to her husband's career, including the Philippine Scouts Heritage Society, the US Cavalry Association, and the Oklahoma Military Academy. In 2018 she received the Congressional Gold Medal on her husband's behalf.

Tricia Aurand is an award-winning screenwriter, media critic, and podcast host. She's a contributor to several popular YouTube channels and cohosts a film-focused podcast, *Beyond the Screenplay*. She also frequently cowrites with two-time Oscar nominee Stephen J. Rivele (*Ali*, *Nixon*). In 2018 her short film *Work* screened at more than forty festivals in twenty countries. Her work has been selected and honored at numerous other festivals and competitions.

In 2016 she cowrote the documentary feature *Lieutenant Ramsey's War* (Talmarc Film Productions and Viewfinder Pictures, in development), the wartime story of Edwin P. Ramsey. A decorated hero of World War II in the Philippines and United States, Ramsey led the last mounted cavalry charge in US Army history and commanded the East Central Luzon guerrilla forces during four years of fighting behind enemy lines after the Japanese invaded the Philippines. Through this project, she learned of Ed's sister, Nadine, one of the remarkable and forgotten women in our nation's history. She lives with her husband, Sam, a director, in Los Angeles.

INDEX

Note: page numbers in italics refer to images.
The photo gallery is listed as pages *G-1* through *G-8*.